Wisconsin Q

HISTORY IN THE STITCHES • 2ND EDITION

MW00997620

ELLEN KORT

Revised by Maggi McCormick Gordon

Photography by Stewart Wolfe

Wisconsin Quilts. Copyright ©2008 by Ellen Kort and Maggi McCormick Gordon. Manufactured in China. All rights reserved. The patterns and drawing in the book are for personal use of reader. By permission of the author and publisher, they may be either hand-traced or photocopied to make single copies, but under no circumstances may they be resold or republished. It is permissable for the purchaser to make the projects contained herin and sell them at fairs, bazaars and craft shows. No other part of this book may be reproduced in any form or by any electronic or mechanical means including information storage and retrieval systems without permission in writing from the publisher, except by a reviewer, who may quote a brief passage in review. Published by Krause Publications, an imprint of F+W Publications, Inc., 700 East State Street, Iola, WI 54990-0001, (888) 457-2873. Revised edition.

11 10 09 08 07 5 4 3 2 1

Distributed in Canada by Fraser Direct, 100 Armstrong Avenue
Georgetown, ON, Canada L7G 5S4
Tel: (905) 877-4411

Distributed in the U.K. and Europe by David & Charles
Brunel House, Newton Abbot, Devon, TQ12 4PU, England
Tel: (+44) 1626 323200, Fax: (+44) 1626 323319
Email: postmaster@davidandcharles.co.uk

Distributed in Australia by Capricorn Link
P.O. Box 704, S. Windsor, VSW 2756 Australia
Tel: (02) 4577-3555

Cover credit: Quilt, *Jo's Garden*, made by Jo Ann Jacobi

Library of Congress Cataloging-in-Publication Data 2007942700

Kort, Ellen
Wisconsin Quilts
ISBN-13: 978-0-89689-592-8
ISBN-10: 0-89689-592-0

Editor: Toni Toomey
Designers: Heidi Bittner-Zastrow and Donna Mummery
Photographer: Stewart Wolfe

kp krause publications
An Imprint of F+W Publications

700 East State Street • Iola, WI 54990-0001
715-445-2214 • 888-457-2873
www.krausebooks.com

This book is dedicated to the long journey of ancestral women quiltmakers, to those who have documented the quilts, and to those who continue to preserve them and carry their stories into the future.

In memorium

Linda Moore   *10/04/44—12/04/06*
Marion Wolfe   *05/07/25 —11/10/07*

ACKNOWLEDGMENTS

Putting a book together is much like creating a quilt. It starts with an idea and moves toward completion piece by piece. This book would not have come to fruition were it not for many people. We are grateful to all the quiltmakers whose work is cultural, artistic, and historical testimony to the need for stories and beauty, and to the owners who preserved the quilts and were willing to share them.

The Wisconsin Quilt History Project drew many dedicated people who served on the steering committee and the past and present board of directors. They have given unselfishly of their time and talents over the years. Our particular thanks go to Sally Boaz, Kim Borisch, Adeline Briggs, Kathleen Briggs, Jeanne Bronikowski, Carol Butzke, Jan Cregar, Elinor Czarnecki, Luella Doss, Jan Fritz, Sue Gyarmati, Sue Heinritz, Kathy Hickman, Ann Hill, Cynthia Holly, Marian Houlehen, Judy Jepson, Elrid Johnson, Betsy Kohler, Jan Lennon, Judy Zoelzer Levine, Betty Llewellyn, Sue Monfre, Jan Montgomery, Linda Moore, Helen Pfeifer, Pam Quebemann, Linda Schmalz, Nancy Schmid, Maribeth Schmit, Peggy Scholley, Sharon Stewart, Kathleen Sweeney, Pat Thompson, Sharon Timpe, Kay Walters, and Marion Wolfe.

To the many generous individuals, guilds, businesses, and community organizations who have given financial support over the years, thank you. We especially acknowledge our major financial supporters:
Armbrust Foundation; Pat and Jay Baker Foundation; Crazy Quilter's Guild; Cera-Mite Corporation; Heller Foundation; Darting Needles Quilt Guild; Marion Wolfe; Dr. Roy G. and Cynthia Holly; North Shore Quilter's Guild; Marshall & Illsley Foundation; Paul Jones; Puelicher Foundation; Nancy K. and Allan Schmid; Wisconsin Quilter's, Inc.; Sharon Timpe; The James A. Taylor Family: a Wausau private foundation; Winifred Woodmansee; Wisconsin Arts Board; Women's Club of Wisconsin

We are grateful to all Wisconsin Quilt History Project cosponsors, supporters, and volunteers who made Quilt History Documentation Days throughout the state possible. We also thank those who assisted with exhibits and provided ideas, support, and encouragement along the way, not least our spouses and families. Our co-sponsors include the following organizations:
Adams County Historical Society, Adams County
Apple River Quilt Guild, Polk County
Around the Clock Quilters, Sauk County
Baraboo Quilt Guild, Sauk County
Barron County Historical Museum, Barron County
Barron County Homemakers, Barron County
Cedarburg Cultural Center, Ozaukee County
Chippewa County Historical Society, Chippewa County
Chippewa County Piecemakers, Eau Claire County
Chippewa Valley Museum, Eau Claire County
Clearwater Quilters, Eau Claire County
Columbia County Historical Society, Columbia County
Cornerstone Quilt Guild, Sauk County
Crazy Quilt Guild, Walworth County
Curtis Corners Quilt Club, Clark County
Darting Needles Quilt Guild, Outagamie County
Door County Historical Society, Door County
Door County Quilters, Door County

Farmhouse Fabrics, Waushara County
Flying Geese Quilt Guild, Fond du Lac County
Frederic Mixed Sampler Quilt Guild, Burnett County
Friendship Quilters, Richland County
Geri's Fabric Patch, Oneida County
Heritage Quilters, Ozaukee County
Hoard Historical Museum, Jefferson County
Juneau County Historical Society, Juneau County
Katie June Quilt Club, Juneau County
Lakeside Quilters Ltd., Winnebago County
Langlade County Historical Society, Langlade County
Lighthouse Quilters, Racine County
Lincoln County Historical Society, Lincoln County
Madison Art Center, Dane County
Manitowoc County Historical Society, Manitowoc County
Marathon County Historical Museum, Marathon County
Marquette County Historical Society, Marquette County
Mead Public Library, Sheboygan County
Milton Historical Society, Rock County
Milwaukee Public Museum, Milwaukee County
New Richmond Preservation Society, St. Croix County
Nicolet Area Technical College, Oneida County
North Shore Quilters' Guild, Milwaukee County
Old World Wisconsin, Walworth County
Old World Wisconsin Quilters, Waukesha County
Outagamie Historical Society, Outagamie County
Pepin County Historical Society, Pepin County
Pewaukee Area Historical Society, Waukesha County
Piece Makers Quilt Guild, Jefferson County

Pierce County Historical Association, Pierce County
Pine Tree Needlers, Waushara County
Pine Tree Quilters, Marathon County
Prairie Heritage Quilters, Dane County
Price County Historical Society, Price County
Price County Quilters, Price County
Quiltessential Quilts, Sauk County
Radley House, Waushara County
Rapid Fingers Quilters, Wood County
Red Cedar Quilters, Barron County
Reedsburg Historical Society, Sauk County
Sheboygan County Historical Society, Sheboygan County
Sheboygan County Quilters, Sheboygan County
South Wood Historical Corporation, Wood County
Southport Quilt Guild, Racine County
Spirit of America, Milwaukee County
Stitcher's Corners, Juneau County
Sunset Stitchers, Fond du Lac County
University Quilters, Eau Claire County
Wakely Inn Preservation, Inc., Wood County
Walworth County Historical Society/Webster House, Walworth County
Wauwatosa Historical Society, Milwaukee County
West Allis Historical Society, Milwaukee County
West Suburban Quilters, Waukesha County
Westby Area Historical Society, Vernon County
Winnebago County Historical Society, Winnebago County
Wisconsin Quilters, Inc., Waukesha County
Wisconsin Historical Society/Pendorvis, Iowa County
Wiseman Family, Outagamie County
Woman's Club of Wisconsin, Milwaukee County

Contents

PREFACE

There is something powerful about making a quilt. If it were possible to unlock the thoughts and feelings of a mother or great-grandmother as she placed each precise stitch into fabric, it would become storytelling pure and simple. The very act of cutting and piecing, stitching, joining, and creating a pattern gives voice to a hands-on art form that women have created and re-created for centuries.

Quilts are versatile. Through the ages they have served as warm blankets, cabin door and window coverings, and crop protection against freezing weather and grasshopper plagues. They have been used to celebrate weddings, to comfort the sick, to bundle babies, and to shroud the dead. They have been made from sugar, flour, and tobacco sacks, as well as ribbons, ball gowns, christening dresses, old shirts, jackets, and fabric scraps that were as dearly traded and as valuable as money.

Their names ring out like a litany of beloved ancestors: Grandmother's Flower Garden, Rose of Sharon, Log Cabin, Crazy Quilt, Star of Bethlehem, Double Wedding Ring.

Quilters do not always know beforehand precisely what it is a quilt may have to say. But what they do recognize is the need to cut and match and sew, and the pleasure and pain of the process itself. A Milwaukee grandmother tells of working long hours into the night to finish a Grandmother's Flower Garden quilt to celebrate the birth of her granddaughter. A Log Cabin quilt, made by a woman whose name is no longer known, is soaked in water and used for protection as people flee the disastrous Peshtigo fire. A Prairie du Chien woman stitches fifty quilts during her lifetime, each one made with bits and pieces of fabric. These Wisconsin women and their quilts are storytellers. And what they release into the world is a voice, a story map of a real and present life that is worth remembering.

Today only a small percentage of quilts made over the last two hundred years survive. Many of these quilts are valued as family heirlooms. An owner's knowledge about the quiltmaker and the circumstances of how and why the quilt was made may be fragmentary. Even when the name of the quiltmaker is known, detailed written accounts of the woman's life and family experiences may never have been recorded, let alone passed down through the generations of a quilt's ownership. Often an owner's knowledge has survived only as personal remembrances and anecdotes from generation to generation.

Documentation of quilts and quiltmakers allows a unique perspective on women's history. Where complete biographies are unavailable, oral histories can augment such personal documents as letters, diaries, and journals. Most of the stories in this book are family histories given to us by the descendants of individual quiltmakers and were presented orally, conversationally with honor and humility. Descendants speak of a particular quilt and its connection to their family heritage, its design, the chosen fabrics, and the skill and workmanship of the maker. They see quilts as a way to understand more about the history of a certain time and an individual woman's place in that history. They have gained insight regarding their own lineage, a sense of kinship through the generations, a way of viewing family values, and an opportunity to explore the present and their own lives juxtaposed against the past. One Waukesha County woman is the latest in eight generations of women who assumed ownership of a treasured ancestral quilt. She sees herself not only as caretaker of the quilt but as part of an inheritance pattern that empowers her as a woman and connects her to the generations of women before her.

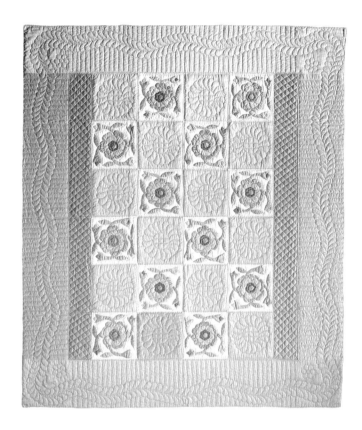

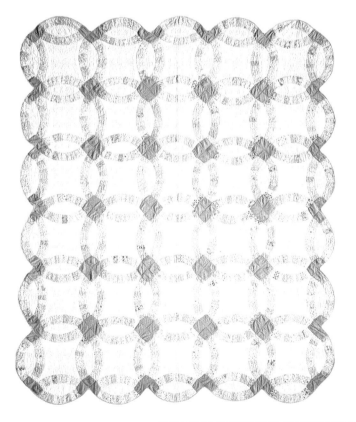

INTRODUCTION

With great honor the Wisconsin Quilt History Project (WQHP) presents *Wisconsin Quilts: History in the Stitches, Edition II* , by author Ellen Kort, revised by Maggi McCormick Gordon and the Wisconsin Quilt History Project. The first book, *Wisconsin Quilts: Stories in the Stitches*, published in 1999, was reprinted once and received the Wisconsin Library Award. This revised edition offers patterns and instructions for blocks from eight of the quilts that were featured in the first book. The quilters who contributed sample quilt blocks are: Jo Ann Jacobi, Jo's GARDEN; Sylvia Adair, FEATHERED STAR; Maggi Gordon, OLD MAID's PUZZLE; Mary Mauer, GRANDMOTHER's FLOWER GARDEN; Karen Moore, VASE OF FLOWERS; Maribeth Schmidt, APPLIQUÉD FLOWERS; Kay Walters, CROWN OF THORNS; Marion Wolfe, ROMAN STRIPE. Sincere appreciation is extended to Maggi Gordon and to all who participated in creating this new edition.

To have been involved with the WQHP from its inception has been my pleasure. Inspired by Shelly Zegart, the founder of the Kentucky Quilt Project, one of the first states in the U.S. to celebrate and exhibit early quilts and to publish a state quilt book, I was determined to organize a similar program for Wisconsin. With the assistance of the late Dr. Robert Bishop, director of the Museum of American Folk Art in New York, we established goals and wrote a mission statement. Cynthia Holly, former director of Wisconsin Quilters, Inc., helped get the project rolling with her enthusiasm and support.

Wisconsin's first Quilt Day was held during the Spirit America Folk Art Festival in Milwaukee in 1987. Dr. Bishop helped in receiving and appraising many of the 150 quilts that were documented on that first successful day. Word spread quickly about the Quilt History Days that were documenting quilts made before 1950. Marion Wolfe created an introductory packet, which helped inquiring groups create local quilt days in their own communities. Quilt History Days were publicized locally, and quilt owners brought their quilts to specific sites. With the help of hundreds of volunteers and seventy local quilt guilds, historical societies, and museums in thirty-nine counties, nearly seven thousand quilts were photographed and documented between 1988 and 1996. WQHP provided quilt preservation guidelines to the owners and helped them to record the history and research characteristics of each quilt.

Fine quilts in traditional patterns, utilitarian quilts, and quilts unique in pattern, design, and workmanship were discovered. Most quilts were made in Wisconsin, or traveled to Wisconsin, and represented quiltmakers with European backgrounds or ethnicity. Only a few quilts, derived from geographic areas representative of distinct European or other ethnicity where families had resided in the same location for four or more generations, reflected distinct patterns, colors, and designs of that ethnicity. Future books will hopefully feature wider selections of quilts made by Native, African, and Latin American origin, as those quilts are being documented in larger numbers now.

In 1998 and 1999, the WQHP cosponsored three quilt exhibits featuring 120 quilts discovered during the research. Exhibits were installed at the Milwaukee Art Museum and the Pabst Mansion in Milwaukee, and at the Kneeland-Walker House in Wauwatosa. These exhibits reflected ten years of research and 150 years of quiltmaking in Wisconsin.

From the seven thousand quilts documented by the project, ninety-eight quilts were selected to be included in this book. The selections, based on story elements, visual presence, and historical background, were made by four researchers, WQHP board members, and the author. Each quilt, individual as it is, speaks for hundreds of others in telling the story of quiltmaking, as well as the historical traditions and contributions to everyday life of Wisconsin women.

An 1850s German farmstead in Cedarburg, Wisconsin, was purchased in 2001 by the WQHP to provide a physical home for its research and growing quilt collection. The seven buildings on the property include a large barn and a stone farmhouse. These help in presenting programs and events to accomplish the goal of establishing a new vision: the Wisconsin Museum of Quilts & Fiber Arts.

The early research mission of the WQHP has expanded to educating the public about the artistic, cultural, historic, and social importance of quilts and fiber arts, as well as preserving the historic buildings located on the landmark farmstead. This includes providing a climate-controlled environment for a research library, textile storage and conservation, classrooms, and exhibition galleries. A substantial capital fundraising campaign exists to create these spaces.

The museum offers a variety of activities. Educational events and programs are presented early spring through late fall. The Quilt and Fiber Arts History Day on the Farm is held in conjunction with the Cedarburg's Strawberry Fest each summer. Year around, the rotating exhibits in the Interim Museum at the Stone Farmhouse showcase different styles of quilts and other fiber arts. Themed exhibits are presented–each focusing on a different fiber arts discipline. The museum shop gallery offers treasures–many one of a kind–for gift giving or personal collection.

The WQHP continues to research textiles. In June 2002, the WQHP presented its first annual opportunity to document all quilts (not only those made before 1950) at the barn on the farmstead. When invited, the WQHP continues to document quilts offsite. One such venue included a Quilt History Day at the Milwaukee Art Museum during the Gee's Bend Quilt Exhibition. In 2005, the WQHP helped to generate the first rug-hooking documentation by cooperating with leaders in that discipline.

The WQHP encourages the documentation of all fiber arts disciplines, and welcomes volunteers to assist us in that endeavor. Our goal is to showcase the importance of textiles in people's lives.

Luella Doss
Founder, Wisconsin Quilt History Project

Chapter 1

Settlement to Statehood, 1848

FACING PAGE: A woven tapestry designed by Lorentz Kleiser, featuring a pictorial map of early Wisconsin. Details include various ethnic groups, native animals, and fish, as well as sites such as the state capital at Madison and Fort Howard at Green Bay. In the southern half of the map, the viewer can identify Cornish lead miners, the badger (Wisconsin's state animal), a Harlequin figure symbolizing the Ringling Brothers Circus, and Swiss, German, and Dutch settlements. Various Scandinavian settlements can be found in the northern portion of the map, as well as the mythical hero Paul Bunyan and his Blue Ox, Babe. To the left of the map are early French, British, and American flags. Below is a historical scene of Jean Nicolet being welcomed by the Winnebagos at Red Banks on Green Bay in 1634. The American eagle is featured at the top of the map, and just above it is the year of Wisconsin statehood, 1848. The Kohler tapestry is on permanent display in the Wisconsin Room restaurant at the American Club resort hotel in Kohler, Wisconsin.

In the Victorian mid-1800s, women were perceived as standing outside of history. They were considered appendages to the dynamic forces of war, politics, and commerce. A woman's world was in the home, where she was to be a submissive wife who would give birth and raise the next generation. She was expected to serve as housekeeper, moral anchor, and spiritual guide as well as helpmate to a husband, whether he farmed or practiced a city trade.[1]

Mary Elizabeth Meade was born in Harrisburg, Pennsylvania, on September 8, 1818. She was the daughter of David—a native of Dublin, Ireland—and Lydia Meade. In 1836, the year Wisconsin achieved territorial status, Mary Elizabeth met Charles Grignon, and they were married in Green Bay on New Year's Day 1837. The first of their eleven children was born in 1838.[2]

Mary Elizabeth and Charles worked together in the planning, construction, and furnishing of their new house, located on the Fox River near Kaukauna. It would become a center of hospitality for family and friends. Mary Elizabeth sewed, kept cows and chickens, and tended a garden. She shared with her husband the responsibility of providing for their large family.[3]

In 1856, as a leader of one of Wisconsin's founding families, Charles was one of several well-known pioneers invited to Madison to share stories of the state's early settlement. Charles was a respected ex-fur trader, soldier, businessman, and government official. The Grignon family's frontier history was longer than that of Mary Elizabeth's family, but her experience was just as important, from both a human and a historical perspective, as was her husband's. Her work, her role, and her status were vital factors in shaping the complex and fundamental institutions of family and culture. But Mary Elizabeth was not invited to the capital to tell her story because she was a woman.[4]

If women were not allowed or encouraged to speak their stories and felt nameless, it comes as no surprise that they would find another way—something tangible and durable, something made with their own hands, like a quilt—that could record their life and be passed from generation to generation. Individual women may not have recognized that a quilt might become a journal to be read by one's descendants, but on some level they knew these quilts as ancestral links, as intricate sets of interlocking stories.

From mothers and daughters to pioneers and storytellers, from workers and political activists to healers and tenders of the earth, women from around the world have earned their place as keepers and transmitters of tradition and ritual. Women's stories have been long overlooked. They often were told consciously or unconsciously through the women's quilts. The making of quilts evolved as an art form that helped define and express women's experiences.

A hand-crocheted silk fringe frames three sides of the Center Medallion quilt. Fanciful grasshoppers, crickets, and flies are embroidered on the pre-printed silk border. This quilt, like other early silk quilts, has a lighter color scheme and is lighter in weight than Victorian-era weighted silk quilts.

Center Medallion (Yankee Puzzle)

Catharine Ann Penniman was born on November 5, 1778, in Braintree (now Quincy), Massachusetts, the daughter of William and Rebecca Edmunds Penniman. Catharine's father was a well-known ship-builder whose shipyard built the Continental frigate *Confederacy*, the first warship owned by the new U.S. government. The shipyard would become a main target of the British during the War of 1812.

Catharine was fifteen years old when she became the bride of twenty-six-year-old Charles Bradford on December 26, 1793, in Boston. Charles was a sea captain who sailed between America and England. He was the great-great-great-grandson of William Bradford, who came to America on the Mayflower and became the first governor of Plymouth Colony.

When Catharine was twenty-four years old, in 1802, she gave birth to a daughter whom she named Catharine Ann. Catharine Ann married Seraphim Masi on November 8, 1825.

She received a silk wedding quilt from her mother, a special quilt that would be passed on through many generations, as would the name Catharine, which would be given to the eldest daughter in each succeeding Bradford generation.

Silk was expensive and had to be imported to the colonies, but this was not a drawback for Catharine. The center panel of the quilt was brought from England by her husband. (The stitching in this panel is not consistent with the other quilt panels and embroidery, which suggests that it may have been pre-embroidered.) Catharine surrounded the central medallion with small hand-pieced triangles of silk and added fanciful embroidery to the pre-printed outer border. In more recent times the set of triangles around the center has been called Yankee Puzzle or Hour Glass, but those names were recorded much later than the quilt, between 1894 and 1929.[5]

The heirloom quilt has become an ancestral storyteller, a bridge to the early days of our country's history and the history of the Bradford family. Each new Catharine has been the caretaker, assuming both the obligation and the honor of keeper of the quilt.

Catherine Bradford Surridge Kollath, the eighth Catharine and the current owner of the quilt, brought it with her when she moved from San Francisco to Wisconsin in 1989. She remembers "how special it was to see the quilt with my great-grandmother, grandmother, mother, and myself all gathered around it. I don't know if I understood the importance of the 170-year-old fabric, but I was aware of how special it was to have four generations of Catharine Bradfords together, celebrating our history…Two things about the quilt remain vivid in my memory: the musty smell of the aged silk and the sound of the threads snapping as it was opened up…Every time we had a viewing, it was discussed as to whether or not we should put the quilt in a museum…We concluded that the point of the quilt was to pass it on to our daughters…Nothing could ever replace the experience of physically wrapping myself in my own history."[6]

Catharine's quilt reflects her Massachusetts heritage. Most New England quilts before 1830 had a medallion format with a T-shaped dropped panel at the foot of the bed to accommodate the heavy posts of early-nineteenth-century beds. Catharine's quilt was exhibited at the 1876 Centennial Exposition in Philadelphia, at the 1893 Columbian Exposition in Chicago, and at the Athena Club in Burlington, Vermont, in 1932.

PATTERN: *Center Medallion (Yankee Puzzle)*
DATE: *1825*
MAKER: *Catharine Penniman Bradford (1778-1827)*
ORIGIN: *Boston, Massachusetts*
FINISHED SIZE: *93½" x 98"*
FABRIC: *Silk*
OWNER: *Catherine Kollath, great-great-great-great-great-granddaughter of the maker*
LOCATION: *Waukesha County, Wisconsin*

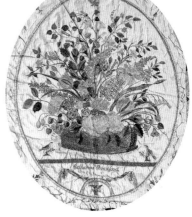

Catharine embroidered her name within the oval of the pre-embroidered silk panel at the center of the quilt.

Quilted cloth has always been used as an insulation against the cold, and the quilted petticoat was first worn as a warm undergarment. In the eighteenth century, women in Europe and England created dresses that opened at the front from the waist to the floor. Exposing part of the petticoat became high fashion. The silk industry in France, England, and Italy produced elegant woven materials, and wealthy Americans in Boston, New York, Philadelphia, Charleston, and other ports imported and copied fashions from abroad.[9]

These dresses—reproduction petticoats, neck and sleeve ruffles—are from the American Textile History Museum's costume collection dating from c. 1790-1807. (Photo courtesy of the American Textile History Museum, Lowell, Massachusetts. Photo by Anton Grassl.)

Freedom Gown
(Medallion with Star Corners)

When Joseph Buckminster's daughter Frances turned eighteen in 1752, he wanted to honor the occasion with a special present. He carefully chose a unique dress, a gift of fashion. The "freedom gown," as this family called it, boasted an attached skirt that was open enough in front to reveal a pink silk quilted petticoat.

Frances married Jonathan Brewer in 1763 and gave birth to a daughter, Susanna, on August 4, 1764.

According to family records, the quilt was most likely made by Susanna, who used pieces of her mother's gown to make quilts for each of her own three children. It was not until the 1830s that the remaining third of the quilted petticoat was used as the center square of a simple medallion quilt. Material from a cousin's blue-green silk dress was used to complete the corners and borders. Susanna started a family tradition of passing on the quilt to the eldest daughter in each generation.[8]

The center medallion was made from a 1752 quilted petticoat.

PATTERN: *Freedom Gown (Medallion with Star Corners)*
DATE: *c. 1830*
MAKER: *Susanna Brewer (1764–1855)*
ORIGIN: *Massachusetts*

FINISHED SIZE: *57½" x 57"*
FABRIC: *Silk, cotton backing*
OWNER: *Susan Marie Bailey*
LOCATION: *Ozaukee County, Wisconsin*

Territorial changes, 1800–1838. (Map adapted from the History of Wisconsin, Vol. 1, and used by permission of the State Historical Society of Wisconsin.)

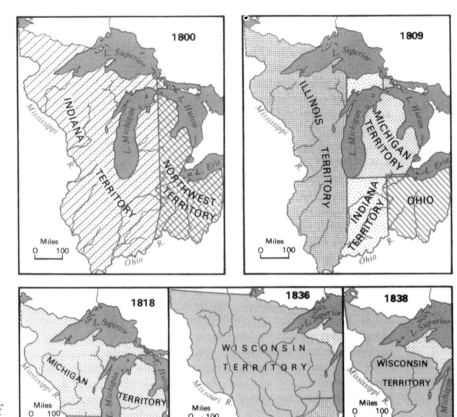

Wisconsin was populated by a number of Native American tribes, including Winnebago, Ojibwa, Potawatomi, Menominee, Dakota, Oneida, Stockbridge, and Ottawa, as well as by fur traders and the military (see the tapestry map on page 12). It was part of the Northwest Territory from 1787 to 1800.[11] It was included as part of the Indiana Territory for the next nine years, the Illinois Territory from 1809 to 1818, and the Michigan Territory from 1818 until the Wisconsin Territory was established in 1836 (see the map of territorial changes on page 23).[12]

When the Erie Canal opened in 1825, it drew people into western New York and raised land values there, so settlers moved westward to cheaper land. The canal connected the New York cities of Albany on the Hudson River and Buffalo on Lake Erie. In Albany passengers crowded onto flat-bottomed boats towed by horses for a ten-day, 360-mile canal trip. In Buffalo settlers boarded a steamer or schooner for the passage through Lake Erie, north on Lake Huron, through the treacherous Mackinac Straits, and south on Lake Michigan to Wisconsin ports.[13] The canal connected the Great Lakes with world markets, creating cheaper and better shipping, and laid open Wisconsin's rich agricultural land.[14]

Between the time the War of 1812 ended and the year 1836, some ten thousand settlers made their way to the raw, virtually trackless new land between Lake Michigan and the upper Mississippi.[15] They came by a variety of routes and modes of travel, including river boat, canal boat, stagecoach, and train. Those from foreign countries spent two to three months crossing the ocean before starting their journey inland to Wisconsin. Settlers made every attempt to arrive in the spring in order to have time to find and clear land, put in crops, and make preparations for winter.[16]

When Wisconsin was created as a territory in 1836, Gov. Henry Dodge instituted a territorial census. The greatest number of settlers were in the southwestern Wisconsin lead region, north of Galena, Illinois.[17]

Settlement across southern Wisconsin followed the routes established by teams hauling lead to Lake Michigan ports, then north into Columbia, Marquette, and adjacent counties in central Wisconsin, and along the Mississippi River north of Prairie du Chien.[18]

Many German immigrants settled north of Milwaukee, in the timber region of Ozaukee and Washington counties, because Yankees had taken the more desirable land and were charging five to ten dollars an acre.[19]

John Kinzie and his wife, Juliette, were among

the early settlers who came to Wisconsin. Juliette Magill Kinzie was born in Connecticut, where her maternal grandfather and great-grandfather Wolcott had been leading statesmen. John's parents were originally from Detroit, and John would eventually follow his father's occupation of fur trader.[20]

Juliette and John were married in 1830 and within a month traveled by boat from Detroit to Fort Winnebago, where John had been serving for two years as the fort's first Indian agent. The fort had been established when the Winnebago war ended in 1828, as a way of guarding the portage between the Fox and Wisconsin rivers. The Kinzies lived at the fort for three years and had their first child there. Juliette was a well-educated young woman, and when an Indian Agency house was finally built in 1830, she wrote of her life in the Wisconsin wilderness: "Our quarters were spacious, but having been constructed of the green trees of the forest…they were considerably given to shrinking and warping, thus leaving many a yawning crevice. Stuffing

the cracks with cotton batting, and pasting strips of paper over them formed the employment of many a leisure hour."[21]

Many other women also recorded diary stories of their families' journey to Wisconsin and the hardships they endured along the way.

Mrs. John Weaver of Augusta, New York, wrote of her husband: "After our marriage, he often had a touch of the Western Fever…we had a flattering account of Wisconsin…just the place for young people to commence life in earnest…an earthly paradise … On the first day of September, 1836, we…bid good-bye to…all that was near and dear to us, and with our small children…started on our journey."[22]

Rosaline Peck and her husband and baby son emigrated to Wisconsin from Vermont in 1836. She was five months pregnant and the first white woman to settle in Madison. This is what she wrote about their arrival: "Well, now, here we are at Madison…sitting in a wagon under a tree, with a bed quilt thrown over my

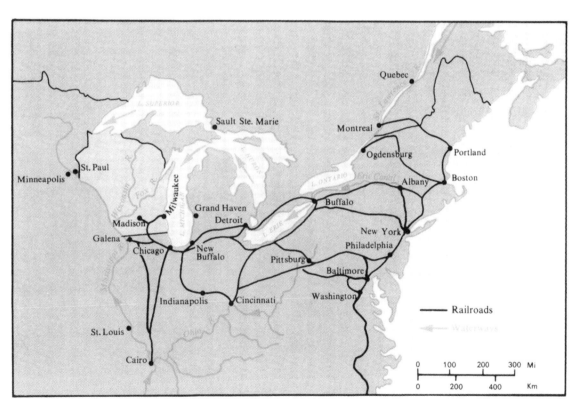

Routes to Wisconsin, 1854. (Map adapted from the History of Wisconsin, Vol. 2, *and used by permission of the State Historical Society of Wisconsin.)*

own and my little boy's head, in a tremendous storm of snow and sleet, 25 miles from any inhabitants on one side, and nearly 100 on the other."[23]

As soon as the Peck's cabin was built, Rosaline offered shelter to any traveler who needed it. She gave birth to a daughter and named her Wisconsiana. Two years later the family moved to a claim in the Baraboo Valley, and the young mother's willingness to help others evolved into a skilled and caring way of treating the sick and setting broken bones.[24]

Illness and death were familiar companions on the journey to the frontier. European immigrants faced a long sea voyage, and the trip from New England to Wisconsin required at least a month before the first railroad provided a link to Chicago. Smallpox, typhoid, and cholera were no strangers on the Wisconsin frontier.[25]

One pioneer mother recalled her family's eighteen-day journey by wagon from Detroit in November 1843. Her four children were sick, and they found overnight shelter with a family along the way. She cried when the woman of the house offered warm biscuits to the children. "It was the first morsel, except one, that we had received without money, in five weeks." The mother and children stayed with her brother while the father claimed land and built a cabin. He returned to find "three of us in one bed and nine of us in a little shanty 12 by 14 feet in size." Two of her four children died of smallpox.[26]

Pioneer life was especially difficult for women and children. Rural women were fortunate if a midwife lived nearby, and most women gave birth alone or with the aid of family or neighbors. They often raised their children on a diet of salt pork, cornbread, and whatever vegetables they could grow. Life insurance companies had little interest in children: a pioneer Milwaukee company set its age limit at fourteen.[27]

Pioneer women who helped settle Wisconsin found needlework a necessity and were responsible for an overwhelming amount of work. Eliza Page was twenty-eight years old when she married Luke Stoughton. Eliza carded wool and spun yarn for blankets. Using linen thread, she wove twelve sheets,

five tablecloths, and a variety of pillowcases, towels, and napkins by hand for her dowry. She learned to cook, make soap, cure meat, and manage a household.

Luke left his bride and their home in Westfield, Vermont, in 1837 and traveled to Wisconsin, where he purchased land seven miles north of Janesville. A year later Luke, Eliza, and their infant daughter journeyed from Vermont to Albany, New York, then by horse-drawn Erie Canal boat to Buffalo and finally across the Great Lakes by steamboat to Milwaukee. While crossing Lake Erie they encountered a violent storm, and when the ship seemed in danger of sinking, the captain ordered some of the freight thrown overboard, including Eliza's treasured dowry.

Loading their remaining goods into oxcarts, Luke and Eliza followed the rough trail from Milwaukee to the land Luke had purchased. In 1847 Luke bought another tract of land on the Yahara River between Janesville and Madison, and built a gristmill and sawmill. This small settlement grew into what is now known as Stoughton, a town named for its founder.[28]

It was often the mill owner who was the first settler in an area. Farmers cleared land, planted crops, and brought their grains to the mill. It became a gathering place and served as an inn, post office, blacksmith shop, and even a church. Getting to the mill sometimes required a full day's journey, but was well worth the effort. The trip meant shopping, visiting, and sharing news. Farm produce was bartered for coffee, spices, fabric, needles, and buttons. Even quilt patterns could be exchanged among farm wives.

Getting needed supplies was often a major difficulty, and women's diaries and letters were filled with stories similar to that of the young Belgian woman who walked sixty miles round trip from her home in Granleigh to the mill at DePere. She set out at 3 A.M. and arrived at 6 P.M. She was given permission to sleep on gunnysacks in the warmth of the engine room before making the trip home the next day, carrying her sack of wheat.[29]

PATTERN: *Triple Feather-Edged Star*
DATE: *c. 1840*
MAKER: *Harriet Dunn*
ORIGIN: *Lancaster, Pennsylvania*
FINISHED SIZE: *81" x 84"*

FABRIC: *Cotton*
OWNER: *Harriet I. Anderson, great-granddaughter of the maker*
LOCATION: *Unknown*

Triple Feather-Edged Star

The Triple Feather-Edged Star quilt, stitched by Harriet Dunn in about 1840, provides a trail of history for a family with a lineage of nine generations in America. According to family records, Harriet was a Quaker living near Lancaster, Pennsylvania. She chose Turkey red, blue, and muslin to piece four large triple feathered-edged stars, a complex pattern that showcased her fine needlework skills.

She named her creation Four Star Colony quilt. The stars were symbolic of the earliest colonies: Jamestown, Virginia; Plymouth, Massachusetts; Portsmouth, New Hampshire; and New York City. As Harriet placed the last stitch to complete her quilt, it was both an ending and a beginning. Her needlework would be valued from generation to generation and find its way to Wisconsin in 1972 through a descendant, its present owner.[7]

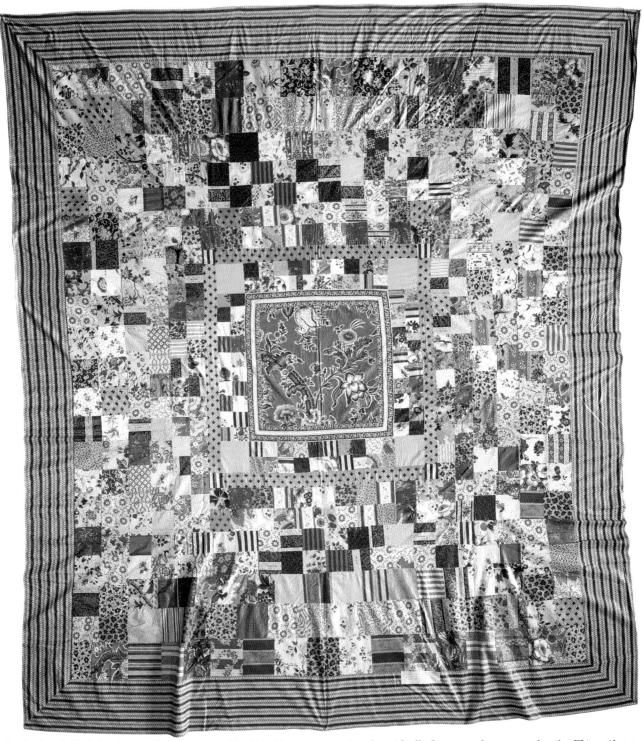

In the first half of the nineteenth century, some English chintzes were printed specifically for use as the centers of quilts. This quilt top showcases English fabrics from the 1830s and 1840s.

PATTERN: *Center Square Medallion*
DATE: *Begun in 1840, finished in 1860*
MAKERS: *Harriet Holmes (Mrs. George) Waller (1834–1934); her mother, Mariah McGeary; her grandmother, Susan Ellis Holmes, and her aunt, Harriet Holmes*

ORIGIN: *Portsea, England*
FINISHED SIZE: *90" x 110"*
FABRIC: *Cotton chintz*
OWNER: *Barbara Vallone*
LOCATION: *Racine County, Wisconsin*

Center Square Medallion

Harriet Holmes of Portsea, England, was six years old when she began to piece the Center Square Medallion quilt top in 1840. She worked on the center portion of the quilt for two years under the careful tutelage of her mother, Mariah McGeary, and her grandmother, Susan Ellis Holmes. Some fabrics were pieced together several times before they were large enough to add to the quilt, and it took Harriet two years to piece the middle section. Her stitches were tiny and perfect—approximately thirty-two to the inch.

In 1861 Harriet married George Waller, and they left England for America. As part of her trousseau, the quilt top was completed by Harriet's grandmother and her aunt Harriet. They added the outer pieces using the English method of working the fabric shape over paper templates.

When the Wallers arrived in America, they traveled to the town of Burlington, Wisconsin. Harriet was uneasy about the Civil War activities taking place there, and the following day she and George walked to Rochester to establish a home.

Harriet was very active in her community and in 1866 founded a girls' school. After George's death on November 11, 1900, Harriet settled in Burlington and contributed to the community in many ways, including the creation of a Christmas Seal campaign and a school nurse program. When she died in 1934, two months before she turned one hundred, flags in the city of Burlington were flown at half-mast for an entire week.[10]

The Wallers were one of many couples who left homes and families to make their way to the new Wisconsin Territory.

Detail of Center Square Medallion quilt.

Harriet Holmes Waller and her husband, George, August 1861, Portsea, England. (Photo courtesy of Barbara Vallone.)

Aunt Kitty's Fantasy (Center Medallion)

Catherine Weekes, who lived in London, England, practiced sewing at an early age, and by the time she helped celebrate Victoria's coronation as queen of England in 1838, she was twenty-six years old and a highly skilled seamstress.[30] Little did she know on that coronation day that she would become a milliner for the queen, creating velvet bonnets in royal blue, fuchsia, green, and somber tones of black and brown. At the end of each day, Kitty, as she was nicknamed, took the remnants of fabric with her to her home on Downing Street. She cut and pieced them into a center medallion quilt and thought of her brother Thomas, who with his boyhood friend George Burchard was sailing the high seas in search of whales.

When war broke out between Mexico and the United States in 1846, Thomas's whaling vessel was confiscated by the U.S. government off the coast of San Diego. As compensation for the vessel's conversion into a warship, the sailors on board were given land grants, many in Wisconsin. In the spring of 1848, Thomas and George claimed their land near the crossroad town of Rathburn, in Sheboygan County. Kitty soon joined Thomas in Wisconsin, bringing with her the quilt made from Queen Victoria's bonnet scraps.

Kitty lived with Thomas and his new bride. She helped clear the land and build a house. In 1855, at the age of forty-four, Kitty culminated a lifetime friendship with George by marrying him and creating a permanent place for her multicolored velvet quilt.[31]

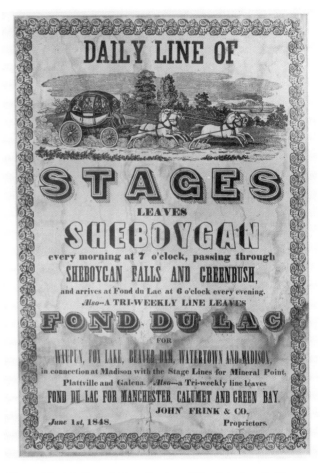

(Stage Schedule Broadside, collection of Fond du Lac Public Library, Fond du Lac, Wisconsin. Photo by Charles E. Sosinski.)

PATTERN: *Aunt Kitty's Fantasy (Center Medallion)*
DATE: *c. 1840–1845*
MAKER: *Catherine Weekes (Mrs. George Burchard, 1811–1895)*
ORIGIN: *London, England*
FINISHED SIZE: *55¾" x 67"*
FABRIC: *Velvet*
OWNER: *Katherine Simmons, great-great grandniece of the maker*
LOCATION: *Unknown*

Catherine served as a milliner to the queen of England and created this quilt of velvet scraps from bonnets she made for Queen Victoria.

PATTERN: *Sunburst Variation*

DATE: *c. 1847*

MAKER: *Ann Jenkins (1827–1887) and her daughters, Phoebe, Mary, Margaret, and Elizabeth*

ORIGIN: *Shipboard—on the Atlantic Ocean*

FINiSHED SIZE: *86" x 89"*

FABRIC: *Cotton*

OWNER: *Margaret Blount, great-great-granddaughter of the maker*

LOCATION: *Columbia County, Wisconsin*

(Transparencies by Gallery Studio, Portage, Wisconsin.)

Detail from Sunburst Variation pictured on page 26.

Sunburst Variation

When the Jenkins family left Cardigan in south Wales and crossed the Atlantic for America in 1847, Ann Jenkins helped pass the time by piecing quilt squares with her four daughters. It was her way of teaching Phoebe, Mary, Margaret, and Elizabeth something practical while measuring the long, hard journey to their new home. They pieced rays of color into Sunburst blocks to be joined together when they reached their destination.

Upon their arrival in America, Ann, William, and the girls were surprised by the distance they still had to travel to the town of Manitowoc, Wisconsin Territory. They made that part of the journey by way of the well-established route through the Erie Canal and the Great Lakes. Some years after settling in rural Manitowoc County, part of the family moved west to Columbia County to join other Welsh immigrants in the town of Caledonia.

Margaret Jenkins married David J. Williams, also from Wales, on November 12, 1856. They settled in the town of Caledonia and had five children: William, Griffith, Sarah, Thomas, and John.[32]

(Transparency courtesy of the Oshkosh Public Museum)

PATTERN: *Autograph (Album) detail*
DATE: *1850–1851*
MAKER: *Pieced by Mrs. Hastings Strickland, quilted by Mrs. Susie Hughes*
ORIGIN: *Bangor, Maine*
FINISHED SIZE: *59" x 81½"*
FABRIC: *Cotton*
OWNER: *Oshkosh Public Museum, Oshkosh, Wisconsin. Donated by Mrs. D. L. Harmon.*
LOCATION: *Winnebago County, Wisconsin*

Autograph (Album)

Autograph quilts, also known as album quilts, were popular in the 1840s and 1850s, during westward expansion. As women left their homelands and families, they were often presented with friendship quilts, pieced and inscribed by friends and relatives they might never see again. Squares cut from the used clothing of their makers were embroidered or inked with names, dates, personal messages, Bible verses, or literary quotes. Autograph quilts were reminders of what had been left behind—tangible memories, ways for women to carry the landscape of home with them into a new world.[33]

Sarah Washburn received an autograph quilt when she left Bangor, Maine, for her new home in Oshkosh in the spring of 1851. It was pieced by her aunt Mrs. Hastings Strickland, quilted by Mrs. Susie Hughes, and signed in ink by her friends and family. Inscribed were the following:

Sarah, sister unexpected was thy flight
But now so ever thy heart is light
Tho in far off Oshkosh you do reside
You're oft in Bangor enjoyed ...
Sis, Lysandee Strickland
Let not thy new friends steal thy heart from thine old ones
Mary A. McQuesten, Bangor, April 1851
Hurrah for the west for Wisconsin hurrah
Tis the land we now seek in the nation afar
O clear are her waters and blue are her skies and fair her
broad lands where the minerals lie
Far away in the west gleams for us a bright star
And there shall our home be Hurrah! O hurrah.[34]
Wm B. Hayford, 1851

Mary Jane brought her Feathered Star quilt to Dodgeville, Wisconsin, from her native England in 1848. (See instructions for making the feathered star block on page 184.)

PATTERN: *Mary Jane's Star (Feathered Star)*
DATE: *c. 1848*
MAKER: *Mary Jane Rule Davies (1825–1912)*
ORIGIN: *Cornwall, England*
FINISHED SIZE: *86" x 86"*

FABRIC: *Cotton*
OWNER: *Gwen Kraemer, great-great-granddaughter of the maker*
LOCATION: *Sauk County, Wisconsin*

Mary Jane's Star (Feathered Star)

Mary Jane Rule Davies left her family in Cornwall, England, on her wedding day, April 25, 1848, to sail for America. She took with her the blue and white Feathered Star quilt she and her mother had made, a keepsake that would remind her of home in the exciting and anxiety-filled days ahead. The rest of the family, including her mother, moved to Australia, and it is unlikely that Mary Jane ever saw them again. Mary Jane and her husband, Joseph, settled in the hill country near Dodgeville, seven miles to the northeast of Mineral Point, where Joseph mined lead and zinc. Many of their Cornish countrymen had settled there as far back as 1832 to work the mines.

As a young bride, Mary Jane found comfort in the Cornish women who lived nearby, women who knew how to make a familiar saffron cake, tea, and quilts. Being welcomed by a sisterhood of women helped Mary Jane establish friendships in a new community.[40]

Caroline Seabury used forty-three hundred diamonds to make sixty-one miniature Star of Bethlehem blocks for her quilt.

PATTERN: *Miniature Stars of Bethlehem*
DATE: *1856*
MAKER: *Caroline Seabury (1818–?)*
ORIGIN: *Iowa County, Wisconsin*
FINISHED SIZE: *92" x 98"*

FABRIC: *Cotton*
OWNER: *Milwaukee Public Museum. Donated by Donald and Mary Krier*
LOCATION: *Milwaukee County, Wisconsin*

Miniature Stars of Bethlehem

Mineral Point, Dodgeville, Plattville, and Shullsburg were just a few of the places that became settlements when thousands of miners came to Wisconsin in search of "gray gold." Lead mining, rather than furs or farming, attracted most early settlers to Wisconsin. As mining flourished so did the population in the southwestern part of the state. During the early 1820s lead prices were high, and there was great demand in eastern markets for lead that could be used in the manufacture of paint. News of abundant ore deposits along the Fever River spread rapidly, and hundreds of miners moved into the area. For the next two decades, Wisconsin's lead region grew in both area and population as new diggings were established and settlements developed around them.[35]

Cornish miners came to Wisconsin in the 1830s following a decline in tin mining in their native Cornwall, England. Wisconsin's mining opportunities had become widely known abroad, and the possibility of owning a mine or working one on shares brought more than seven thousand Cornishmen to Mineral Point. By 1840, when the surface ore was depleted, it was the Cornish who provided the technological expertise for shafting and drainage.[36]

Because timber was scarce on the open prairie, many miners built sod huts or dug makeshift houses into the sides of hills. Some people say it was these houses, which resembled the den holes of badgers, plus the strength and ingenuity of the miners that gave Wisconsin residents the nickname "Badgers."[37]

Daniel Parkinson, who settled his family at New Diggings in Lafayette County, recalled that newcomers were so intent on making money by mining that they "could not take time to erect for themselves and families even a comfortable dwelling place. Instead of houses, they usually lived in dens or caves; a large hole or excavation being made in the side of a hill or bluff, the top being covered with poles, grass, and sods … Families lived in apparent comfort and the most perfect satisfaction for years, buoyed up by the constant expectation of soon striking a *big lead*."[38]

The lure of the lead mines brought eighteen-year-old Caroline Prideaux and her new husband, William, from Cornwall, England, to Mineral Point in 1836. The region was expanding daily with new immigrants. Working in the lead mines was often dangerous, and by the middle of the 1840s Caroline was widowed with three small children to care for. In 1849 she married S. F. Seabury, a Yankee Vermonter. In 1856, the year after her eldest daughter, Julia, married, Caroline pieced a remarkable Miniature Stars of Bethlehem quilt. She made sixty-one miniature Star of Bethlehem blocks with tiny hand stitches, using forty-three hundred diamonds. The quilting was profuse, with every half inch of the quilt covered by stitches, ten to the inch. Caroline must have been proud of her work, for she signed it twice on the front: "C. Seabury, Mineral Point: March 4th, AD 1856."[39]

This seven-inch block contains seventy-two diamonds measuring ⅝" per side. Adjacent to the block is the maker's signature: "C. Seabury, Mineral Point: March 4th, AD 1856."

Betsey made two outstanding appliqué quilts based on the wildflowers of Wisconsin, including tulips, marigolds, campanulas (bluebells), morning glories, dicentras (bleeding hearts), pansies, calendulas, peonies, and tradescantias (coneflowers). Both quilts are in museums—one in Wisconsin and the other in California.

PATTERN: *Flowers and Urn*
DATE: *c. 1850s*
MAKER: *Betsey M. Seelye Sears (1813–1901)*
ORIGIN: *Jefferson County, Wisconsin*
FINISHED SIZE: *88″ x 95″*

FABRIC: *Cotton*
OWNER: *Fort Atkinson Historical Society, Hoard Historical Museum. Donated by Nellie Sears Roberts, great-granddaughter of the maker*
LOCATION: *Jefferson County, Wisconsin*

Flowers and Urn and Floral Appliqué

Betsey and Silas Sears bundled their four children into an open, ox-drawn wagon to get from Detroit to the Wisconsin homestead of Betsey's brother in November 1843. They came from New York by way of an Erie Canal boat and a Great Lakes steamer as far as Detroit. The Searses were almost out of money and still had a long way to go before reaching Wisconsin in the "far west." Mud, cold, snow, and rumors of a smallpox epidemic frightened the young mother as she tried to keep her children warm. She wrote in her diary, "It seemed as though I must sink down and die."

In December they were welcomed to the small house of her brother's family near Prairieville, now Waukesha. Silas left almost immediately to look for a home site. Within nine days of his departure, Betsey and the two youngest children were overcome with deadly smallpox. She wrote of her husband's return: "When he came, there we were in a pile, three of us in one bed and nine of us in a little shanty 12 by 14 feet in size ... on Sunday, at eleven o'clock, the little girl died; on Monday, at twelve o'clock her little brother followed her. It had always seemed to me that if I should ever lose a child, I could never let it out of

my arms; but now two of my loves were dead ... They must be hurried into the ground as quick as possible, and I was not able to see them buried. But God strengthened my almost exhausted endurance, and I became resigned to my fate."

On January 1, 1844, two weeks after the burials, the Sears family moved into their own small log cabin in Bark Woods, now known as Sullivan, in Jefferson County. During the bitter winter they survived on turnips, dried apples, bread, and flour gravy. Thirty-year-old Betsey had been a seamstress all her life, and by early spring she was determined to sell some of her needlework. She walked fourteen miles through mosquito-infested woods to a prosperous farm, where a Mrs. Davenport bought fourteen yards of her hand-knit lace and a floor cloth for $3.50. This money bought eight bushels of ground winter wheat, enough to get the Searses through the remaining cold spring. Betsey sold her shawl and a large pair of tailor's shears to help pay for their first cow.

Two years later, when Betsey was seven months pregnant, their ten-year-old son died of influenza and Silas was "taken by the ague" (malaria) and was unable to work. Betsey and her twelve-year-old son, Lowell, harvested the corn and potatoes by themselves and prepared the winter's firewood. The only mention she made in her diary regarding her pregnancy was, "On the 29th of November, 1846, a little Badger boy, weighing eleven pounds, came to our fireside."

By 1848 Silas had sold the homestead and built an inn in the newly platted town of Rome. Betsey's brother Ambrose Seelye laid out the town and recorded it in September 1848. The Searses named their new inn Live and Let Live. It was their home for the next seven years. In 1855 Silas built a frame house on the outskirts of Rome, not far from their first house in Bark Woods.

The same year they settled into their new home, Betsey made something for herself: Floral Appliqué, a quilt of her own design with flower

Quiltmaker Betsey M. Seelye Sears (seated on the left) and her family in front of the home Betsey and Silas built in Rome, Wisconsin. (Photo courtesy of Maurine May.)

With the exception of the binding, all of Betsey's "laid work," as appliqué was then called, was done with close buttonhole stitches rather than hidden stitches. "I remember my mother telling me the story of how my great-great-grandmother Betsey made the design for her flower quilt by picking flowers and then taking them apart petal by petal to be sure she had it right," remembers Mary Jane Reckahn.

bouquets. She added her signature, "By Mrs. Betsey M. Sears, aged 42 years, 1855." In that same decade she made another quilt, Flowers and Urn, unsigned, with similar design motifs.

Silas died four years after they moved into the frame house, and Betsey continued to make quilts for the rest of her life. She often used poetry to describe events of her life and her increasing support of prohibition. In her later years she operated a small printing business in Rome, where she handset type and printed her own treatises, handbills, and cards of local businessmen. The Flowers and Urn quilt remains in Jefferson County, at the Hoard Historical Museum.[41]

OUR WALK AT HOME
By B. M. Sears, Rome Wisconsin

Perhaps you may think it a strange subject of talk!
To be telling about such a common stone walk;
But this walk you see, (but yet it's not common.)
Although it's not handsome, has been laid by a woman.
When you enter the gate in front of the house
Now I know that this will your wonder arouse.
Although it may be a strange thing to relate;
But as sure as you live we've at last got a gate.
When you enter the gate the first thing that you see
Right there in the walk is the great letter B.
Go two or three feet further ahead and then,
The next that you'll see is the great letter M.
Then a little further on you will find I should guess
If I am not mistaken'd the great letter S
Although these great letters are of no great fame:
Yet they are the initials of that woman's name ...
Then look to the right and as sure as you are alive;
It will read eighteen hundred and fifty and five.
This walk that we see is all laid with small stones,
Some dark ones some light ones all native each one.
These stones I have gathered from road sides and hills,
From pastures and rivers from cellars and wells:
I have been with my husband to get them together,
And here they lay spread out exposed to the weather
How oft I've set down and looked over this walk,
And thought of the pains and the labor and talk
That I've had on this spot since these stones were laid down
With that loving one, but he's gone to his crown ...[42]

Quiltmaker Betsey M. Seelye Sears in the late 1890s, when she was in her mid-eighties. (Photo courtesy of Dorothy May.)

The California quilt features appliquéd garden flowers, including fritillarias, poppies, sunflowers, roses, and coreopsis. A gift from Helen Adelsberger, Betsey Sears's great-granddaughter, the quilt is part of the permanent collection of Heritage Park, City of Santa Fe Springs, California. (Photo courtesy of Heritage Park, City of Santa Fe Springs, California.)

PATTERN: *Floral Appliqué*
DATE: *c. 1855*
MAKER: *Betsey M. Seelye Sears (1813–1901)*
ORIGIN: *Jefferson County, Wisconsin*
FINISHED SIZE: *80" x 86"*

FABRIC: *Cotton*
OWNER: *Heritage Park, City of Santa Fe Springs, California. Donated by Helen M. Adelsberger, great-granddaughter of the maker*
LOCATION: *Santa Fe Springs, California*

Chapter 2

Statehood Through the Civil War, 1848-1865

The citizens of territorial Wisconsin approved a state constitution in 1848, an important step toward gaining statehood. As quickly as railroads were built, settlers followed, including a rapidly growing population of immigrants from foreign countries. Handbooks of advice were common. Some warned against the evils of New York, urging new arrivals to head west with measured speed.

Wisconsin's foreign-born population increased five-fold between 1850 and 1890. Part of the influx was due to the efforts of the state's Commission of Emigration, which was established in 1852, and the propaganda distributed by land speculators.[1] Germans were by far the most numerous of non-English-speaking immigrants, followed by Norwegians and Canadians of French descent.

Hoping to escape German taxes and bureaucracy, the German-born population of Wisconsin rose to 124,000 in 1860, accounting for ten percent of the German migration to the United States. By 1885, about one-third of Wisconsin's population was of German background. German immigrants were drawn to the climate, soil, and topography of Wisconsin and were market-conscious enough to appreciate Milwaukee's waterway connection to the Atlantic seaboard.[2]

Many foreigners who had already settled in the state wrote to family members in Europe, encouraging them to come to the new land. German immigrant George Adam Fromader settled in Jefferson City in the Wisconsin Territory. He wrote long, informational letters to his friends in Bavaria in case any might join him there. The following excerpt is dated January 15, 1847:

"Please tell our relatives and friends about this letter or make a copy of it, for it is impossible to write such a long letter to each one. We send cordial greeting to all and beg you to answer us…
You dear friends, good night!
I have accomplished the voyage
That I intended to take
And have come to a good land.

Early Wisconsin farmhouse. (Photo courtesy of the Oshkosh Public Museum, Neg. 3215.)

I thank God for this way
Of getting a free life.
I have much wood and good land,
Were you here you would have it too.
I live here happily
And wish you could have it the same way.
Good night, all you friends!
Germany is a vale of tears."[3]

Driven mainly by economic need, some forty thousand Norwegians, including farmers, laborers, and others, came to America between 1840 and 1860. Seventy percent of the Norwegians in the United States lived in Wisconsin by 1850. They usually came from a farming background, and Wisconsin seemed more like their homeland than most other states. They tended to settle in colonies, spreading up the Rock River and westward from Stoughton and Madison.[4]

Jannicke Saehle, a young unmarried woman, arrived in Koshkonong Prairie in 1847. She worked as a servant for a Norwegian family, the Torjersens, and told her brother of her earnings in a letter home: "I have now received from Torjersen for my services, three acres of land for cultivation for three years, and it is now planted with winter wheat—if God will give me something to harvest."[5]

Despite the diversity of immigrants, Wisconsin was a Yankee state. New England did not have enough land to support its rapidly growing native population and huge influx of foreigners, so many people journeyed westward. They often had a line of credit from back East to help them get started. Yankee settlers were activists and quickly settled in to become speculators, lawyers, editors, preachers, merchants, and the politicians of newly formed communities.[6]

British families, especially the English and the Scots, came to Wisconsin and settled easily among the Yankees. Both cultures were relatively well educated and enterprising, and the newcomers often chose business professions as well as farming. The largest single group of British immigrants comprised the Cornish miners, who settled in the lead region of Wisconsin.[7]

The Irish were often identified as Catholic and poor. Wherever there was construction work, such as the building of plank roads, canals, or railroads, the Irish could be found. Although some turned to farming, most chose an urban setting close to their church.[8]

Smaller nationality groups also joined Wisconsin's rich ethnic mix, each with its own history and cultural heritage. The Swiss and Dutch numbered 1,244 and 1,157, respectively, in the 1850 census.[9]

Along with the influx of settlers came improved lands, roads, schools, a growing economy, and taxpayers. In 1852, Wisconsin became the first state to establish a foreign immigration office, located in New York City. It was created to encourage immigration and to work closely with steamship agents and railroad companies.[10]

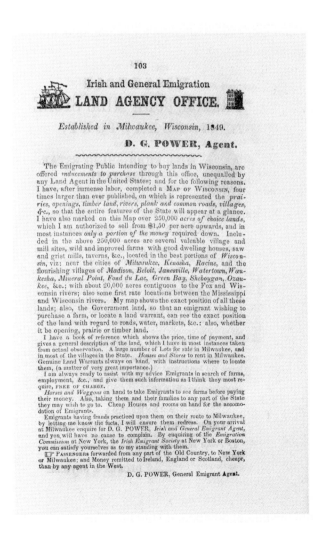

Advertisement for land in Wisconsin. (Courtesy of the State Historical Society of Wisconsin, WHi(x3)33833.)

Julia Ann Hanbest made a fine quilt for her approaching marriage to Robert Patterson in Philadelphia in 1849.

Oak Leaf and Reel

PATTERN: *Oak Leaf and Reel*
DATE: *1849*
MAKER: *Julia Hanbest Patterson (1830–1867)*
ORIGIN: *Philadelphia, Pennsylvania*
FINISHED SIZE: *71½" x 74"*

FABRIC: *Cotton*
OWNER: *Doris Hefferon, great-granddaughter of the maker*
LOCATION: *Racine County, Wisconsin*

Julia Ann Hanbest made a fine quilt for her approaching marriage to Robert Patterson in Philadelphia in 1849. The pattern she chose, Oak Leaf and Reel, was a popular wedding quilt design and one many of her friends had also made. In early literature the oak leaf symbolized strength and fertility. Julia stitched her quilt in the well-liked red and green color scheme of the day.

Not yet twenty, Julia and her new husband moved from Philadelphia to St. Louis. Julia died there after the birth of her second daughter. The new baby, named Elizabeth, was raised by Robert's parents in Elkhorn, Wisconsin. Elizabeth was given Julia's wedding quilt, a keepsake made by a mother she never knew. [11]

Quiltmaker Julia Ann Hanbest Patterson, St. Louis, Missouri, c. 1860. (Photo courtesy of Doris Hefferon.)

Red and green was a common color scheme in homes from 1830 to the end of the nineteenth century. It was used for everything from walls and draperies to carpets and table covers. Red and green cotton fabrics had become available and affordable for quilt makers by 1840. Wisconsin quiltmakers, like their sister quilters in Ohio, Kansas, and Pennsylvania, incorporated these strong colors into their bedrooms in the form of floral appliqué and pieced quilts. The trend, believed to have originated in the mid-Atlantic region, was carried by quilters along migration routes. European immigrants were influenced by American tastes, and a red and green quilt was the perfect way to combine their love for bright colors and traditional folk designs.

Sarah pieced this quilt when she was eighteen years old and finished it before her marriage to Isaiah Kettlewell.

Feathered Star with Wild Goose Chase Center

PATTERN: *Feathered Star with Wild Goose Chase Center*

DATE: *1850–1860*

MAKER: *Sarah Robinson Kettlewell (1834–1921)*

ORIGIN: *Waushara County/Winnebago County*

FINISHED SIZE: *94" x 99"*

FABRIC: *Cotton*

OWNER: *Barbara Beaman, great-granddaughter of the maker*

LOCATION: *Green Lake County, Wisconsin*

Sarah Robinson knew her birth mother only through the stories told by Mrs. Hunter, the woman who raised her. Even though the information regarding the circumstances of the first few months of Sarah's life haunted her, she also treasured the story of her mother's love. In 1835 Sarah's mother left England to sail for America. The young mother, who had only one hand, took her infant daughter with her. During the long journey she realized that she might never be able to properly care for a baby in a rough new world. When they arrived in America she carefully considered what was best for her child. With unselfish love and courage she gave her daughter to Mrs. Hunter, a woman she had met on board ship, a woman Sarah's mother felt could provide better care than she could offer.

Having been taught essential needlework skills by Mrs. Hunter, Sarah pieced an intricate feather-edged star quilt when she was eighteen years old. She used a Turkey red and yellow-green color combination popular among young women in 1852. The quilt was finished by the time she married Isaiah Kettlewell. She took it with her to their first home, a farm in central Wisconsin, in the Waushara/Winnebago County area.

Sarah gave birth to eleven children, and when one of the children was injured, she gave her treasured quilt to the doctor as payment for his fee. A member of her family eventually saved enough money to reclaim the quilt for Sarah. Several of the Kettlewell children died during a diphtheria epidemic, and those who remained valued the well-used quilt and its story.[12]

Lack of colorfast dyes and the need to set colors were problems for quilters, but help could be found in cookbooks or newspaper and magazine articles that featured household hints. The popular color combination of red, green, and white called for fabrics whose colors would not run. In the 1836 *The American Frugal Housewife*, Mrs. Child wrote, "An ox's gall will set any color—silk, cotton, or woolen. I have seen the colors of calico, which faded at one washing, fixed by it. Where one lives near a slaughter-house ... the gall can be bought for a few cents."[13]

Women often dyed fabric using the madder root to achieve a bright, or "madder," red color for making quilts and exchanged the recipes. The following recipe appeared in the 1887 *White House Cookbook*: "To each lb. of goods, alum 5 ounce, red or cream of tartar, one ounce. Put in the goods and bring the kettle to a boil for ½ hour; then air them and boil ½ hour longer; empty the kettle and fill with clean water. Put in bran, one peck; make it milk-warm and let it stand until the bran rises. Then skim off the bran and put in ½ lb. madder. Put in the goods and heat slowly until it boils and is done. Wash in strong suds."[14]

Quilt maker Sarah Robinson Kettlewell.

Mr. and Mrs. Hunter, who raised Sarah Robinson. (Photos courtesy of Barbara Beaman.)

Rachel's quilt, four large blocks set together, is typical of mid-nineteenth-century quilts.

PATTERN: *Whig Rose Four Block*
DATE: *Early 1850s*
MAKER: *Rachel Jane Hobby Silkman (1825–1919)*
ORIGIN: *Pleasantville, New York, and Milwaukee, Wisconsin*

FINISHED SIZE: *92¼" x 90"*
FABRIC: *Cotton*
OWNERS: *Sara M. and John Stover, great-grandson of the maker*
LOCATION: *Ozaukee County, Wisconsin*

Whig Rose Four Block

Rachel Jane Hobby Silkman traveled by way of the Erie Canal to Wisconsin in 1849 and carried with her the beginning of a red and green quilt. She and her husband, John, moved to Milwaukee from Pleasantville, New York. They settled on the eastern bluffs of the city overlooking Lake Michigan, in an area that came to be known as Yankee Hill. It was a lively city where chickens scratched in the dirt and cows were still driven to pasture through even the most fashionable streets.

Rachel finished her quilt in Milwaukee in the early 1850s. She was a fine needlewoman, and her appliqué stitches were nearly invisible.[15] The four large blocks she set together were a typical format for quilts made in the mid-1800s. One name for her pattern was Whig Rose, an indication of sympathy for the Whig Party, under whose banner William Henry Harrison won the presidency in 1840. Though women could not vote, they were not ignorant of political issues, and they sometimes used quilt patterns to express their views. As early as 1845 a pattern similar to Rachel's was called the Democrat Rose; thus both parties claimed the design.[16]

Whig Rose with Sashing

Elizabeth Jenkinson was raised near Fairwater, in Fond du Lac County, on a farm her parents carved out of the wilderness when they moved south from Canada in 1846. Her father, Robert, was born in County Wicklow, Ireland, but was of English heritage. Her mother, Georgianna Pomenville, was French Canadian. Lizzie, one of nine children, helped with the farm chores as well as the household tasks. Her father served as county sheriff in 1852 and county treasurer in 1854, and was allowed to pasture his cows and other livestock on the courthouse lawn. Lizzie milked the cows every day and used some of the milk to make pumpkin pies for prisoners in the county jail.

Lizzie married Brian Fergus O'Laughlin on January 28, 1856. Brian was born in Kilfenora, County Clare, Ireland, and arrived in Wisconsin in October 1849. The couple had twelve children, and Lizzie taught all six of her daughters to sew. According to Lizzie's descendants, her 1850's red and green Whig Rose quilt was one of several quilts made by the women in the family near Fond du Lac. It has been passed on and "lived in" by generations of Lizzie's descendants. The quilt was mended through the years, sometimes by hand and sometimes by machine, each generation making its own contribution to the quilt. It still remains in Wisconsin, with a great-granddaughter.[17]

PATTERN: *Whig Rose with Sashing*
DATE: *c. 1850s*
MAKER: *Elizabeth Jenkinson O'Laughlin (1836–1914) and female relatives*
ORIGIN: *Fond du Lac County, Wisconsin*
FINISHED SIZE: *78¼" x 64¼"*
FABRIC: *Cotton*
OWNER: *Rosemary Gerharz, great-granddaughter of the maker*
LOCATION: *Milwaukee County, Wisconsin*

The faded green fabric of Elizabeth's quilt gives the checkerboard pattern and sashing greater prominence than on most Whig Rose quilts.

PATTERN: *Rose Wreath*
DATE: *c. 1858*
MAKER: *Mary C. (Mrs. Abel) Slocum (c. 1817–?)*
ORIGIN: *Rock County, Wisconsin*
FINISHED SIZE: *88" x 88"*

FABRIC: *Cotton*
OWNER: *State Historical Society of Wisconsin.*
Donated by F. B. Potter.
LOCATION: *Dane County, Wisconsin*

Rose Wreath

Mrs. Abel Slocum made a Rose Wreath quilt for her daughter Ella's hope chest in 1858. The Slocum family lived on a farm in Lima Township in Rock County. Lima was a settlement of easterners and Irish, and the tradition of fine quilt making there was strong.

Mrs. Slocum's quilt was done with wreaths of stuffed red roses and plump stuffed buds. Her quilting was elaborate—small, even, and profuse. In small red cross-stitches, she signed her quilt "Mrs. M. C. Slocum; Lima, Rock Co. Wis. 1858."

PATTERN: *Star of LeMoyne with Pieced Border*
DATE: *1858*
MAKER: *Esther Garthwaite (1841–1860)*
ORIGIN: *Rock County, Wisconsin*
FINISHED SIZE: *80" x 69½"*

FABRIC: *Cotton*
OWNER: *Milton Historical Society. Donated by Lucille Schwartz, great-granddaughter of the maker*
LOCATION: *Rock County, Wisconsin*

Star of LeMoyne with Pieced Border

Sometimes a quilt is like a sealed letter that must be read intuitively. In 1858, Esther Garthwaite, seventeen, unmarried, and pregnant, was forbidden by her family to marry the father of her coming baby. The rejected young man headed west, and Esther stayed with her family in a small log cabin in south-central Wisconsin. She felt isolated in the town of Milton, a community of moral Yankee Baptists. As she awaited the birth of her child, she pieced and quilted a Star of LeMoyne quilt, deliberate work that kept her sheltered and busy. Esther gave birth to a son and named him Charles but would not live to raise him. She came down with "fever" and died soon after the baby was born. Charles was raised by his grandparents, Mercy and Henry Garthwaite. The connecting thread from mother to child was her carefully stitched star quilt.[18]

Hattie had begun piecing this Log Cabin quilt by 1860, when she was eight years old.

PATTERN: *Log Cabin*
DATE: *c. 1860*
MAKER: *Harriet Cadelia Shepherd (1852–1934)*
ORIGIN: *Dodge County, Wisconsin*
FINISHED SIZE: *72" x 64½"*
FABRIC: *Cotton and wool*
OWNER: *State Historical Society of Wisconsin. Donated by Mrs. Katherine Stone Moore*
LOCATION: *Dane County, Wisconsin*

Log Cabin

Most girls in the 1800s were taught to sew even before they were taught to read. It was not unusual for a young girl to start her first quilt at the age of five, a quilt often made for a doll or a newborn sister or brother. Stella Howard, a young seamstress, received a prize at the Rock County Agricultural Society Fair in 1853. A notice of it read, "Miss Stella Howard, daughter of Sheriff Howard of Janesville, only six years old; patchwork; quite superior; and the committee would encourage such efforts. 1st Premium, $1.00."[19]

Harriet Cadelia Shepherd, known most of her life as Hattie, began sewing at an early age. She was born in Saylesville, in Dodge County, in 1852. By the time she was eight years old, Hattie had begun piecing a Log Cabin quilt from soft brown calicoes. She hand-pieced strips of cottons, interspersed with wool, to a muslin foundation. Hattie positioned the Barn Raising set of blocks to represent barn beams lying on the ground before the walls were "raised" and the sides closed in.

In 1874 Harriet married Charles Whitman Sayles, and they had a daughter, Nell. Nell's daughter, Katherine Stone, started a hope chest when she was fifteen, and at that time she was given her grandmother Harriet's quilt. She also acquired her grandmother's "button string" and felt sure that many of the old buttons came from dresses used in the quilt.[20]

See page 192 for construction pattern.

PATTERN: *Crown of Thorns*
DATE: *1860*
MAKER: *Maria Ambrose
Gochenaur (1833–1912)*
ORIGIN: *Richland County,
Wisconsin*
FINISHED SIZE: *90" x 62"*
FABRIC: *Cotton*
OWNER: *Ellen Gochenaur
Noehre, great–great–
granddaughter of the maker*
LOCATION: *Unknown*

Crown of Thorns

Maria Ambrose Gochenaur's strength would be tested in a way she could not have guessed when she and her husband, Levi, and their new baby moved from Indiana to join Maria's parents in Orion, Wisconsin, in 1855. Levi left Maria and the baby with her parents for the winter and traveled to Forest Township, forty-five miles to the northwest, to clear land and build a cabin. It was not until spring that he was able to return for his family.

One of Maria's favorite stories was of the day she found red fabric at the general store. When she told Levi she considered it the most beautiful fabric she had ever seen, he bought the entire bolt. She became known for the red dresses she wore and the bright red curtains in their new cabin. It was this red fabric that she also used to make her Crown of Thorns quilt in 1860. By then she was the mother of four children, and making a needed quilt was a welcome respite after a long day of physical chores.

In the thirteenth year of their marriage, Levi became ill with tuberculosis and died on the day he turned forty. Maria raised their four children, ran the farm, and continued to sew. She died in 1912, at the age of seventy-eight.[21]

Postage Stamp

Using English Paper Piecing, Charlotte created a quilt of 6,372 squares, each the size of a postage stamp.

PATTERN: *Postage Stamp*
DATE: *1850–1865*
MAKER: *Charlotte Baker (Mrs. William) Waller (1800–1885)*
ORIGIN: *Sussex, England*
FINISHED SIZE: *65" x 82"*
FABRIC: *Cotton*
OWNER: *Burlington Historical Museum. Donated by Mrs. and Mr. George Healy, grandson of the maker*
LOCATION: *Racine County, Wisconsin*

Charlotte Waller of Sussex, England, began her Postage Stamp quilt in the 1850s. The quilt was so named because it was constructed of one-inch squares, each the size of a stamp. She worked from her scrap bag, which contained tiny print calicoes. The predominant color was brown, with enough variety to make both light-and dark-colored blocks. She carefully cut squares of fabric and basted them over one-inch squares of paper. For paper she used old letters, and the fine script is still visible today. Charlotte sewed the squares together with tiny stitches, a method that came to be known as English Paper Piecing. With patience and persistence she created a quilt of 6,372 squares.

Charlotte's son George had an illustrious career in the British navy. He fought in the Crimean War of 1853 to 1856, during which he met Florence Nightingale and was impressed by her skill and kindness in nursing the wounded. When George returned home from the war, he received a letter of commendation from Queen Victoria. He carried the letter with him when he left England and brought his new bride, Harriet, to Wisconsin in 1861 (see pages X–X).

In the fall of 1865, George returned to Sussex to visit his aging mother. When he left six months later to return to America, she presented him with her Postage Stamp quilt—a tangible link between English and American homelands.[22]

For at least two decades prior to the Civil War, Wisconsin residents exhibited strong antislavery feelings. Wisconsin became an important link in the Underground Railroad, assisting escaped slaves on their way to Canada and freedom. The Wisconsin Supreme Court nullified the federal Fugitive Slave Law of 1850 after Sherman M. Booth, an abolitionist newspaper editor, led a mob that forcibly freed a fugitive slave from a Milwaukee jail.[23]

Alexander Randall, an outspoken abolitionist, was Wisconsin's governor when the Civil War began. He converted a large agricultural exposition ground in Madison into a military camp and quickly mobilized men into service. Camp Randall would become a training site for more than seventy thousand of the almost ninety-two thousand men Wisconsin furnished to the Union army.[24]

Nancy Derby of Oshkosh was a schoolteacher for thirteen years and kept a diary of personal history and daily events. Her journal reveals that she was born on August 30, 1830, had two sisters, Mary and Hattie, and came to Oshkosh from Calais, Maine. She married George Derby on July 5, 1852. Their first child, Willie, was born on September 1, 1855, and a daughter, Lizzie, was born on February 11, 1862.

(Courtesy of the State Historical Society of Wisconsin, WHi(x3)2710.)

Although Nancy's diary is filled with events close to home, she also chronicled her concern regarding the war:

January 1, 1857—*There is quite a commotion to the South now. There are signs of the Negroes rising to regain their freedom. Would that they could be set at liberty. It would save much bloodshed, would do away with so much political strife.*

August 5, 1857—*Mary and I met with the sewing circle at Mrs. Mills. There were thirty ladies in all.—had a very pleasant time.*

October 14, 1857—*Pleasant. We are invited to a quilting tomorrow over to Mrs. Fowlers.*

December 3, 1857—*Mary came home last night. She went down to help mother quilt. We had a surprise party in evening.—24 besides ourselves.*

January 9, 1858—*There is a "sewing bee" at Mrs. Robbthoms in afternoon....*

November 22, 1860—*Mrs. Page put in her quilt today.*

January 1, 1861—*This bids fair or promises to be the most unhappy and troubled year of our National life. I hear that preparations for war are being made and hate and malice seems [sic] to be the prevailing passions. I cannot and dare not foresee the end.*

April 25, 1861—*I called Mrs. Jewell to learn about the flags. The ladies are making them of silk on sewing machines. Red, white and blue and stars put on and appropriate mottoes.*

May 20, 1861—*The girls are quilting for Mrs. Powell today.... Some of the ladies are going round begging for Mrs. Powell's people-some give money & some shoes & stockings & cloth-others give groceries. People seem to give liberally.*

September 24, 1861—*Lucy came up in morning to assist me with my quilt.*

October 2, 1861—*Mary and I went to the "Ladies Society" in afternoon. It met at Mrs. Scott's. We had a very pleasant time. There were only fifteen ladies present.*

December 10, 1861—*Oh this is a dreadful thing. We little realize it in all its magnitude of wretchedness. Brother fighting against brother and father against son. God grant that in the end it may all work out for good and not the destruction of this once glorious country.*

December 31, 1861—*Hattie and I put in my quilt today and I look for mother-She thought of coming down to help me, and going to a Watch meeting.*

January 8, 1862—*I have put in Willie's quilt today and he is proud of it.*

January 9, 1862—*Mary came down to help me quilt this morning.*

January 14, 1862—*Lucy came up in morning and has been quilting for me all day on Willie's quilt.*

January 15, 1862—*Lucy staid with us last night and is helping me again. Evening. Lucy has gone home. We took the quilt out today and I am binding it this morning.*

August 13, 1862—*Drums commenced to beat early this morning and volunteers are pouring in fast. Men dread to be drafted and so they enroll their names voluntarily.*

September 23, 1862—*It seems the Wis. 2nd was cut up badly—only some 60 men left out of a thousand men. I pity their sad friends at home.*

September 24, 1862—*Col. Scott has returned wounded, so they come wounded and crippled.*

September 30, 1862—*This is a terrible thing. We do not realize it in all its awful reality. O the orphans and widows that will be left to mourn, left to the cold charities of the world. People talk of the enormous debt the country will be burdened with and dread the taxes the coming year, but what is money in comparison to the sacrifice of human life...*

November 9, 1863—*I have put a quilt into the frame today. It seems like old times to see a quilt in process of manufacture. Quiltings are almost out of date, but many are the good sociable times we have had quilting in our childhood's home.*

November 12, 1863—*The Ladies Fair at Chicago has closed. It was a success and has realized the sum of $6,276.62 for the Soldier's Relief and the Freedman's Relief Societies. Both of which are truly deserving charities. Success to all such undertakings.*[25]

Quilt maker Mary Shove Ellis, c. 1900. (Photo courtesy of Geneva Watts.)

PATTERN: *Prairie Star and Autumn Leaf*
DATE: *c. 1865*
MAKER: *Mary Shove Ellis (1845–1937)*
ORIGIN: *Pottawatomie County, Kansas*
FINISHED SIZE: *70" x 72½"*

FABRIC: *Cotton*
OWNER: *Geneva Watts and Rodney Watts, distant relatives of the maker*
LOCATION: *Racine County, Wisconsin*

Prairie Star and Autumn Leaf

Far to the west of Wisconsin, in the raw territory of Kansas, twenty-year-old Mary Shove hand-pieced Prairie Star blocks. She chose the red and green color scheme so popular throughout the country during the 1860s and set the blocks alternately with a pattern that came to be called Autumn Leaf. The bed covering was to become her wedding quilt. Her quilting reflected the high standards of the pre-Civil War times—many tiny, close stitches covering the surface and outlining shapes. A distant relative of Mary's brought this quilt to Wisconsin after the Civil War.

Civil War Eagle and Flowers

Mary's quilt was never used. She displayed it at fairs and won many blue ribbons. It was recently sold at auction for a record price.

PATTERN: *Civil War Eagle and Flowers*
DATE: *Early 1860s*
MAKER: *Mary Bell Shawvan*
ORIGIN: *Dodge County, Wisconsin*
FINISHED SIZE: *82½" x 81½"*
FABRIC: *Cotton*
OWNER: *Private Collection*

Mary Bell's memorial quilt was passed on to succeeding generations, along with her husband's pension papers and the advice, "Never part with the quilt."

The thousands of Wisconsin wives and mothers who were left with no breadwinner during the Civil War became dependent on support from their communities and the state legislature—help that very often never materialized. Women, children, and older men took on the hard labor of working their farms.[27]

Mary Bell—or Polly as she was known to her friends—and John Shawvan were married in 1854 and began farming in Dodge County near Iron Ridge, southeast of Horicon. By 1860 Polly had given birth to six children. Even though John was in his early thirties and had substantial family obligations, he enlisted in response to the Union's call to arms. He mustered in from Milwaukee in October 1861 and was assigned to Company B of the 1st Wisconsin.

The young mother assumed full responsibility for running the farm, managing the household, and caring for her children. She could not know what ordeals her husband might be experiencing, but she felt connected to him somehow by creating a quilt for them to share when he returned home. The Civil War Eagle and Flowers design was her own, strongly patriotic and symbolic of pride in the Union cause. The tension she felt about the war made its way into small, precise stitches and intricately designed floral sprays.

Under the command of Col. John C. Starkweather, Company B was sent to Tennessee and into the bloody battle of Chickamauga in 1863. The battle took place on the banks of a creek known by Indians as the "river of death." True to the name, the conflict became the most destructive battle of the war to that date, save for Gettysburg. John Shawvan had been a flag bearer for other battles, but this was to be his last. He was wounded on the second day of fighting and died two days later, at the age of thirty-four. Polly and the children were left without a husband and father, and Polly had to rely on a Civil War widow's pension to support them.[28]

On April 27, 1861, Wisconsin Governor Alex Randall issued the following request: "To the Ladies of Wisconsin: The great demand throughout the country for blankets render it extremely difficult to furnish enough, immediately, for the health and comfort of the soldiers who are ordered into service. Any contributions of blankets and quilts, made for the use and benefit of the soldiers, until purchases can be made will be most thankfully received."[29]

Women often sent their sons and husbands off to war with a quilt from home. One woman attached a note to the quilt she was donating to an unknown soldier. It read: "My son is in the army. Whoever is made warm by this quilt, which I have worked on for six days and most of six nights, let him remember his mother's love."[30]

A quilt made by women in Green Bay in 1864 was sent to the army and found twenty years later in the cabin of an African-American family living near Bentonville, Arkansas. Eight blocks of the quilt remained, each bearing the name of its maker in indelible ink. One square contained this message:

> If rebels attack you, do run with the quilt.
> And safe to some fortress convey it;
> For o'er the gaunt body of some old secesh
> We did not intend to display it.
> Twas made for brave boys, who went from the West;
> And swiftly the fair fingers flew,
> While each stitch, as it went
> To its place in the quilt,
> Was a smothered
> God bless you boys, too.[31]

Wisconsin women, accustomed to working for missionary and sewing societies, quickly organized soldiers' aid societies. They stretched pieces of linen or old tablecloths over plates and scraped them with sharp knives into fluffy piles of lint, to be used as absorbent cotton in field hospitals. They sewed comfort-bags, or hussies, and filled them with needles, thread, buttons, yarn, and pins. Often a small bottle of quinine was added for medicinal purposes. They also knit mittens, gloves, and socks and collected vegetables to be sent to the army to help prevent scurvy. The

Chicago branch of the Sanitary Commission was organized on October 17, 1861. Because of its convenient location, it became the channel through which most of the supplies from Wisconsin were sent to the front.[32]

When Louis P. Harvey was elected Wisconsin's governor in 1862, the nation was already involved in the Civil War. Louis drowned four months after assuming office, and his wife, Cordelia, was appointed sanitary agent. She spent the war years working in Southern hospitals as a way of tempering her own grief. She distributed needed supplies, compiled accurate rosters, and facilitated proper care for the wounded. She visited every soldier from Wisconsin and gave each a treat from the basket she carried with her. She came to be known as the Wisconsin Angel.[33]

The Civil War emergency also created opportunities for women at home who were eager and willing to contribute to the war relief. Millions of articles, including bandages, quilts, blankets, and salves, were collected and sent to the troops by soldiers' aid societies throughout the state.

A small group of Milwaukee women, inspired by Lydia Ely Hewitt, addressed the need to provide for disabled and homeless soldiers returning from the war. The organization established a soldiers' home in Milwaukee, one of the first homes for war veterans in the nation. With the help of women across the state, almost $101,000 was raised at a soldiers' home fair in Milwaukee. A huge banner at the fair proclaimed, "The only national debt we can never repay is the debt we owe the Union soldiers."[34]

Thomas Nast's woodcut depicted women of the Sanitary Commission and was printed in Harpers Magazine, *April 9, 1864. (Courtesy of the State Historical Society of Wisconsin.)*

When the Civil War ended, the Rouse family packed this quilt and their possessions into a covered wagon. With their oldest son, Henry, they headed for new land in Chickasaw County, Iowa.

Quiltmaker Jane Orr Rouse and child, Walworth County, Wisconsin, 1864.
(Photo courtesy of Kathlyn Rouse Hickman.)

PATTERN: *Stars of Bethlehem*
DATE: *1861–1865*
MAKER: *Jane Orr Rouse (1837–1913)*
ORIGIN: *Walworth County, Wisconsin*
FINISHED SIZE: *69" x 78"*

FABRIC: *Cotton*
OWNER: *Kathlyn Rouse Hickman, great-granddaughter of the maker*
LOCATION: *Milwaukee County, Wisconsin*

Stars of Bethlehem

The guns of the Civil War were just beginning to sound and the young men of Walworth County were leaving when Jane Orr Rouse started a quilt in 1861.

Jane and Anthony Rouse were one of many farm families who had helped make Wisconsin the wheat basket of the nation by the early 1860s. Jane, of Scottish descent, had just given birth to her second son. In between her many household chores, she took care of the children and worked on her quilt. She used brown fabric from her husband's shirts, small print shirtings from young Henry's and Will's nightclothes, and a pink vine print from her own garments. She cut the leftover fabrics to create four Star of Bethlehem blocks and joined them to form a

quilt top. Jane saved a small bit of Turkey red print and green calico from her scrap bag with which to fashion a three-sided border and added a few red diamonds to each star.

The glamour and fervor of men marching off to war dimmed, and the Rouse family felt immense sadness as their community began to bury its Civil War casualties. Jane's Stars of Bethlehem quilt was destined to become a memorial quilt when Will died shortly before his first birthday and her third son, Martin, died of "brain fever" at the age of two. He was buried next to Will in Old Pioneer Cemetery, and the memory of the boys' short lives was recorded forever in the diamonds of their mother's quilt.[26]

Rose Wreath and Double Irish Chain

Lucy's quilt includes delicate stuffed work on the roses and embroidered details on the flowers. She appliquéd the leaves in the miniature corner wreaths with small buttonhole stitches.

PATTERN: *Rose Wreath*
DATE: *1865*
MAKER: *Lucy Hephzibah Sayles Gilbert Netherwood (1841–1918)*
ORIGIN: *Dane County, Wisconsin*
FINISHED SIZE: *81½" x 81½"*
FABRIC: *Cotton*
OWNER: *Martha Curless, granddaughter of the maker*
LOCATION: *Unknown*

Diagonal quilting lines, ⅛ inch apart in the white spaces and crossing in the center of each small square, show Ann's excellent quilting skills.

PATTERN: *Double Irish Chain*
DATE: *1865*
MAKER: *Ann Roxy Sayles (1845–1900)*
ORIGIN: *Dane County, Wisconsin*
FINISHED SIZE: *79" x 70¾"*
FABRIC: *Cotton*
OWNER: *Marge Syoen, great-great grandniece of the maker*
LOCATION: *Kendall County, Illinois*

Young girls and their mothers, husbands, brothers, and sons were all touched by the war. But in spite of it, the day-to-day tasks continued. Lucy Sayles Gilbert had already lost her brother Mordecai in the Civil War when she began her Rose Wreath quilt, and within months her older brother, Harrison, would lose a leg in the battle of Vicksburg.

Lucy's husband, Thomas, had joined the Union army with her brothers in August 1861. All three were assigned to Company E of the 8th Infantry. When Mordecai died in August 1862, Lucy, with her infant daughter, Addie, at her side, continued making quilts with her sisters, Ann and Polly of Cross Plains, in honor of a brother who gave his life for the Union.

Thomas was killed in Alabama in 1865, less than two weeks before the end of the war. Lucy remained in Oregon, Wisconsin, and purchased a home in 1866. She married a Civil War veteran, Charles Netherwood, in 1868 and had six more children. Lucy's last surviving granddaughter, Martha Curless, continued to live in the house Lucy bought in Kendal County, Illinois, and always displayed her grandmother's Rose Wreath quilt on a bed.

Lucy's sister Ann made a Double Irish Chain quilt while her sisters worked on other pieces during the war. The quilt was completed in 1865, and Ann signed it twice, once on the front and again on a back corner. Ann never married, and the quilt was passed down to descendants of her sister Sarah. The present owners of the Rose Wreath and Double Irish Chain quilts made by Lucy and Ann were not aware of their relationship until the quilts were photographed and displayed in a State Historical Society of Wisconsin quilt exhibit in 1983.[35]

Multicolor Pineapple

Elizabeth's quilt reflects the wide variety of cotton prints manufactured during the nineteenth century, including a "pinwheel" printed patchwork.

PATTERN: *Multicolor Pineapple*

DATE: *After 1864*

MAKER: *Elizabeth Lindredge Weekes Humphreys (1831–1915)*

ORIGIN: *Grundy County, Illinois*

FINISHED SIZE: *76" x 76"*

FABRIC: *Cotton*

OWNER: *Robin Engl, great-great-granddaughter of the maker*

LOCATION: *Waukesha County, Wisconsin*

Thomas Weekes married Elizabeth Lindredge in Illinois in the 1850s. Their life together ended during the Civil War, when Thomas died in a prison in Richmond, Virginia.

In order to support herself and two sons, Elizabeth opened a millinery shop in Morris, Illinois, in 1864. She was considered a fine seamstress and built a steady clientele. She used the narrow strips of reds and browns, muted blues, and tiny shirtings left over at the end of the day to create the whirling blocks of the Pineapple pattern. The design formed by the graded colors also resembled the blades of prairie windmills standing sentinel on neighboring farms.

Elizabeth remarried and, with her new husband, John Humphreys, moved to a farm in Blackstone, Illinois, taking her quilt and bag of scraps with her. After her second husband's death, Elizabeth and her daughter Edith Elizabeth again packed the Pineapple quilt and joined Elizabeth's two oldest sons in Nebraska, where they had walked from Illinois to stake claims to new land.

The name Elizabeth was handed down in each succeeding generation as a tribute to the first Elizabeth, the maker of the quilt. Edith Elizabeth's daughter Bess, who lived in Illinois, cared for the quilt until she was ninety-two. In 1988 she presented the quilt to her granddaughter, and once again the quilt and its family story made a journey, this time to Wisconsin.[36]

Quilt maker Elizabeth Lindredge Weekes Humphreys, fifty-eight years old. (Photo courtesy of Robin Engl.)

Even though many women joined the work force during the war, not everyone could find a means of support. The following excerpt is from a letter written by Mrs. Clara Bowen of Genesee, Waukesha County, addressed to the Military Relief Fund:

"I have one babe just three months old, and no one to do anything, and out of wood; no shoes to my feet, and but very little to eat. Is not this hard, to have my husband taken away from me, and not one cent to help myself with?"[39]

Wisconsin soldiers served with distinction in every major battle of the Civil War. The famous Iron Brigade, composed of Wisconsin, Indiana, and Michigan volunteers, was hailed as the "dyingest" brigade in the Union army. The Calico Boys of the Iron Brigade's 6th Wisconsin Volunteer Infantry included men like James P. Sullivan, a farmer-turned-volunteer who carried a canteen of fresh milk into battle.[37]

Gottlieb and Elisabeth Torke, Sheboygan, Wisconsin, c. 1870. (Photo courtesy of Leona Torke Kane.)

Elisabeth Torke was only 21 years old and struggling to care for her two baby girls alone. She managed their Sheboygan County homestead while her husband, Gottlieb, served with the Calico Boys. His letters home were filled with concern for Elisabeth and the children and were interspersed with directions for managing the farm. Following are excerpts of the letters, written between December 1864 and February 1865, as translated from the original German by their owner, Leona Torke Kane:

"About the turnips, when you think they will not keep, give them up and feed them all away before they rot; and with the potatoes pull them out if there should be a little snow and before the ground has frozen hard…then carry 10 or 15 bushels into brother Wilhelm's cellar. That you should do on a nice warm day so that you don't freeze on the way…

"Cut the turnips up in small pieces for the cattle so that no accident happens. You can also cut some for the sheep…

"You wrote me that you want to sow in the clearing, but I advise you to let the clearing be, and don't take upon yourself that trouble and work. You have enough land within the big fence, where you clear off the land and plow good…remember that I am not at home and you have lots of hay to make. If you want, you can fence in a corner of the clearing and plant rutabagas…

"If it is God's merciful will and I come home again, then we have still the hope to celebrate next Christmas together. Oh, that dear God may have pity on our country and give us peace…"

Gottlieb survived the war and returned home to Elisabeth and their family. The Torkes had nine more children.[38]

Appliquéd Roses

PATTERN: *Appliquéd Roses*
DATE: *1865*
MAKER: *Sarah Ide Howe (1831–1907)*
ORIGIN: *Dane County, Wisconsin*
FINISHED SIZE: *70" x 89"*
FABRIC: *Cotton*
OWNER: *State Historical Society of Wisconsin.*
   Donated by Miss Margaret Shelton
LOCATION: *Dane County, Wisconsin*

Sarah Ide Howe was fortunate that her husband was a physician and far from the dangers of the battlefield. They lived near the town of Oregon, where Dr. Isaac Howe practiced medicine and built a drug and grocery store. Sarah purchased the exact fabrics she needed to make a spectacular Appliquéd Roses quilt in 1865. Her quilt was opulent, with plump roses, tiny buttonhole stitches, and quilting measuring 11 stitches to the inch.

Circuit Rider (Birds and Flowers)

Catherine's quilt has borders on only two sides and was made for a single bed pushed against a wall.

PATTERN: *Circuit Rider (Birds and Flowers)*
DATE: *1860–1880*
MAKER: *Catherine Blockwitz Umbreit (1839–1896)*
ORIGIN: *Green Lake County, Wisconsin*
FINISHED SIZE: *76" x 79½"*

FABRIC: *Cotton*
OWNERS: *Pat and Jim Simonsen, great-grandson of the
  maker*
LOCATION: *Eau Claire County, Wisconsin*

Women found solace in quilting through hard times and loneliness. Even those whose husbands did not go to war found powerful meaning in the gathering, the assemblage, and the stitching of fabric.

Catherine Blockwitz left her home in Germany when she was four years old and came to America with her mother and sisters in 1843. They joined their father in New York and five years later moved to the town of Manchester, near Green Lake, to farm. On March 1, 1860, Catherine married a young German by the name of Traugott Umbreit, who kept a detailed diary most of his life. He was pleased with Catherine and praised her in his journal: "My wife was known as a very industrious farm girl who knew how to cook, bake, wash, sew, milk cows, chop wood, dig, and bind. She could adapt herself to anything. That is the way I knew her. It must have been God's guidance and will that we married."

Traugott became a minister and was licensed to preach by the Wisconsin Conference of the Evangelical Church on May 4, 1865. He accepted the call as a circuit rider and served many missions throughout Wisconsin, mostly in the Milwaukee and Madison areas. Even though he was often invited to stay in homes along the way, it was a solitary existence. While her husband was on the road, Catherine stayed busy and in her spare time created her Birds and Flowers quilt using a pattern and colors from her German heritage.[40]

Wedding picture of quilt maker Catherine Blockwitz Umbreit and Traugott Umbreit, 1860. (Photo courtesy of Jim Simonsen.)

Star of LeMoyne with Appliqué Border

PATTERN: *Star of LeMoyne with Appliqué Border*
DATE: *Mid-1860s*
MAKER: *Cornelia Guepner*
ORIGIN: *Pittsburgh, Pennsylvania*
FINISHED SIZE: *93" x 93"*

FABRIC: *Cotton*
OWNER: *Cornelia Rowell Greve, granddaughter of the*
original recipient of the quilt
LOCATION: *Ozaukee County, Wisconsin*

Cornelia Rowell Greve, left, and her Aunt Cornelia, Milwaukee, Wisconsin, 1934. (Photo courtesy of Cornelia Greve.)

Margaret Guepner Taylor, who received the Cornelia quilt when she and her husband moved to Cincinnati in the mid-1860s. (Photo courtesy of Cornelia Greve.)

Cornelia Guepner tried to maintain a sense of normalcy as she worked on a Star of LeMoyne quilt during the waning days of the Civil War. She was pleased with the effect of the combination of double pink seaweed and blue diamonds in the hand-pieced stars covering the center of the quilt. It is not known if Cornelia was related to Margaret Guepner Taylor, but Cornelia's finished quilt became a gift to Margaret when Margaret and her husband moved to Cincinnati from Pennsylvania at the close of the Civil War.

Margaret named her first daughter Cornelia, who became the owner of the quilt. In 1917 Cornelia Taylor moved to Hartland to live with her sister, Grace Taylor Rowell, Grace's husband, and their daughter Cornelia. When Cornelia Rowell was in her early twenties, she received the treasured quilt from her aunt. Cornelia said, "I always knew about the quilt and remember my Aunt Neal (Cornelia Taylor) talking about it. She said that my Grandmother Margaret called Cornelia Guepner, the quilt maker, her best friend. The quilt was thought of as a very precious keepsake, a treasure, and was never used. For many years it was kept in a trunk. Long before I received the quilt, my mother put a label on it with the date it was made and all the Cornelias' names. We always called it the Cornelia quilt."[41]

Tumbling Blocks

PATTERN: *Tumbling Blocks*
DATE: *c. late 1870s*
MAKER: *Martha Ruth Hamilton Gourley (1846–1924)*
ORIGIN: *Big Run, Pennsylvania*

FINISHED SIZE: *76½" x 74½"*
FABRIC: *Silk, velvet, cotton*
OWNER: *Ann Hill, great-granddaughter of the maker*
LOCATION: *Milwaukee County, Wisconsin*

Quilts often become a medium for stories that might otherwise never have been passed from one generation to another. Martha Ruth Hamilton Gourley thought of the many lives that had been lost as she pieced a Tumbling Blocks quilt in the late 1870s, after the Civil War had ended. She thought of her childhood sweetheart, George Gourley, who ran away from home at the age of sixteen to join the Union forces. George was in the army for four years and spent the last nine months in Georgia's Andersonville Prison. The conditions there were deplorable, and many young men died. George came home desperately ill. Martha and George finally married in 1872, but George never fully recovered. The quilt and its story became a part of life for Ann Hill, Martha's great-granddaughter, in Wisconsin when she acquired it in 1964.[42]

Martha Ruth Hamilton Gourley's album, thimble, and diary. (Photo courtesy of Ann Hill.)

Lone Star

A 1943 quilt made from a Civil War uniform.

PATTERN: *Lone Star*
DATE: *1943*
MAKER: *Mary Catherine Trussoni Garvalia*
 Levendoski (1899–1970)
ORIGIN: *Vernon County, Wisconsin*

FINISHED SIZE: *69" x 92"*
FABRIC: *Wool*
OWNER: *Marilyn Leum, niece of the maker*
LOCATION: *Vernon County, Wisconsin*

Sometimes quilts have been made long after a particular event. They serve as juxtaposed fragments, enabling the viewer to witness personal stories that reach beyond the edges, beyond generational boundaries. And so it is with a unique quilt made from an old Civil War uniform. Although the quilt was made in 1943 by Mary Catherine Levendoski, its story began fifty-four years earlier, when her father, Lorenzo Trussoni, left Italy and made his way to America. He married and settled in Genoa, overlooking the Mississippi River in western Wisconsin. Mary was the second of nine children born to the Trussoni family. She grew up and married Vincent Garvalia in 1919. They had five children. When Vincent died in 1942, Mary remained on the Garvalias' farm, worked the land, and raised her five boys. She married Fredrick Levendoski in 1948.

Times were hard on the farm near Genoa, and Mary was grateful that she could sew and make her own quilts and other household furnishings. When she was forty-four years old, World War II had just begun, and fabric was scarce. Her neighbor offered an old Civil War uniform found in their attic as possible quilt material. Mary soaked the blue uniform in cold water for three days to remove the bloodstains of Joseph Woodward, Company D, 3rd Wisconsin Regiment, who had been wounded in battle. (The first recruits from Wisconsin were outfitted in gray uniforms, the same color as troops from the South. Joseph must have been wounded in 1862 or later, after Northern troops had been issued blue uniforms.) Mary cut the blue fabric into diamonds and pieced them with matching black diamonds to make a Lone Star design, preserving the uniform of a soldier who fought in a war so long ago…a soldier she never knew.[43]

Wisconsin's woolen industry was strongly affected by the call for wool during the Civil War. With the shortage of southern cotton and the need for army blankets and uniforms, Wisconsin's coarse fleeces were in high demand. Appleton Woolen Mill, utilizing the Fox River's inexpensive power source, became known for the manufacture of Union army uniforms.[44]

On September 23, 1861, the acting secretary of war sent a directive to the governors of all the loyal states: "The department respectfully requests that no troops hereafter furnished by your State for the service of the government be uniformed in gray, that being the color generally worn by the enemy. The blue uniform adopted for the Army of the United States is recommended as readily distinguishable from that of the enemy."[45]

Chapter 3

Urbanization and Industrialization, 1865-1885

Between 1870 and 1890, the number of Wisconsin female industrial workers rose from 3,784 to 12,751. Besides maintaining homes, women found a variety of ways in which to become wage earners. In Milwaukee, the manufacture of clothing, including knits, gloves, hats, and caps, employed sixty-seven hundred women pieceworkers, some working at home rather than in factories. Tailors also often farmed out their piecework to women at home. Women edged their way into male-dominated fields, including those of factory-made clothing, hosiery, and knitting mills.[1]

Retailing and the office and counting rooms of businesses and manufacturers remained male domains at the end of the Civil War decade. Just ninety-eight women in Wisconsin worked as clerks and accountants in retail stores, according to an 1870 occupational census. Change came slowly as more women moved into retail; and after the invention of the first practical typewriter in Milwaukee in the 1870s, women also became office stenographers, typists, clerks, and copyists.[2]

Teaching was considered a more genteel occupation for women. By 1874, women outnumbered men by two to one in the classroom, and by 1890 the number of female teachers had almost doubled. Average wages for men teaching in country districts in 1874 were $47.44 per month, while women earned $32.13.[3]

The Industrial Revolution in the United States had its beginnings when some of women's textile work was removed from the home. Mechanized spinning and weaving was followed by factory-produced cloth, and those developments had a profound impact on quilting. Cotton was less costly, and printed cottons

became standard fare for American quilters.[4] By 1900 more than two-thirds of the world's silk was woven in the United States, and mass production made silk fabrics affordable for quiltmakers.[5]

The sewing process and quiltmaking would be forever altered by the advances in fabric-dyeing techniques and the commercial production and distribution of textiles and sewing supplies. As women shifted from square-cut styles to more fitted fashions, cut-away fabric from store-bought cotton made remnants readily available for pieced quilts.[6]

Printed patterns and the invention of the sewing machine made dressmaking less labor intensive and influenced the design revolution in nineteenth-century American quiltmaking.[7] Elias Howe, a New England mechanic, invented the sewing machine in 1846. It would take the combined efforts of several companies, including the Singer Company, and Howe to make it available to clothing manufacturers. The larger market of at-home women became a successful one once Victorian men were convinced that women could operate machines and would not "run wild" after being freed from the labor of hand-sewing. Women embraced the first home appliance made readily available to them, a "metal workhorse" that revolutionized women's sewing.[8]

Many late-nineteenth-century quiltmakers used their sewing machines to construct quilt tops and did the finishing by hand. This mixture of hand and machine sewing appears repeatedly in quilts made in the last quarter of the nineteenth century. By the turn of the century, many families owned a sewing machine; women knew how to use them efficiently and took them enough for granted that they again returned to appliquéing and quilting by hand.[9]

Appliquéd Flowers

Ann Balson made this quilt to celebrate the birth of her first grandchild. See page 190-191 for construction pattern.

PATTERN: *Appliquéd Flowers*
DATE: *1869*
MAKER: *Ann Treleven Balson (1810–1896)*
ORIGIN: *Fond du Lac County, Wisconsin*
FINISHED SIZE: *80½" x 82"*
FABRIC: *Cotton*
OWNERS: *David and Beverly Batson. David is the nephew of Lucille Batson, the great-granddaughter of the maker*
LOCATION: *Fond du Lac County, Wisconsin*

Quilts that have been preserved over the years have a mysterious beauty that is part of the past. It may be a piece of fabric or a certain color or stitch that reminds us that quilt makers were women much like ourselves. Their lives, however, were very different from ours.

Ann and James Balson and their seven-year-old son, John, left Cornwall, England, in 1843 to cross the Atlantic and claim land in Fond du Lac County, Wisconsin. They joined the Treleven boys, Ann's brothers, who had staked claims there the previous year. Ann had buried two babies in England before their first birthdays and would bury two more in Wisconsin. Her only surviving child, John, was her firstborn.

In 1869 Ann worked the Appliquéd Flowers quilt for John in celebration of his first son, Alvin. She chose Turkey red, golden orange, and yellow-green for the stylized flowers and leaves. Her fine quilting stitches measured ten to the inch. The quilt became a family heirloom. Since 1925 the Treleven and Balson families have held annual reunions in Fond du Lac County, where the quilt is displayed in honor of Ann and her strength and courage in making a new home in America.[13]

Quiltmaker Ann Treleven Balson, Fond du Lac, Wisconsin, c. 1868-1873. (Photo courtesy of Lucille K. Balson.)

Rob Peter to Pay Paul

Eliza bartered fresh eggs at a dry goods store for the fabric for this quilt.

PATTERN: *Rob Peter to Pay Paul*
DATE: *c. 1870*
MAKER: *Elizabeth Thoermer Baeten (1852–1944)*
ORIGIN: *Brown County, Wisconsin*
FINISHED SIZE: *61" x 70"*

FABRIC: *Cotton*
OWNER: *Helen M. Ley Flanagan, granddaughter of the maker*
LOCATION: *Brown County, Wisconsin*

Elizabeth Thoermer was the eldest of five sisters in her Irish immigrant family and a dedicated quiltmaker. The Thoermers lived near Wrightstown, in northeastern Wisconsin, where Eliza stitched quilts while waiting for her father to return from the Civil War.

Eliza fell in love with John Baeten, a tall man from Holland. They planned to be married when he returned from the Dakota Territory, where he had gone to stake a 160-acre claim under the Homestead Act. Eliza quilted while she waited for her fiancé, and in early 1870 she pieced a red and white curved-seam Rob Peter to Pay Paul quilt for her hope chest. She acquired the fabric at a dry goods store in exchange for fresh eggs. Eliza was the most diligent of the Thoermer sisters in preparing a hope chest and put her finest hand-stitches into her quilt. She had a collection of hand-sewn trousseau quilts and gave several to her youngest sister, Rose, who married before Eliza.

By the time the red and white quilt was completed, John had returned to Wrightstown. He and Eliza were married in January 1881 and planned to leave for the Dakota Territory in the spring. But when the snow had melted and the wagon, team, and supplies were readied, Eliza refused to leave Wisconsin. Being the oldest daughter, Eliza was given the family farm in Brown County, where she and John farmed and raised a family.[10]

Helen Flanagan of Green Bay, granddaughter of Elizabeth Thoermer Baeten, remembers the thirteen years her grandmother lived with her family following her grandfather's death and the stories she told. "My grandmother talked about her Irish relatives and how the women helped one another. They walked or hitched a horse and cart and came to one another's homes to sew, quilt, bake bread, or work at anything that needed to be done. They brought their babies, their children, sewing materials, seeds, hoes, axes, and plenty of news to be shared. If someone was sick or having a baby, they came and stayed as long as necessary. There was always at least one woman who was a midwife. Sometimes, if the weather turned stormy or very cold, some of the women stayed all night and left early in the morning. They did a lot of quilting during the night by lamplight."[11]

The Baeten family, Wrightstown, Wisconsin, c. 1920. Quiltmaker Elizabeth Thoermer Baeten is seated at far right; her husband, John Baeten, is seated at far left. (Photo courtesy of Helen Ley Flanagan.)

Folk Animals and Flowers

*With the help of her four sons, Eva Kraus made this special wedding quilt for her daughter Sevina.
Eva lived to be 101 years old.*

PATTERN: *Folk Animals and Flowers*

DATE: *c. 1870*

MAKER: *Eva Frank Kraus (1827–1928)*

ORIGIN: *Iowa County, Wisconsin*

FINISHED SIZE: *69" x 89½"*

FABRIC: *Cotton*

OWNER: *Kathleen Hanold, great-granddaughter of the maker*

LOCATION: *Milwaukee County, Wisconsin*

Eva Frank had just turned fourteen when she married Martin Kraus, a hired man on her parents' small farm in Germany. They lived with her parents and helped work the farm. When her parents died, the couple immigrated to America with their two children, John and Elizabeth.

They left Germany in 1849. Eva was three months pregnant, and they were convinced that the three-month ocean journey would be over in time for the baby to be born in America. But halfway across the Atlantic the schooner lay helplessly becalmed, and in spite of daily prayers for wind, the journey took six months. Food supplies were depleted, illness was rampant, and half of the fifty passengers died. Near starvation, Eva gave birth to a daughter, Julia, but was unable to produce milk for the infant. The baby might have died were it not for a young Jewish mother who nursed Eva's baby as well as her own on the last days of the ocean journey.

As the ship sailed within sight of America, the Kraus's three-year-old daughter, Elizabeth, died. Eva and Martin did not want her buried at sea, and they requested permission to keep her body until the ship landed. She was laid to rest in a small grave in New York. Only then did the Kraus family start their long overland journey west.

Wedding picture of Sevina Kraus and Henry Harms, Iowa County, Wisconsin, 1870. (Photo courtesy of Kathleen Hanold.)

Seven more children were born to Eva and Martin in southwestern Wisconsin, where Martin cleared the land and built a log cabin. In 1870, as Eva's daughter Sevina was planning her wedding to Henry Harms, her mother asked Sevina's four brothers to help make a Folk Animals and Flowers wedding quilt. Bill, Coon, Ernest, and Leonard each drew an animal to be added to the pots of flowers that surrounded the two center blocks Eva had already completed. Eva chose red, yellow, and green fabrics reminiscent of the German folk art of her childhood.

Henry commissioned the preacher, who earned part of his living as a skilled woodworker, to build a wedding bed. Henry and Sevina lived with his parents until they had saved enough money to purchase land near the Wisconsin River. They built a large two-story home complete with a huge porch and second-floor balcony.

The quilt, a special gift from mother to daughter, still rests today on the same hand-carved bed.[12]

This quilt survived the Peshtigo fire and was used as a protective covering during the catastrophe.

PATTERN: *Log Cabin, Dark and Light Diamonds*
DATE: *c. late 1860s*
MAKER: *Name unknown*
ORIGIN: *Marinette County, Wisconsin*
FINISHED SIZE: *68" x 88"*
FABRIC: *Wool, cotton twill*
OWNER: *Elinor Czarnecki, who purchased the quilt from a descendant of the maker's husband*
LOCATION: *Dodge County, Wisconsin*

Log Cabin, Dark and Light Diamonds

Peshtigo Harbor, located on Lake Michigan's Green Bay, was the place at which some new immigrants disembarked from the Great Lakes schooner or steamer that had brought them to Wisconsin. By the 1860s they could travel by railroad six miles inland, to the settlement of Peshtigo. That same railroad carried lumber and other goods to be shipped by water to eastern markets.

Sometime in the late 1860s, the wife of an engineer at the Peshtigo Harbor Railroad made a scrap quilt in the Log Cabin pattern, a quilt that would be warm and serviceable for Wisconsin winters. It was a utility quilt, made of wool and cotton in stripes, checks, plaids, and prints. The heavy blocks were pieced together and tied over a rust-colored, pinstriped back. The quilt maker, whose name is unknown, was more concerned with practicality than beauty and could never have imagined how important the quilt would become or how it would be remembered.

In the summer of 1871, the entire country was

The Newberry family lost twelve members whose names are listed on each side of this gravestone in the Town of Drover Cemetery. (Photos by Linda S. Moore.)

Grave marker of a victim of the Peshtigo fire, at the Town of Grover (formerly Sugar Bush) Cemetery, three miles south of Peshtigo.

parched by prolonged drought. It was a common practice for hunters, lumberjacks, railroad workers, and farmers to burn tree stumps and rubble. But because of the unique combination of drought and strong October winds, several such fires raged out of control, blazing a wide path from Appleton, Wisconsin, to Menominee, Michigan. By Sunday, October 8, residents of Peshtigo sensed doom in the hot, eerie calm that surrounded the village. Gray ash from distant fires filtered onto wooden sidewalks, and the sky was a smoke-filled bronze. As evening settled, a terrifying roar exploded to the southwest.

Flames driven by gale-force winds turned homes and people alike into instant torches. As the city was consumed by fire, many fled in terror, hoping to reach the waters of the Peshtigo River.[14]

According to Stella VanBogart, curator of the Peshtigo Fire Museum, "When the wind came up, many people were in bed, and all they could do was try to get to the river, and within one hour the entire city was gone."

The Peshtigo Harbor Railroad engineer, husband of the quilt maker, wet down the nearest cloth he could reach, which was the Log Cabin quilt, and placed it over his head. He loaded his train with people and drove back and forth to the harbor over and over again. His courage and quick thinking—and the quilt's wet, protective surface—saved many lives that night. The two railroad engines were consumed by flames, and all that remained were the boilers of the two locomotives. Iron tracks were twisted, and the wooden ties under them were powdered into ash. But the quilt survived, a tattered emblem of one of the worst natural catastrophes in the history of the Middle West.

The notorious Chicago fire also occurred on October 8. It overshadowed the Peshtigo fire in spite of the fact that five times as many people died in Wisconsin. An estimated twelve hundred people perished, but the true total will never be known.[15] Almost twenty-five hundred square miles were burned, wiping out entire towns on both sides of Green Bay. Whole farmsteads and isolated logging camps were erased, leaving no trace of life. Many of those who survived died later of injuries or starvation.[16]

Wesley Dukel was six years old at the time of the fire and at the age of ninety-three still remembered it as the worst forest fire in American history. "When the balls of fire started coming down that night, my mother and father took us down to the spring. We lay down on the ground. They wrapped us with wet quilts. A ball of fire hit the house, and it burned. But my sister saved the sewing machine. She wrapped it in wet blankets."[17]

Rev. Peter Pernin, a Catholic priest, later wrote in his journal, "Clothing and quilts had been thrown into the river, to save them, doubtless, and they were floating all around. I caught at some that came within reach and covered with them the heads of the persons who were leaning against or clinging to me."[18]

Annie designed a quilt in red, white, and blue fabric to commemorate the 1876 centennial.

PATTERN: *Streak of Lightning*
DATE: *1876–1877*
MAKER: *Annie Kiesling Miller (1858–1938)*
ORIGIN: *Jefferson County, Wisconsin*
FINISHED SIZE: *65" x 75"*
FABRIC: *Cotton*
OWNER: *Hoard Historical Museum, Fort Atkinson, Wisconsin. Donated by Hazel Leonard, granddaughter of the maker.*
LOCATION: *Jefferson County, Wisconsin*

Streak of Lightning

The United States of America celebrated its centennial in 1876. Picnics, parades, and baseball games were held in large and small communities across Wisconsin. Women worked diligently to make sure the state was well represented at the Centennial Exposition in Philadelphia. They organized Women's Centennial Clubs throughout the state, and Mrs. J. G. Thorpe was appointed to the chair.[19] One of the needlework pieces that resulted was a centennial medallion incorporating the Beloit College seal. It was stitched on satin, with silk and velvet, by Mrs. S. B. Bodtker of Beloit and displayed in a gilt frame.[20]

During the summer of 1876, eighteen-year-old Annie Kiesling became engaged to marry Peter Miller. Annie designed a quilt for her hope chest and wanted to use red, white, and blue fabric to commemorate the

centennial. She persuaded her father, who was partial to Mr. Bullwinkle's store, to let her buy new fabric for the quilt top from the fine selection of calicoes at Mrs. Weber's dry goods store in nearby Helenville.

Annie and Peter were married on March 11, 1878, and settled on a farm near Fort Atkinson in Jefferson County. They felt at home among their German neighbors, who welcomed them with customs the young couple found comforting and familiar. The completed Streak of Lightning quilt was proudly displayed over the corn-husk mattress on the Miller rope bed for many years, long enough for Annie's granddaughter Hazel to remember sleeping under it as a child. The quilt was an integral part of the sixty-four years that Annie and Peter were married and was bequeathed to Hazel after Annie's death.[21]

Carrie Howe was a milliner who pieced her vibrant optical-illusion quilt top from silk and velvet scraps.

PATTERN: *Baby Blocks*
DATE: *Begun 1877, completed c. 1880*
MAKER: *Carrie Brownlow Howe (1860–1937)*
ORIGIN: *Rockford, Illinois, and Walworth County, Wisconsin*
FINISHED SIZE: *72" x 90"*
FABRIC: *Silk and velvet*
OWNER: *Karen A. Varhula, great-granddaughter of the maker*
LOCATION: *Walworth County, Wisconsin*

Baby Blocks

In an era when ready-to-wear garments were not available, most women made their own clothing and gradually turned dressmaking and millinery into trades that could be carried out at home. With the rising standard of living, new methods of textile production, and the affordability of sewing machines, dressmaking and millinery ranked as the fourth most popular occupation for women in the 1880s. By the year 1900, almost eighty-three thousand American women earned their living by making hats, and at least twelve thousand were proprietors of their own shops.[23]

Carrie Brownlow lived with her parents in Illinois, fifteen miles south of the Wisconsin border. She worked in a small milliner's shop throughout the summer of 1877 and at the age of sixteen was an excellent seamstress. Her stitches were tiny and sure, and the hats she created were fashionable and in demand. At the end of each day the owner of the shop allowed Carrie to

gather the scraps of fabric. From these scraps Carrie cut diamonds for a Baby Blocks quilt, a common pattern in Victorian England using a single repetitive shape throughout. She pieced the dark-, medium-, and light-colored blocks so that they rippled out from the center of the quilt top in concentric rectangles.

In December 1877, not long after Carrie's seventeenth birthday, she married Will Howe, a young farmer who shared her English Baptist heritage. Will had established a farm in Geneva Township, in Walworth County, Wisconsin. Carrie took her partly finished quilt top and bag of scraps with her and finished it in her new home. In 1902 Carrie and Will moved to nearby Elkhorn, where Will worked in a grocery store. Eleven years later he bought the store and renamed it Howe Groceries. Carrie helped her husband run the store until his death, when their son took over the business.[24]

Mariner's Compass

Great skill and patience were required to piece the narrow points of this unique quilt.

PATTERN: *Mariner's Compass*

DATE: *1876*

MAKER: *Johanna Quillinen Lane (c. 1835–?) and her daughter Elizabeth Ann Lane (1857–1944)*

ORIGIN: *Monroe County, Wisconsin*

FINISHED SIZE: *73½" x 83"*

FABRIC: *Cotton*

OWNER: *Wisconsin Quilt History Project. Donated by Mary Ellen Werner, great-granddaughter of the maker*

LOCATION: *Ozaukee County, Wisconsin*

Elizabeth Ann Lane Ebert had been a widow for thirty-three years when this photo was taken in 1914. (Photo courtesy of Mary Ellen Werner.)

Elizabeth Ann Lane, known as Lizzie, began teaching school when she was only fourteen years old. During the centennial year of 1876, at the age of nineteen, Lizzie and her mother, Johanna Quillinen Lane, made a trousseau quilt for Lizzie's upcoming marriage. The nation's birthday was reason enough to celebrate, but it was the young girl's wedding to Frederick Ebert on July 11 that had both women stitching an intricate Mariner's Compass, a design so unusual it might have been of their own creation.

Lizzie and Frederick moved to their farm home in Monroe County, taking the mother-daughter wedding quilt with them.

A year later Lizzie gave birth to a baby girl, Mary Ellen. Within four years Frederick had died, and Lizzie was forced to sell the farm and move to Tomah. She became a bookkeeper in order to support herself and her daughter. She never remarried, and the colorful quilt became a reminder of both her mother and her husband.[22]

Basket Weave

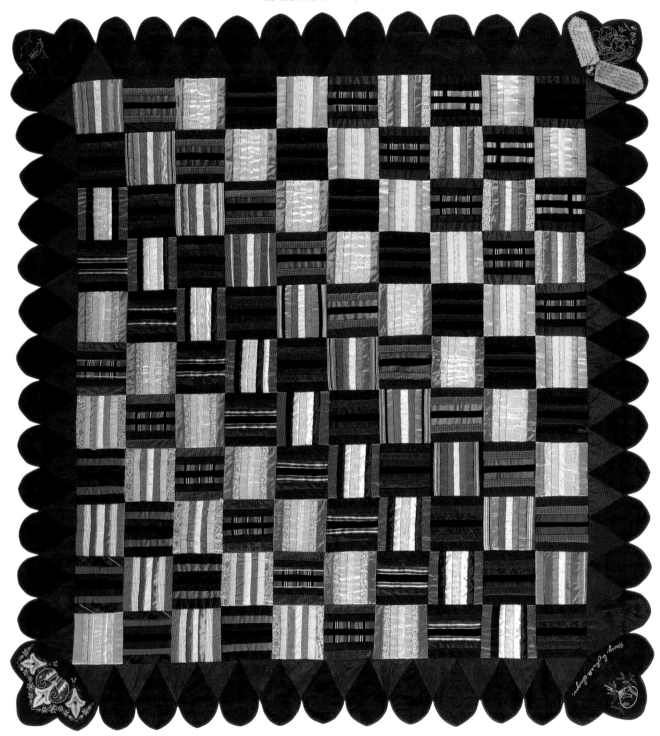

(Transparency courtesy of the Oshkosh Public Museum)

PATTERN: *Basket Weave*
DATE: *1883*
MAKER: *Mary E. Jewell Sawyer (1842–1910)*
ORIGIN: *Winnebago County, Wisconsin*
FINISHED SIZE: *62¼" x 57¼"*
FABRIC: *Silk, velvet brocade, satin*
OWNER: *Oshkosh Public Museum, Oshkosh,*
  Wisconsin. Donated by Edgar Sawyer.
LOCATION: *Winnebago County, Wisconsin*

Mary E. Jewell Sawyer (Photo courtesy of the Oshkosh Public Museum.)

Both Edgar P. Sawyer and his father, U.S. senator Philetus Sawyer, were pioneer residents of Oshkosh and can be credited with much of its growth and prosperity. Philetus Sawyer served in the state assembly at Madison and was in the national House of Representatives for ten years. He was involved in the lumber industry, became mayor of Oshkosh in 1863, and founded a bank for the city. His son Edgar never entered politics, but he followed in his father's footsteps in community service, as well as by supervising the family's landholdings and mills. The Sawyer homestead on Algoma Boulevard is now the Oshkosh Public Museum.[25]

In 1864 Edgar married Mary E. Jewell, the daughter of Henry Jewell, also a former mayor of Oshkosh and a member of the state legislature. They had two children, Nia and Phil. Mary was highly respected, not only for her community involvement, but also as a quilter. In 1883, in honor of her son's tenth birthday, she pieced a Basket Weave quilt with a handwritten message:

> *I know not what to others seem*
> *These patches gay and somber,*
> *To me they bring of life a dream,*
> *Wherein my darlings wander*
> *Too soon, alas! They leave behind,*
> *Their childish toys and graces;*
> *Then let me gaze on these dear scraps,*
> *While memory shows their faces.*
> *M. E. J. Sawyer*[26]

Mary's name can also be found on other quilts, including an autograph quilt top that, even though it was never completed, bore special verses and names of members of the Sawyer and Jewell families.[27]

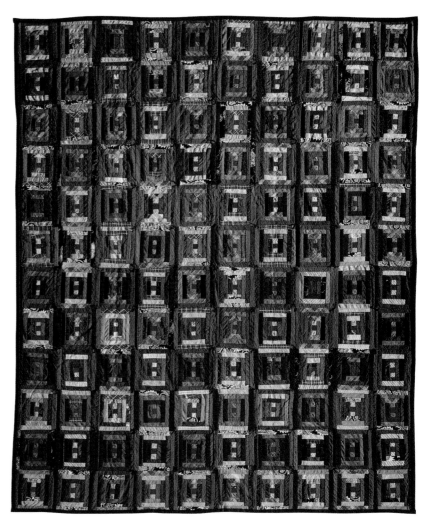

PATTERN: *Log Cabin, Courthouse Steps*

DATE: *1880–1885*

MAKER: *Karen Andersdatter Hagendahl (1825–1895)*

ORIGIN: *Waupaca County, Wisconsin*

FINISHED SIZE: *62¾" x 74½"*

FABRIC: *Wool, brocade*

OWNER: *Cynthia Holly, purchased from Carmen Barnes, granddaughter of the maker*

LOCATION: *Waupaca County, Wisconsin*

Log Cabin, Courthouse Steps

A steady procession of Danes, hoping to find economic freedom, came to Wisconsin during the last half of the nineteenth century. The largest urban group settled in Racine County, and a large rural settlement was established in central Wisconsin's Waupaca County. Danes maintained strong family ties and their proud culture by forming societies and organizations to preserve their language, literature, and music.[28]

Karen Andersdatter Hagendahl was an expert seamstress and embroiderer in the queen's service in Copenhagen before she and her husband, Carl, crossed the North Atlantic to Quebec in 1865. They traveled through the Great Lakes to Chicago and by stagecoach to Oshkosh, arriving just in time for the city's grand Fourth of July celebration. One of the Hagendahls' first impressions of their newly adopted country came from the large crowds of finely dressed people.

The family journeyed northwest and settled in the Waupaca area, where Carl built a house with the traditional detached summer kitchen in the back. In addition to her farm tasks, Karen made the family's clothing and quilts and taught her daughter, Martha Cecelia, how to sew.

Martha was six years old when the Hagendahls came to America. She became a schoolteacher when she was sixteen and taught for nine years. When Martha married a fellow Dane, Niels Jensen, in the spring of 1885, she was already considered an old maid at the age of twenty-five. Karen made a Log Cabin quilt in honor of her daughter's wedding, using strips of wool salvaged and gathered from men's suits, vests, and ties. In 1890 Karen and Martha pooled their resources and skills and opened a dressmaking establishment in Waupaca, offering young girls the opportunity to learn how to sew.[29]

Mary Jane made this quilt for her only child, Carrie.

PATTERN: *Blue and White Pineapple*
DATE: *1886*
MAKER: *Mary Jane Roberts Vernam (1849–1931)*
ORIGIN: *Clark County, Wisconsin*
FINISHED SIZE: *70" x 82"*
FABRIC: *Cotton*
OWNER: *Yvonne Bradley Yeager, great-granddaughter of the maker*
LOCATION: *Chippewa County, Wisconsin*

Quilt maker Mary Jane Roberts Vernam, Neillsville, Wisconsin, c. 1880. (Photo courtesy of Yvonne Bradley Yeager.)

Blue and White Pineapple

In 1886, following the tradition of her mother and grandmother, Mary Jane Vernam began hand-piecing a quilt in indigo blue prints and muslin. Mary Jane and her husband, Dallas, a tavern keeper, lived in the west-central Wisconsin town of Neillsville, near the Black River. The dry goods store on Hewitt Street sold tools, harnesses, sacks of sugar, and other necessities, as well as fabric. There Mary Jane chose a variety of colorfast indigo blue and white prints and a length of black and white pinstriped fabric for her Pineapple wedding quilt. She made it for her only child, Carrie, who married Wilder Newell on December 8, 1886. Carrie later made a gift of the quilt to her own daughter.[30]

Embroidered Penny Squares

A detail of the quilt that takes its name from the stamped squares purchased for a penny each.

PATTERN: *Embroidered Penny Squares*
DATE: *1888*
MAKER: *Margaret Porter Radcliffe (1863–1945)*
ORIGIN: *Milwaukee County, Wisconsin*
FINISHED SIZE: *70" x 80"*
FABRIC: *Cotton*
OWNER: *West Allis Historical Society. Donated by Margaret Jane Park, granddaughter of the maker*
LOCATION: *Milwaukee County, Wisconsin*

Quiltmaker Margaret Porter Radcliffe, West Allis, Wisconsin, c. 1928. (Photo courtesy of the West Allis Historical Society Collections.)

Margaret Porter, of Scottish and English heritage, grew up on Walker's Point, a finger of land extending through the swampy Milwaukee River valley, in an enclave that was more Yankee than the rest of Milwaukee, where the German language was heard more and more on the streets, and where German culture would soon dominate the city. Margaret was well educated and familiar with the social graces expected of a young city woman.

Margaret married James Edward Radcliffe and had the first of their three children in 1887. They named their first daughter Margaret. As the new mother cared for her infant, she began work on a quilt. The quilt was in Redwork, a then-popular style of red embroidered designs on eight-inch squares of muslin. The stamped squares could be purchased for a penny each and became known as Penny Squares.

The Radcliffe family moved from Milwaukee to West Allis when Margaret was forty-one years old. Her husband was the owner of Radcliffe Manufacturing Company, where Margaret did the bookkeeping while her children were in school. She was an advocate of education and a tireless organizer of groups and campaigns for various causes. She served as president of several women's clubs, on library and bank boards, and as a delegate to the International Congress of Women in 1920. She organized the Home Industries Association, which helped poor women in West Allis make goods in their homes and sell them. Margaret also organized Wisconsin's first Parent-Teacher Association and the Milwaukee Sentinel Cooking School, which gave women the opportunity to learn proper food preparation, nutrition, and entertaining.[31]

Embroidered Fund-Raiser

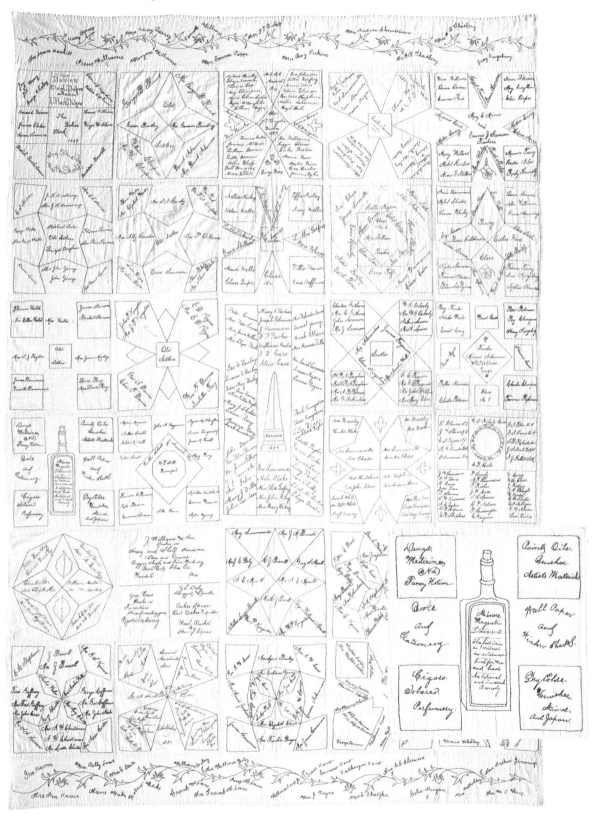

The Necedah Methodist Women's Society made a quilt to raise money for the refurbishment of their one-room church.

PATTERN: *Embroidered Fund-Raiser*
DATE: *1889*
MAKER: *Necedah Methodist Women's Society*
ORIGIN: *Juneau County, Wisconsin*
FINISHED SIZE: *54" x 76"*
FABRIC: *Cotton*
OWNER: *Necedah United Methodist Church*
LOCATION: *Juneau County, Wisconsin*

Throughout generations of quiltmaking, women used ingenuity and creativity in a wide variety of ways, including the making of quilts to raise money for specific causes. The names of people or businesses were embroidered on such quilts in exchange for payment. The quilt was then auctioned off, used as a raffle prize to raise additional funds, or sometimes presented to a leader in the community. Fund-raising quilts have done their part in raising money for everything from building churches and schools to supporting women's suffrage and furnishing orphanages. Although the money raised seems small by today's standards—three hundred to five hundred dollars per quilt—it was enough to establish a church, which could be built for seven hundred dollars in the late 1800s.[32]

In 1889, in the small lumbering town of Necedah, near the Wisconsin River in north-central Wisconsin, Alanzo Stillman carefully lettered the last of 502 signatures onto eleven-inch squares of muslin. Alanzo's wife had suggested he volunteer his penmanship for the Necedah Methodist Women's Society fund-raiser. The society had decided to make a quilt to help raise the needed money for refurbishing their small, one-room church, which had been built in 1857. Anyone who wanted to have his or her name lettered and then embroidered on the quilt could do so for ten cents.

The names were arranged by Sunday school classes, from the Cradle Roll to the more adult Pansy Class. Local businesses, including the pharmacy and dry goods store, supported the project by paying to have their names added, along with the goods and services they provided. One business used the tag line, "No whiskey sold here."

After all the names had been embroidered in red thread by the church women, the quilt was sold at auction to raise additional money. Mrs. John Kingston, wife of a pioneer lumberman of the area who had helped to establish the original Sunday school in 1852, was the highest bidder. By 1893 the church had been re-roofed and wallpapered and painted inside, due in large measure to the creative efforts of the women's society.

After many years the quilt was given to Alanzo Stillman's granddaughter Elizabeth Bussell, and she donated it to the Necedah United Methodist Church. The quilt's journey has come full circle; it is an important keepsake of Necedah's early years. People doing family research often come to look for names embroidered on its surface.[33]

Necedah United Methodist Church, Necedah, Juneau County, Wisconsin, as it looked in 1889. (Sketch by Creeko Creations, Johnson Creek, Wisconsin.)

Pyrotechnics and Family Tree

Ellen began piecing circular blocks in 1880. One hundred years later, her great-granddaughter Margaret Dopp Schliepp incorporated eighteen of the blocks into a Family Tree quilt.

PATTERN: *Pyrotechnics and Family Tree*
DATE: *c. 1880–1895, original blocks; c. 1980-1985,*
   additions and completion
MAKERS: *Ellen Lane Dopp (1819–1895) and*
   Margaret Dopp Schliepp (b.1916)
ORIGIN: *Portage County, Wisconsin*
FINISHED SIZE: *77" x 93½"*
FABRIC: *Cotton*
OWNERS: *Susan and Glenn Rasmussen, great-great-*
   grandson of the maker of the blocks
LOCATION: *Champlin, Minnesota*

Margaret Dopp and Glenn Rasmussen on their wedding day, June 8, 1940. This photo was taken on the steps of the Dopp Methodist Church, Portage County, Wisconsin. Glenn died in 1966, and Margaret married August Schliepp in 1969. (Photo courtesy of Margaret Dopp Rasmussen Schliepp.)

Ellen Dopp, in her early thirties with young children to care for, came with her husband, Henry, from Duchess, New York, to the farmland of central Wisconsin. In the spring of 1853, Henry and his brother William decided to leave Waukesha County and move their families 150 miles northwest, to Portage County.

Both Dopp families quickly began the rigorous work of clearing land and building homes. Their homesteads grew in proportion to their families, and they built a small country schoolhouse, called the Dopp School; a Methodist church, known as the Dopp Methodist Church; and a country graveyard—the Dopp Cemetery.

Through the years of raising five children, Ellen pieced quilts. In 1880, with her children gone

from home, she began piecing an unusual and intricate pattern called Pyrotechnics. Tiny triangles exploded like fireworks into rolling wheels of color in each of the unique circular blocks. It took great skill to make each one lie round and flat. Ellen completed twenty-three blocks, which she planned to make into a quilt. But in 1895, Henry died, and Ellen followed four months later. They were buried next to each other in the Dopp family cemetery.

Ellen's blocks were folded in a tea towel and placed in a trunk that was given to her only daughter. After the daughter's death, the trunk and its contents were passed on to Ellen's son Charles, who in turn gave the trunk to his oldest son, Robert. Robert kept the trunk, and the quilt blocks inside, wrapped in the tea towel, for another fifty years. In early 1940 he gave the trunk to his niece, who was Ellen's great-granddaughter, Margaret Dopp Rasmussen Schliepp.

Margaret grew up on a farm just two miles from the homestead, attended Dopp School, and was married to Glenn Rasmussen in the Dopp Methodist Church in 1940. Glenn died in 1966, and Margaret married August Schliepp in 1969. She was a mother, homemaker, and teacher. It was not until she had retired from teaching that she opened the trunk and considered making a quilt from Ellen's blocks, still wrapped in the tea towel. In 1980, one hundred years after Ellen had started piecing Pyrotechnics, Margaret used eighteen of the blocks to frame an elaborate family tree of her paternal grandfather's ancestors and descendants.

She placed Ellen's and Henry's names in the roots of the tree, their son Charles on the tree trunk, Uncle Robert and her father on the branches, herself and her sister on the apples, their children on the blossoms, and her grandchildren on the leaves. Five years passed between the time Margaret unwrapped the tea towel and the moment when she placed the final stitch in the quilt—a quilt that can be defined as a continuing legacy, a gift from one generation to the next.[34]

REMNANTS
FOR CRAZY PATCHWORK

SADIE'S SILKEN SHOWER OF SATIN SAMPLES

ART in needle-work is on the advance. We know the ladies delight in odd pieces of silk and satin,— "CRAZY QUILT" making is VERY POPULAR. We are sure we have a bargain that all ladies will now delight in. Bright, handsome, odd-shaped, and pretty colored goods accumulate very fast at all NECKTIE FACTORIES; for years have been burdened and over-run with remnants of many RICH GOODS. We have thousands of pieces of silk and satin on hand which we are going to give you a big trade on. People at a distance have hard times getting the right assortment to put into sofa-pillows, quilts, etc., and we can help you out now. We are going to dispose of this immense lot RIGHT OFF. Our packages contain from 99 to 168 pieces of the best quality assorted goods, and we want to get a lot introduced into every home; then you can order as you like for your friends, and MAKE MONEY doing our work and helping yourself also. Remember these pieces are carefully trimmed, and especially adapted to all sorts of fancy, art, and needle work. Many ladies sell tidies, fancy pillows, etc., at a great price made from these remnants. Order one sample lot now for only 25c. It would cost many dollars bought at a store. GRAND OFFER: If you order our great assorted lot AT ONCE, we will give you, absolutely FREE, five skeins of elegant embroidery silk, all different bright colors. This silk is worth nearly the price we ask for the remnants; but we know if you order ONE lot we will sell many in your locality, so make this liberal offer. Three lots for 65c.; five for $1.00. BEST WAY. We send ONE of the above complete assorted lots FREE to all who send 25 cents for 6 months subscription to "COMFORT," the best Home Monthly now published, or if you send for more than one lot as above, "COMFORT" goes for one year.

COMFORT PUB. CO., Box 115, Augusta, Maine.

BETTER YET. To all answering this ad. before 30 days we will also send 6 pieces of elegant PLUSH FREE. They come in Red, Blue, Green, Old Gold, etc.

This advertisement was printed in Ladies' World *magazine in September 1892.*

Chapter 4

New Lifestyles, 1875-1900

Along with urbanization and industrialization came another hallmark of the Victorian era: leisure time and more emphasis on decorative work.

In Victorian times, women assumed the responsibility of creating and maintaining well-decorated homes. They looked to books and magazines for guidance on interior design and decorating. They took to heart what was considered tasteful and copied fashionable decor by creating elegant accessories from everyday household objects. Decorative labor, or "fancywork," made it possible for a woman to furnish her home in an elegant and creative manner.[2]

Rural women were just as interested in fancywork as urban women, but they didn't have access to the same plush fabrics. Many found that less expensive materials, such as canvas and muslin, could be just as creatively decorated.[3]

The nation's Centennial Exposition, held in Philadelphia in 1876, was more than just a celebration. For women across the country who took part by providing items for the exposition, needlework took a step forward into what became known as the decorative arts movement. Art schools, decorative arts societies, and women's exchanges were established across the country, and women were encouraged to view their needlework as artistic as well as practical. Crazy quilts and outline embroidery quilts are believed to have been a direct response to the decorative arts movement and became popular and widespread in Wisconsin as well as throughout the nation.[4]

Each individual quiltmaker, although following a trend, gave expression to her own life experience and tried to make a quilt that was strong and clear and beautiful, something artistic that sustained her.

Crazy quilts reached their peak of popularity in the late nineteenth century and were made by sewing fancy fabric pieces, usually silk, onto a larger piece of lighter-weight foundation fabric. The quilts reflected the availability of silk fabric then being produced in America. It is believed that the term "crazy" referred to the irregular and unusual shapes of the individual fabric patches, much like crazed china when the glaze cracks and forms an odd, random pattern.[1]

Crazy Quilt with Crescent Moon

Esther Bate was in her sixties when she created a crazy quilt of silk, velvet, and embroidery.

PATTERN: *Crazy Quilt with Crescent Moon*
DATE: *c. 1890s*
MAKER: *Esther Heald Bate (1831–1911)*
ORIGIN: *Dane County, Wisconsin*
FINISHED SIZE: *69" x 71"*

FABRIC: *Silk, velvet*
OWNER: *Dr. Richard C. Haney, great-great-grandson of the maker*
LOCATION: *Walworth County, Wisconsin*

Quiltmaker Esther Hamlin Heald Bate (below) and her daughter, Beda Alice Bate (left), Black Earth, Wisconsin, 1888. (Photos courtesy of Dr. Richard C. Haney.)

Esther Heald was sixteen years old in 1847, when she left Maine with her mother to join her father and sisters in south-central Wisconsin. They arrived by way of the Erie Canal and the Great Lakes. At nineteen Esther completed teachers' training in Madison and began her teaching career in one-room country schools in northwestern Dane County. George Bate, superintendent of schools in the town of Berry, interviewed Esther for a teaching position in 1858 and was impressed with her eight years of experience and good moral character. He not only hired her, but also married her six months later. Because schoolmistresses were not allowed to teach after marriage, Esther devoted her life to being a homemaker and mother.

Through their years together, first on a farm east of Black Earth and then in town after 1870, Esther was involved in school activities, temperance meetings, and other community issues. Her ready wit was evident as women discussed concerns about "demon rum" and the need for women to be allowed to vote. During this time Esther raised a son and daughter and continued to pursue her hobbies of quilting and other needlework. After teaching her daughter Beda the intricacies of fine sewing, Esther and Beda opened a millinery shop in Black Earth in the early 1870s. Esther was in her sixties, widowed, and had married children when she created a crazy quilt of velvets, silks, and shimmering embroidery and tied over heavy wool. Beda's husband, Ed Wolferman, used the quilt for many years on the kitchen daybed, where he rested after doing his chores. [5]

Esther Heald Bate, her husband, George, and their children, William and Beda, in front of their home in Black Earth, Wisconsin, during the 1870s, several years before Esther made her crazy quilt. An extra room was later added to the house to accommodate a millinery shop for Esther and Beda.

Crazy Quilt with Corner Fans

Margaret used silk floss, silk chenille, metallic yarn, and oil paint on silk and silk velvet to complete a unique crazy quilt. (Transparency courtesy of the Milwaukee Art Museum.)

PATTERN: *Crazy Quilt with Corner Fans*
DATE: *1883*
MAKER: *Margaret Beattie (1860–?)*
ORIGIN: *Rock County, Wisconsin*
FINISHED SIZE: *64½" x 76"*
FABRIC: *Silk, velvet*
OWNER: *Milwaukee Art Museum, purchased with funds from Marion Wolfe, Mrs. Helen L. Pfeifer, and Friends of Art*
LOCATION: *Milwaukee County, Wisconsin*

Quiltmaker Maggie Beattie (seated at far right), Stoughton, Wisconsin, c. 1883. Dora Atkinson (standing at far right) signed the quilt and became Maggie's sister-in-law in 1886. (Photo courtesy of the Milwaukee Art Museum.)

Schoolmistress Maggie Beattie of Janesville, in south-central Wisconsin, worked on her crazy quilt in the early 1880s, when the popularity of crazy quilts was at its peak. Maggie added delicate painting on velvet and embroidered animals, flowers, and Kate Greenaway figures in intricate stitches on multicolored silks, velvets, and velveteens.

When Maggie completed the quilt, she embroidered the date, April 26, 1883, on the last block and added the quilt to her trousseau. She returned to her hometown of Stoughton in 1886 to become a bride, but the marriage was short lived, and she maintained her maiden name of Beattie. She had no children and bequeathed the quilt to a friend, Ida Mae Skinner. In 1997 the Milwaukee Art Museum acquired the quilt, an excellent example of the opulent needle art popular at the end of the nineteenth century, for its collection.[6]

Kate Greenaway was a popular English artist, and many of her illustrations could be found in children's books in the last half of the nineteenth century. In 1879 and 1880 *Harpers Bazaar* and *Godey's Lady's Book* featured embroidery patterns that were inspired by her book *Under the Window*, published in 1878. Most of the Greenaway figures were of children rolling hoops, sitting, or playing musical instruments.[7] They were featured in farm magazines, from which quilters could order tissue stamping patterns.

A Kate Greenaway pattern from the July 23, 1881, issue of Harpers Bazaar.

Crazy Quilt with Flowers

When Sarah Goodrich came home from China for a visit, she received this gift quilt, which she took with her when she returned to her missionary wor

PATTERN: *Crazy Quilt with Flowers (detail)*
DATE: *1885*
MAKERS: *Friends of Sarah Clapp Goodrich*
ORIGIN: *Milwaukee County, Wisconsin*
FINISHED SIZE: *71½" x 71½"*

FABRIC: *Silk, velvet*
OWNER: *Wauwatosa Historical Society. Donated by Mr. and Mrs. Luther Carrington Goodrich, son of the recipient*
LOCATION: *Milwaukee County, Wisconsin*

Some of the silk blocks embroidered by Sarah's friends were pre-inked. (Photo courtesy of Judy Zoelzer Levine.)

Luther Clapp family, Wauwatosa, Wisconsin, 1862. From left to right: Harriet Priscilla, Reverend Clapp, Emma, Grace, Mary, Mrs. H. P. Clapp, Sarah, and Wardlaw. (Photo courtesy of the Wauwatosa Historical Society.)

In 1845 a prominent Wauwatosa pioneer family, Rev. Luther Clapp and his wife, Harriet Priscilla Clapp, settled just west of Milwaukee, where he established the First Congregational Church of Wauwatosa. Sarah, the fifth of six Clapp children, was born ten years later and raised with a strong appreciation of service to others. In 1879, when Sarah was twenty-four years old and had completed college and postgraduate work, she decided to travel to China as a missionary. It was a courageous decision and an uncommon opportunity for a woman. She married a fellow missionary, Rev. Chauncey Goodrich, in 1880. They remained in China and raised four children. Sarah founded a school in Tungchou, China, which was named Goodrich School for Girls in her honor.

In 1885, on one of her return visits to Wauwatosa, Sarah's friends gave her a Crazy quilt that they had made for her as a special gift. They embellished their squares with fancy herringbone and meandering feather stitches, using multicolored pearl cotton or six-strand floss.

Sarah took the quilt back to China as a link to friends who cared about her on the other side of the world. She taught at the Union Theological School in Peking and remained in China until she died in 1923. The quilt was given to the Wauwatosa Historical Society in 1985 by Sarah's son Luther Carrington Goodrich, then professor emeritus of Chinese at Columbia University.[8]

"The Crazy Quilt" appeared in the October 25, 1890, issue of *Good Housekeeping* magazine and is an anonymous poet's humorous view of the crazy quilt fad spreading across the country. Following is the first stanza:

Oh, say, can you see, by the dawn's early light,
What you failed to perceive at the twilight's last gleaming?
A crazy concern that through the long night
O'er the bed where you slept was so saucily streaming;
The patches so fair, round, three-cornered and square
Gives proof that the lunatic bed-quilt is there.
Oh, the crazy-quilt mania triumphantly raves,
And maid, wife and widow are bound as its slaves.[9]

Map of the United States

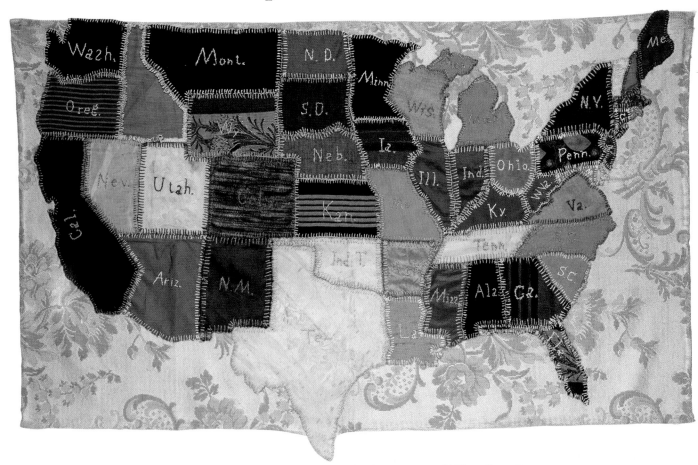

This quilt was a school project made by thirteen-year-old Clara Sawtell.

PATTERN: *Map of the United States*
DATE: *1891*
MAKER: *Clara Elizabeth Sawtell (Mrs. Clarence Harrington, 1878–1953)*
ORIGIN: *Milwaukee County, Wisconsin*
FINISHED SIZE: *16¼" x 28"*
FABRIC: *Velvet, silk, brocade, wool*
OWNER: *West Allis Historical Society. Donated by Claire Harrington, daughter of the maker*
LOCATION: *Milwaukee County, Wisconsin*

Quiltmaker Clara Sawtell, fourteen years old, Milwaukee County, Wisconsin. (Photo from the collection of the West Allis Historical Society.)

In 1891 thirteen-year-old Clara Elizabeth Sawtell worked diligently on her geography lesson. She had to draw and name the forty-four states and four territories of the United States. Instead of using paper, Clara chose to do her project in wool cloth and embroidery, including an even buttonhole stitch around each state, in the same style as the popular crazy quilts. She knew that in 1890 the United States had created an official division of the Oklahoma Territory, making "twin territories"–an Indian Territory in the eastern portion and the Oklahoma Territory in the remaining region. She dutifully embroidered this division on her map quilt. (It would not be until 1907 that Oklahoma, made up of both regions, became the forty-sixth state of the Union.)

Clara spent her early years in a one-room country school near her home on Beloit Road and by the early 1890s attended the new Fifth District School in North Greenfield, Wisconsin (now called West Allis). The school, with its arched windows and elegant belfry, stood near the banks of Honey Creek, overlooking Mukwonago plank toll road. The plank road was an early stagecoach route used by Clara's grandfather, Dr. Sawtell, to make house calls to rural patients.

Clara received her high school diploma from North Greenfield School, went on to normal school (teacher training college), and was a teacher for five years before marrying Clarence Harrington. She was active in community education, the West Allis Woman's Club and Garden Club, and women's suffrage. Her legacy is still honored in the Fifth District School building, which today houses the West Allis Historical Society and where the map quilt she made as a young girl still hangs.[10]

Fifth District School, North Greenfield (today West Allis), Wisconsin, which Clara attended in the early 1890s. It now houses the West Allis Historical Society. (Photo by Richard Eells, from the collection of the West Allis Historical Society.)

Old Maid's Puzzle

Louisa was twenty years old when she worked from her scrap bag of clothing remnants to piece this quilt. See page 180-181 for construction pattern.

PATTERN: *Old Maid's Puzzle*
DATE: *1889*
MAKER: *Louisa Hanneman (Mrs. Henry Gilow, 1869–1946)*
ORIGIN: *Ozaukee County, Wisconsin*
FINISHED SIZE: *72" x 76"*
FABRIC: *Cotton*
OWNER: *Patricia Webster, great-granddaughter of the maker*
LOCATION: *Door County, Wisconsin*

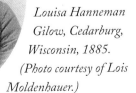

Louisa Hanneman Gilow, Cedarburg, Wisconsin, 1885. (Photo courtesy of Lois Moldenhauer.)

Old Turner Hall, Hamilton, Wisconsin, constructed of local fieldstone in 1867. (Photo courtesy of the Edward A. Rappold Collection of the Cedarburg Cultural Center.)

While the crazy quilt dominated the quilt patterns of the 1890s, the cultural life that emerged reflected the diverse ethnic groups that had settled in Wisconsin during the last half of the nineteenth century. Irish, Germans, Swiss, Norwegians, Danes, and Dutch were just some of the newcomers who added their heritage to the expanding mix of traditions in the Badger State.

Washington and Ozaukee counties in southeastern Wisconsin were heavily populated by German immigrants who worked diligently to clear stones from the fields. By 1889 tidy farms were evident throughout the wooded kettle moraine, spreading farther and farther onto flatter land along Lake Michigan. Fieldstones were used to construct many of the buildings in the small town of Hamilton, one of the earliest settlements in Ozaukee County. The town of Cedarburg, located near Hamilton, was Louisa Hanneman's birthplace in 1869. Her parents had come to America from Germany in the 1850s seeking religious freedom.

Louisa was twenty years old in 1889 as she worked from her scrap bag of clothing remnants to piece an Old Maid's Puzzle quilt. Loose-fitting, gray-blue Mother Hubbard dresses were in vogue. Louisa added trimmings from their excess hems, her father's worn shirts, and some highly valued Turkey red fabric to her collection of scraps. She boiled empty flour sacks to remove the ink-printed labels so she could use them in her quilt, an everyday piece made for her hope chest. Braided rugs, and sheets and pillowcases edged with her own handknit lace, were also added and served her well over the years.

Louisa married Henry Gilow in 1891, and they lived on the Gilow family homestead in Hamilton, on a small farm complete with cows, pigs, chickens, and gardens. While Henry supplemented his farm work by becoming a cheesemaker, shoemaker, basket weaver, and maker of phonograph records, Louisa continued to make quilts and taught her daughter and granddaughter to sew.[11]

Weathervane

Effie completed her quilt before the birth of her fifth child and died shortly after.

PATTERN: *Weathervane (detail)*

DATE: *1890*

MAKER: *Effie Jane Latson Klinck (1860–1891)*

ORIGIN: *Polk County, Wisconsin*

FINISHED SIZE: *62" x 73½"*

FABRIC: *Cotton*

OWNER: *Charmaine Vande Berg, great-granddaughter of the maker*

LOCATION: *Fond du Lac County, Wisconsin*

As a teacher in the one-room country school in Comer in the early 1880s, Effie Jane Latson was responsible for a wide variety of duties. She started the fire in the schoolhouse stove in the morning, made sure the privy was clean, taught all eight grades together, and swept the floors at the end of the day. When she married Joseph Klinck, she left her teaching position as was required.

Effie and Joseph moved to Clam Falls, on the banks of the Clam River in northwestern Wisconsin, where lumbering was the major industry. Effie, thirty years old and expecting her fifth child, made a special quilt for herself and Joseph. She used reds and browns from her scrap bag to piece nine-inch blocks in a Weathervane pattern. She completed the quilt just before the birth of their son Robert on January 6, 1891. The women who helped with the birth brought in fresh straw for the mattress to make her more comfortable. Effie developed a fever and died within two days. Her family attributed her death to "milk fever," which was then believed to be caused by the cold and dampness of the new straw.

It was impossible for Joseph to care for the children because of his lumberjack and postmaster jobs, so they were raised by several aunts and uncles. As his children grew older and moved west, to Washington, Idaho, and the Dakotas, Joseph followed and settled in Oregon. He never remarried, but carried Effie's quilt with him as he traveled, a reminder of his wife and their enduring love.[12]

IOWA COUNTY, WISCONSIN
RULES FOR SCHOOLTEACHERS – 1872

Teachers each day will fill lamps and clean chimneys.
Each teacher will bring a bucket of water and a scuttle of coal for the day's session.
Women teachers who marry or engage in unseemly conduct will be dismissed.
Any teacher who smokes, uses liquor, frequents pool halls, or gets shaved in a barbershop will give good reason to suspect his worth, intention, integrity and honesty. [13]

Howlett School, Black Wolf, Wisconsin, 1902. (Photo courtesy of the Oshkosh Public Museum.)

Flying Geese and LeMoyne Star

Helena chose a diagonal set to make a striking quilt.

PATTERN: *Flying Geese and LeMoyne Star*
DATE: *1895*
MAKER: *Helena Lau Mueller (1869–1955)*
ORIGIN: *Ozaukee County, Wisconsin*
FINISHED SIZE: *74" x 84"*
FABRIC: *Cotton*
OWNER: *Edna Gierach, granddaughter of the maker*
LOCATION: *Washington County, Wisconsin*

Quiltmaker Helena Lau Mueller, 1942, in her garden in Grafton, Wisconsin. (Photo courtesy of Edna Gierach.)

Helena Mueller loved to quilt. When she wasn't canning, tending her garden, baking, or knitting, she was cutting pieces of fabric or placing tiny stitches in her quilts. The quilt she made in 1895 was created with dramatic colors: navy, rusty red, blues, and tans. Helena chose a difficult diagonal set that made the pattern even more striking. The earliest recorded name of this pattern is Cradle quilt, attributed to *Hearth and Home*, by Wilma Smith. Another early name is Fox and Geese, and in recent times Flying Geese and Lemoyne Star have been used.[14]

Helena looked forward to afternoon quilting parties, which she or her neighbors hosted at their farm homes. The quilters didn't stay late at these gatherings; their German work ethic dictated that they return home early enough to make the evening meal for their families.[15]

Country Crazy

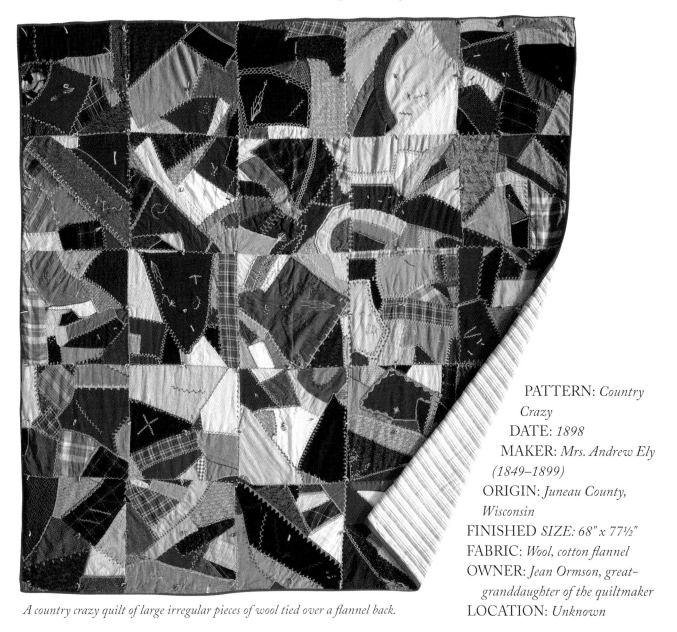

A country crazy quilt of large irregular pieces of wool tied over a flannel back.

PATTERN: *Country Crazy*
DATE: *1898*
MAKER: *Mrs. Andrew Ely (1849–1899)*
ORIGIN: *Juneau County, Wisconsin*
FINISHED *SIZE: 68" x 77½"*
FABRIC: *Wool, cotton flannel*
OWNER: *Jean Ormson, great-granddaughter of the quiltmaker*
LOCATION: *Unknown*

Crazy quilts had appeared in central Wisconsin by the late 1890s. Country crazy quilts, made of large, irregular pieces of wool, corduroy, and sometimes cotton tied over a cotton flannel back, were especially popular in the area. They were embellished with minimal embroidery and often filled with wool batting to provide extra warmth during cold winters. They were practical bedcovers made mostly by farm women from salvageable parts of men's clothing.

Mrs. Andrew Ely, a mother of seven who lived in the central Wisconsin town of Mauston, made such a crazy quilt of wool suitings backed with striped flannel in 1898. She signed and dated her quilt in the center block.

Mrs. Ely's youngest daughter, Florence, was married to Orland S. Loomis, who was elected to the Wisconsin governorship in 1942, but died before his inauguration.[16]

Remember the *Maine*

*A patriotic memorial quilt made by
mother and daughter.*

PATTERN: *Remember the* Maine
DATE: *1898*
MAKER: *Mrs. Matthew Mary Disch
and Mary Disch*
ORIGIN: *Kenosha County, Wisconsin*
FINISHED SIZE: *76" x 97"*
FABRIC: *Cotton*
OWNER: *Kenosha County Historical
Society and Museum. Donated by
Ellen Disch, a descendant of the
maker*
LOCATION: *Kenosha County,
Wisconsin*

On February 15, 1898, an
explosion ripped apart the battleship *Maine*
as it lay anchored in Havana's harbor. It
was in Havana to protect Americans from
rioters. There were two opposing factions:
those who wanted Cuba's complete
freedom from Spain, and those who wanted
a return to Spanish rule. The American public blamed
Spain for the loss of 260 American lives on board ship, and
protests of "Free Cuba" rang out in many American cities.
By April, the United States had declared war on Spain, and
the battle cry became "Remember the *Maine.*"

In Kenosha, nestled along the shores of Lake
Michigan, memorial ceremonies were held in Kenosha
Park Square. Members of the Kenosha Woman's Club
made banners and other tributes to the Maine. One such
memorial was made by forty-seven-year-old Mary Disch
and her twenty-three-year-old daughter, also named Mary.
Mother and daughter worked together to create a vivid
quilt in red, white, and blue proclaiming "Free Cuba" and
"Remember the *Maine.*" The fact that, as women, they were
not allowed to vote for the politicians who made national
decisions did not alter their determination to express their
patriotism. They did it proudly with needle and thread.[17]

On May 19, 1898, Kenosha's *Telegraph-Courier* newspaper
reported that five hundred people had gathered at the
city's Chicago Brass Mill to cheer the unfurling of a
twenty-foot-long American flag. The speaker paid tribute
to President William McKinley and "declared that his
name would be remembered as the greatest defender of
the nation's honor and the nation's flag." Children sang and
marched, and women were chosen to raise the flag. The first
flag ever flown from the spire of a church in Kenosha was
raised simultaneously at St. Matthew's, symbolizing "the
church's support of the army and navy in the defense of
national honor."

A Memorial Day observance at the cemetery, as
reported on June 2, was led by Mrs. S.O. Brower. Twelve
young boys dressed in sailor suits presented speeches
in honor of "the brave boys who went down with the
Maine."[18]

Chapter 5

Progressivism, 1900-1929

Women took a giant step into the public arena in the early 1900s, replacing the Victorian belief that a woman's only place was in the home. It was the beginning of a new era. Political and social reform known as the progressive movement was in full swing. The movement was an attempt to return power to the people and remove government officials who were influenced by corporate contributions and political favors. It was led by fundamentally conservative men, such as Wisconsin governor Robert M. La Follette, Theodore Roosevelt, and Woodrow Wilson.[1]

The reform movement cut across party lines, and the prevailing attitude of political equality and social justice helped revive women's suffrage. Women's continuing campaign for the right to vote and their strong participation in the war effort in 1917 proved once and for all their initiative and adaptability. President Wilson endorsed the suffrage amendment in 1918, and on June 10, 1919, Wisconsin and Illinois became the first states to ratify the Nineteenth Amendment. Women were allowed to vote in the 1920 presidential election. The role and status of American women would be forever altered.[2]

The early 1900s brought changes in home life as well. Free mail delivery to rural areas made the Sears, Roebuck catalog available to homes and farms across the land. In spite of the easy access to factory-made blankets, spreads, and accessories, for many rural women with large families, quiltmaking was still a necessity. They made heavy tied quilts from scraps of men's clothing and often called them "comforts." Such quilts provided warmth during cold winters and could be put together quickly—knotted in a day as opposed to being quilted, which could take many months. Marie Schwartz shared her memories of living in Germantown in 1904, as an eighteen-year-old:

"I quilted with a group of girls my age. My quilting bees were fine parties. Even the boys came to some of them, and everyone sang and joked while we girls did the quilting. Some of the hostesses served real dinners, and every bee ended with a midnight lunch…

When we were girls, we used to cut up old dresses and use the fabric that wasn't worn. Then when the quilt was done, you could look at it and remember which pieces came from your baby dress, which from your mother's dress, and so on…

Calico—now they call it percale—used to cost four cents a yard, and gingham was about eight cents. I remember getting some for twelve cents a yard and thinking that was a terrible price…"[3]

Rural mail carrier, Wisconsin, 1902. (Photo courtesy of the Oshkosh Public Museum.)

A quilt made from leftover pieces of Ringling Brothers circus costumes. See page 178-179 for construction pattern.

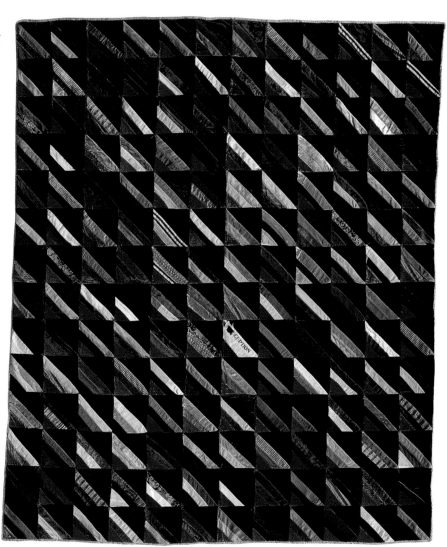

PATTERN: *Roman Stripe (Shadows)*
DATE: *c. 1908*
MAKER: *Letitia Finn Patterson*
ORIGIN: *Sauk County, Wisconsin*
FINISHED SIZE: *58" x 69"*
FABRIC: *Satin, velvet*
OWNER: *Nancy Norgord,
   granddaughter of the maker*
LOCATION: *Winnebago County,
   Wisconsin*

*Quilt maker Letitia Finn,
Evansville, early 1890s. (Photo
courtesy of Nancy Norgord.)*

Roman Stripe (Shadows)

In 1906, when the five Ringling brothers created the world's most spectacular circus, they chose their hometown of Baraboo, Wisconsin, as its summer quarters. In the winter, the great Ringling showmen loaded their equipment and animals—including huge elephants and dancing bears—on a train and traveled from Baraboo throughout the country to perform and entertain. Watching the animals parade to the train station to be loaded one by one was an exciting event that inspired many a child to dream of becoming a ringmaster or trapeze artist.

It was not surprising that the five brothers—Al, Otto, John, Alf, and Charley—started their own circus. As young boys, they gave variety shows in their backyard and advertised them by parading up and down the streets in a goat cart. In 1882, along with his brothers, Al organized the Ringling Bros. Classic Comic and Concert Company. They changed the theme to "circus and caravan" when they added a bear,

The five brothers who created the Ringling Brothers Circus launched the venture from their Baraboo hometown in 1884.

a monkey, an eagle, a hyena, a kangaroo, a pair of lions, and two elephants. By 1892 they had unseated the nation's leading circus, Barnum and Bailey, which they eventually bought. The circuses merged in 1917 and moved to Florida. Baraboo is now home to the

Circus World Museum, which is operated by the State Historical Society of Wisconsin.[6]

Letitia Finn Patterson was a dressmaker in Baraboo in 1908 and developed a special friendship with Mrs. Gorman, who lived next door. Mrs. Gorman was also a dressmaker and sewed costumes for the Ringling Brothers Circus. The two women enjoyed trading fabric remnants. Letitia's five-year-old daughter, Genevieve, would run next door to Mrs. Gorman and bring back leftover pieces from the fancy circus costumes for her mother to use in her quilts. Among those pieces were remnants of Skinner satin (a prized, lustrous brand also used in baseball uniforms) and plain and checked velvets in dazzling colors.

Letitia made a Roman Stripe quilt with the circus fabrics and stitched other quilts, too—often of woolens from sample books provided by local tailors. At least twenty-seven of her quilts survive, ranging from the crazy quilts and log cabins of the 1880s to the cotton Dresden Plates and Grandmother's Flower Gardens of the 1930s.[7]

Ringling Brothers Circus wardrobe department. (Photo courtesy of Circus World Museum, Baraboo, Wisconsin.)

Anna's quilt is edged with an unusual scalloped wool border and tied over a black wool backing. (Slides courtesy of Jane Dean.)

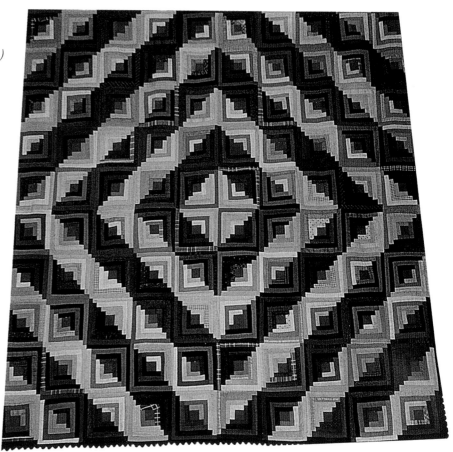

PATTERN: *Log Cabin, Barn Raising Variation*
DATE: *c. 1900–1910*
MAKER: *Anna Figi Wild (1863–1954)*
ORIGIN: *Green County, Wisconsin*
FINISHED SIZE: *80" x 80"*
FABRIC: *Wool*
OWNER: *Jane Dean, great-great-granddaughter of the maker*
LOCATION: *Ozaukee County, Wisconsin*

Log Cabin, Barn-Raising Variation

By 1900, Swiss immigrants had been living in Green County for fifty-five years. The rugged hills of the southwestern part of Wisconsin closely resemble the Swiss canton of Glarus, and the entire area was dotted with neat farms and cheese factories. The Swiss thrived on the acreage they called New Glarus.[4]

Anna Figi was born in New Glarus in 1863, one of fourteen children in her family. Her parents had been among the immigrants who came to America in 1845 to escape a devastating famine in Switzerland. Starting with one cow per family, by the late 1800s the Swiss had built healthy herds of Brown Swiss and Holstein cattle and ended their days of hardship.

Anna was nineteen when she married John Wild, and they had four children. In addition to caring for the children and tending a large vegetable garden,

Anna was an active member of the Swiss Reformed Church and helped establish the Ladies Aid Society, or *Frauen Verein*. Anna did her quilting both at home and in the church. Quilt making fit perfectly with her thrifty, industrious nature. John built quilting frames for Anna, and she held many quilting bees at her home, where neighbor women gathered to tie quilts. Frames were also set up at the church, where a group of expert needlewomen quilted what they called fancy quilts.

Anna was proud of her quilts, and every spring she hung them on the clothesline to air and for all to see. She then folded and stored them in a chest for the summer. She made enough quilts to give each of her granddaughters pieced quilts of wool, including a Log Cabin, Barn Raising variation. She also pieced quilts of cotton for all of her grandsons.[5]

PATTERN: *Bricks (Postcards)*
DATE: *1913*
MAKER: *Anna Luhn Fromm (1865–1947)*
ORIGIN: *Washington County, Wisconsin*
FINISHED SIZE: *74" x 79"*
FABRIC: *Wool, cotton flannel*
OWNERS: *Gladys and Raymond Hron, grandson of the maker*
LOCATION: *Washington County, Wisconsin*

Quilt maker Anna Luhn Fromm on her eightieth birthday, West Bend, Wisconsin, April 26, 1945. (Photo courtesy of Raymond Hron.)

Bricks (Postcards)

Bricks, or Postcards, was a practical quilt pattern that was popular in Wisconsin from 1900 to 1915. It was a favorite of quilt makers who were of German heritage. Wool rectangles salvaged from tailors' samples or cutaways from men's suits were sewn together randomly or in carefully placed patterns of color. Inspired by crazy quilts, quilt makers often added feather-stitch embroidery to the corners of the bricks or as a complete outline. The heavy, dark-colored quilts were both economical and warming for cold winter bedrooms in Wisconsin farm homes.

Anna Fromm made a Bricks or Postcards quilt in 1913. She made a special trip from her dairy farm in Washington County to nearby West Bend to get fabric from Charles Haebig's tailor shop. For a few pennies she purchased Mr. Haebig's outdated wool suit samples and bought a new piece of red cotton flannel for the back. It took her an entire winter of evenings, after the rest of the family was asleep, to embroider a gold featherstitch around each alternating light and dark rectangle. She carefully embroidered the year, 1913, in a gold chain stitch on one of the bricks. Anna lived to be eighty, and the quilt was one of many that she stitched in her lifetime.

Two years before she died, Anna met and approved of the woman her grandson Raymond planned to marry. She did not live long enough to attend the wedding, but she left instructions with her daughter Edna to give the 1913 Bricks quilt to the young couple on their wedding day in June 1949.[8]

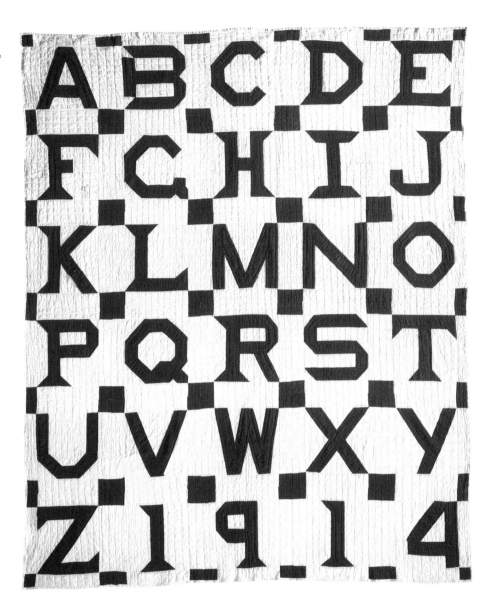

Emma Kruger made this alphabet quilt for her eleven children.

PATTERN: *Alphabet*
DATE: *1914*
MAKER: *Emma Janke Kruger (Mrs. William Kruger, Sr. 1879–1958)*
ORIGIN: *Marquette County, Wisconsin*
FINISHED SIZE: *69" x 84"*
FABRIC: *Cotton*
OWNER: *Teresa Posthuma, granddaughter of the maker*
LOCATION: *Marquette County, Wisconsin*

Alphabet

Emma Kruger sewed quilts on her treadle sewing machine in her Wisconsin farm home near Westfield, in Marquette County. Emma raised eleven children and created a special Alphabet quilt for them when she was thirty-five years old. It's likely she used it to teach her children their letters. During a family shopping trip to Westfield, Emma purchased new fabric at the Hengfuss General Store, choosing a dramatic combination of white muslin for the background and Turkey red for piecing the large letters. She pieced the date, 1914, at the bottom of the quilt.

Varying lengths of quilting stitches suggest that the quilt was worked on by more than one person. The colorfast red fabric is bright in spite of many launderings.[9]

Stars of Bethlehem

The stars, sashing, and border of this quilt were hand-pieced with tiny stitches. The quilting stitches, by contrast, are four to the inch, suggesting the work of two different people.

PATTERN: *Stars of Bethlehem*
DATE: *1910–1915*
MAKER: *Christine Marie Hogenson Jacobson (1879–1961)*
ORIGIN: *Walworth County, Wisconsin*
FINISHED SIZE: *78″ x 79″*
FABRIC: *Cotton*
OWNER: *Roslyn H. Waddell, niece of the maker*
LOCATION: *Dane County, Wisconsin*

Quilt maker Christine Marie Hogenson Jacobson, c. 1910. (Photo courtesy of Roslyn H. Waddell.)

Norwegian immigrants created the Norwegian Ridge settlement in the Spring Lake Township of Pierce County, in northwestern Wisconsin, in the last quarter of the nineteenth century. The Hogensons joined the settlement when they bought a farm there in 1879, the year of their daughter Christine's birth. In the early 1900s Christie was sent to nearby Spring Valley to apprentice with a woman who taught her a variety of needlework skills, including the making of Battenberg lace and hardanger.

Christie was an excellent student and in 1910 planned a quilt for her hope chest. She saved enough money from her job as a seamstress to purchase new fabric from the dry goods store in Spring Valley. She chose "red, oil boiled calico" at nine and a half cents a yard, the best soft, bleached muslin at eleven cents per yard, and a piece of vibrant blue fabric for her Stars of Bethlehem quilt.

The quilt was completed several years before her marriage to Charlie Jacobson in 1919. Christie spent the rest of her life on their farm, located a mile from the Hogenson homestead. She walked the mile to her parents' farm several times a week to visit her brother Henry's four children. Christie and Charlie never had children of their own, so the quilt was given to her niece Roslyn.[11]

Kentucky Crossroads

President James Garfield's widow, Lucretia, contributed
a block to this quilt, which Agnes Allerton conceived as a
wedding gift for Margaret and Robert Blackwood.

PATTERN: *Kentucky Crossroads*
DATE: *1913*
MAKERS: *Friends of Mrs. Samuel Allerton*
ORIGIN: *Walworth County, Wisconsin*
FINISHED SIZE: *87" x 88"*
FABRIC: *Cotton*
OWNER: *Betty Blackwood Host, daughter of the*
  Blackwoods
LOCATION: *Walworth County, Wisconsin*

*Agnes Allerton,
Lake Geneva,
Wisconsin, early
1900s. (Photo
courtesy of Betty
Blackwood
Host.)*

"The Folly," the summer home of Samuel and Agnes Allerton on Lake Geneva, Wisconsin, where Margaret Cronin Blackwood was employed. (Photo courtesy of Betty Blackwood Host.)

Margaret Cronin Blackwood, Lake Geneva, Wisconsin, c. 1913. (Photo courtesy of Betty Blackwood Host.)

Agnes Allerton and her husband, Samuel, lived on an estate on the north side of Lake Geneva in south-central Wisconsin, a popular location for the lavish homes of early industrialists from Chicago as well as Wisconsin. Samuel provided Agnes with a beautiful home and a large household staff. Agnes's personal maid, thirty-five-year-old Margaret Cronin, married Robert Blackwood, the foreman of the Allerton estate, on April 2, 1913. Agnes invited her friends, many with political and financial power, to help make a blue and white Kentucky Crossroads wedding quilt for the couple. President James Garfield's widow, eighty-year-old Lucretia, contributed a block.

In 1914, following the birth of their first baby, Margaret and Robert received a letter of congratulations from Mrs. Garfield.[10]

Appliquéd Floral Medallion

Mary Besau Leanna presented this quilt to her grandson Fred and his bride, Martha.

PATTERN: *Appliquéd Floral Medallion*

DATE: *c. late 1800s, early 1900s*

MAKERS: *Alice Huebner Besau (1835–?) and her daughter Mary Besau (Mrs. Edward Leanna, 1858–1938)*

ORIGIN: *Brown County, Wisconsin*

FINISHED SIZE: *75" x 90"*

FABRIC: *Cotton*

OWNER: *Judy Roehl, great-great-granddaughter of Mary Besau Leanna*

LOCATION: *Oneida County, Wisconsin*

Quilt maker Mary Besau Leanna (seated at left) and Martha Leanna who was given the quilt as a wedding present (seated at right, holding her son Edward), Bay Settlement, Brown County, Wisconsin, 1920. (Photo courtesy of Judy Roehl.)

The quilt's center medallion shows Alice's and Mary's fine sewing skills. See pages 188–189 for construction pattern.

In 1916, when Mary Besau Leanna was fifty-eight years old, she presented a treasured family quilt to her grandson Fred Leanna in celebration of his upcoming marriage on November 24. The quilt had been made by Mary and her mother, Alice Huebner Besau, in the late 1800s or early 1900s, while they lived in a rural Green Bay area, then called Bay Settlement, near Lake Michigan. Mary's mother was of German descent, and the Besau name on Mary's father's side was common among Munsee-Stockbridge Native Americans in Wisconsin and may be a clue to his heritage.

Mary and her mother chose the Appliquéd Floral Medallion design for the quilt in Turkey red, forest green, orange gold, and Prussian blue fabrics, a common choice of the 1850s. The elder woman's Germanic background might have influenced the design of coxcomb-like flowers extending from a red, eight-pointed center. The two women completed the quilt with several borders and delicate appliqué.

The quilt was in excellent condition, with the markings for the clamshell quilting still visible, when Mary presented the quilt to her grandson Fred and his bride, Martha, in their Bay Settlement home. Martha carefully packed the quilt away and used it only for important family occasions. This was her way of preserving its beauty and its link to her husband's grandmother and great-grandmother.

In 1974 Martha wrote a note to her eldest son, Edward, asking him to keep the quilt and pass it on to his eldest daughter, Judy Roehl. Judy intends to give the quilt to her granddaughter Leanna Christine Ohlson.[12]

An adaptation of the quilt, made in 2001–2002 by Jo Ann Jacobi, is featured on the cover of this book. It was raffled through Wisconsin Quilters Inc. and won by Ruth Ann Mathwig of Oshkosh.

PATTERN: *Fanny's Favorite*
DATE: *c. 1918*
MAKER: *Unknown*
ORIGIN: *Milwaukee County, Wisconsin*
FINISHED SIZE: *35" x 48"*
FABRIC: *Cotton*
OWNER: *West Allis Historical Society. Donated by Myrtle E. Leonard*
LOCATION: *Milwaukee County, Wisconsin*

Fanny's Favorite

This quilt was made by an unknown Wisconsin quilter about 1918 and is representative of the designer patterns featured in newspapers and needlecraft magazines. The top was created from scraps of Mother Hubbard blues, checks, and stripes in a pattern that the 1922 edition of *Ladies Art Catalog* referred to as Fanny's Favorite.[13]

Anna incorporated her initials and those of her son Albert in a quilt that could also spell laughter.

PATTERN: *Pieced Initials—AH*
DATE: *c. 1917–1919*
MAKER: *Anna Sophia Koch Horn*
   (1865–1932)
ORIGIN: *Shawano County, Wisconsin*
FINISHED SIZE: *83½" x 91¾"*
FABRIC: *Cotton*
OWNER: *Merlin Horn, grandson of*
   the maker
LOCATION: *Waupaca, Wisconsin*

On the right is quilt maker Anna Sophia Koch Horn (Mrs. John Horn), town of Angelica farm, Shawano County, Wisconsin, c. 1920. (Photo courtesy of Nelda J. Klevesahl.)

Pieced Initials—AH

Anna Horn, like generations of women before her, felt the weight of days when her son Albert went off to war. He served for two years, 1917 and 1918, as a machine gun instructor at Camp Hancock in Augusta, Georgia, during World War I.

Anna was a Shawano County farm wife, a mother of nine who had lost two of her children before Albert left to serve his country. Fear and worry were as much a part of her existence as the daily farm chores. If women could have designed a way to suppress their fears, it might have been in the relentless rhythm of their quilting stitches. Anna's wartime quilt, pieced from plaids and calico prints, incorporated the letters A and H, both her own and Albert's initials.

The quilt remained in Anna's home until Albert married in 1920. It was kept at Albert's farm home near Oshkosh until shortly before his death, when it passed to his sister Martha Westphal of Shawano. She later gave it to Albert's daughter Viona Horn Ginnow, who in turn passed it on to her brother Merlin Horn of Waupaca. His intention is to present this unique quilt to his granddaughter Ashley Horn, who carries the initials sewn into it.[14]

Norma Kruschke was eighteen years old in 1922 and living on Sheboygan County farm when she wrote in her diary, "When brother Alvin was gone during the war in 1918, he sent each one of us at home a picture of himself as a sailor boy. I could never forget those war days and all the songs I sang. I sang 'Keep the Home Fires Burning' the night Alvin left, at Cascade, at a Loyalty legion."[15]

The present owner is the granddaughter of the highest bidder, who was awarded the quilt when it was auctioned as a fund-raiser for the Red Cross.

Red Cross Autograph

PATTERN: *Red Cross Autograph*
DATE: *1918*
MAKERS: *Members of the Brush Creek Farmer's Equity/ Brush Creek Red Cross, Monroe County, Wisconsin*
ORIGIN: *Monroe County, Wisconsin*
FINISHED SIZE: *70" x 75"*
FABRIC: *Cotton*
OWNER: *Audrey Giles*
LOCATION: *Dane County, Wisconsin*

Cpl. Albert G. Willgrubs, twenty-eight, Sparta, Wisconsin, 1920. Albert's father, Henry, placed the highest bid for the Red Cross Autograph quilt. (Photo courtesy of Audrey Giles.)

Motivated by a sense of patriotism and urged by such magazines as *Ladies' Home Journal*, *Harpers Bazaar*, *Woman's Home Companion*, and *Colliers*, Wisconsin women joined and raised money for the Red Cross in the days leading up to World War I.[16] Even before men were fully committed to war duties, women were hard at work for the organization. They formed chapters throughout the state, made Red Cross supplies, and conducted canning and food conservation classes.

As Wisconsin men were called to arms, Wisconsin women replaced them in the labor force. Women also contributed overseas; by June 6, 1917, registered nurses were being called into service. Wisconsin was the first state to recognize the need for such nurses during the war.[17]

The farm women of Brush Creek Valley, in the rural coulee region of west-central Wisconsin, gathered monthly as an extension group of the Farmer's Equity organization. The meetings served as a social get-together, a way to provide neighborly support and exchange the latest local and national news. In 1917 the women's concern was for the war in Europe and the departure of their own sons to the battlefront. On July 1 of that year the following appeal from the State Council of Defense, the first in the nation, was issued to the women of Wisconsin: "Every woman can render important service to the nation in the present emergency. She need not leave her home or abandon her home duties to help the armed forces. She can help to feed and clothe our armies and help to supply food to those beyond the seas by practicing effective thrift in her own household."[18]

Magnus Swenson, food administrator for Wisconsin, requested that citizens set aside Tuesday, September 18, 1917, and each Tuesday thereafter during the war as a meatless day. He also asked that every Wednesday be set aside as a wheatless day and that the people of Wisconsin abstain from the use of bread and pastries on that day as a way of conserving the wheat supply.[19]

The American National Association of the Red Cross was formed on May 21, 1881. One of its founding members was Clara Barton. In her honor, a Clara Barton Rose quilt pattern was "patented" in 1934 by the Rock River Cotton Company of Janesville.[20]

Albert G. Willgrubs, one of many Brush Creek boys who enlisted in 1917, took his basic training at Camp Douglas as part of Wisconsin's famed Red Arrow Division. The following year the Farmer's Equity wives decided to make an autograph quilt to be auctioned off as a way of raising money for the Red Cross. The idea may have come from an article in a 1917 issue of *Modern Priscilla* suggesting that as much as $1000 could be raised for the Red Cross by charging for signatures on an autograph quilt.[21] The Farmer's Equity women embroidered their members' names, plus a blue star next to each one who had a son fighting in Europe. The quilt was dated "June 15, 1918, Brush Creek Red Cross" in red embroidery.

Many families gathered for the auction, and Henry J. Willgrubs placed the highest bid of $100. The Willgrubs never used the quilt, and it became a symbol of pride for their son Albert, who survived two major battles in France and received a Purple Heart for his battlefield injuries. Albert's daughter now owns the quilt.[22]

Flags of the World

A quilt made from cotton flannel cigar box advertising premiums.

PATTERN: *Flags of the World*
DATE: *c. 1917–1918*
MAKER: *Mary Schipper Rusboldt (Mrs. Charles Rusboldt, 1872–1958)*
ORIGIN: *Manitowoc County, Wisconsin*
FINISHED SIZE: *74" x 50"*
FABRIC: *Cotton flannel*
OWNER: *Mrs. Kurt W. Mueller, daughter of the maker*
LOCATION: *Manitowoc County, Wisconsin*

The decorative arts movement that coincided with the 1876 Centennial Exposition in Philadelphia inspired women to beautify their homes by making and displaying their own fancywork. One trend was to use leftover or disposable items to embellish household articles. At the time, cigar ribbons, cigarette silks, and cigar flannels with printed advertisements were used in the merchandising of tobacco. They were colorful, fashionable, and a free resource that women could collect and incorporate into their quilts. They had a unique impact on quiltmaking.[23]

Cigarette silks, called "silkies," and cigar flannels were introduced about 1900. The silkies were usually made of satin and issued in series of lithographed designs: flags, butterflies, flowers, animals, birds, baseball players, US presidents, and other famous people. Flannels were adorned with a succession of flags, Indian blankets, and oriental rugs. Flannel inserts were common only in the United States, but silks were readily available in South America, Canada, England, and other places.[24]

By 1880 cigar smoking had become America's favorite form of tobacco use. Thousands of small cigar factories were scattered throughout the United States, including Charlie Bieberitz's factory in Manitowoc. The cigars were hand rolled and tied in bundles with ribbons so that the cigar maker, who was paid by the bundle, would receive the correct wage. Even in a small private establishment such as Bieberitz's, the cigars were either tied with ribbons or packed into cigar boxes. Women collected the ribbons and often used them in quilts. By 1900, when cotton flannel pictorial squares were being inserted into cigar boxes as advertising premiums, women had begun adding them to their collections.

Charles Rusboldt lived south of the Manitowoc River, in the Polish-German section of town. He smoked cigars—big, fat, aromatic ones rolled from the best brown tobacco leaves. Charlie walked three blocks to visit his friend Charlie Bieberitz and to bring home boxes of his favorite cigars. The hand-rolled cigars were packed in brightly labeled wooden boxes for the Cameo and Dutch Masters cigar companies.

Charlie Rusboldt's wife, Mary, was forty-five years old in 1917. Two of her sons were in the armed services during World War I: Walter in the air force and Erv in the navy. Mary carefully saved the flannel squares—including a series depicting international flags—from the cigar boxes and made the Flags of the World quilt. She did it to preserve the collection rather than to showcase any fancy stitching. Mary joined all of the flag blocks by hand and proudly placed an American flag in the center. She began the quilt in 1917, the same year the tobacco companies discontinued the advertising flannels. In order to complete the quilt Mary added a Detroit baseball team flannel with the signature of player Marty Kavanagh.

Mary's daughter Jeanette still lives in Manitowoc and remembers watching her mother make the quilt. At Sunday afternoon gatherings at the Bieberitz home, the women visited while the men played cards and smoked cigars. Charlie Bieberitz gave Mary broken or scarred tobacco leaves, which she used in her closet as a moth repellent and in chicken nests to prevent lice. Jeanette knew her mother as a strong and resourceful woman who never had the opportunity to learn to read and write. One of Jeanette's favorite stories recalls the birth of her mother's fourth child, a premature first daughter. Mary placed the tiny baby in a blanket-lined cigar box on an open oven door to keep her warm. She tended both the baby and the ongoing fire continuously for six weeks until the child gained strength.[25]

Cigar Ribbons

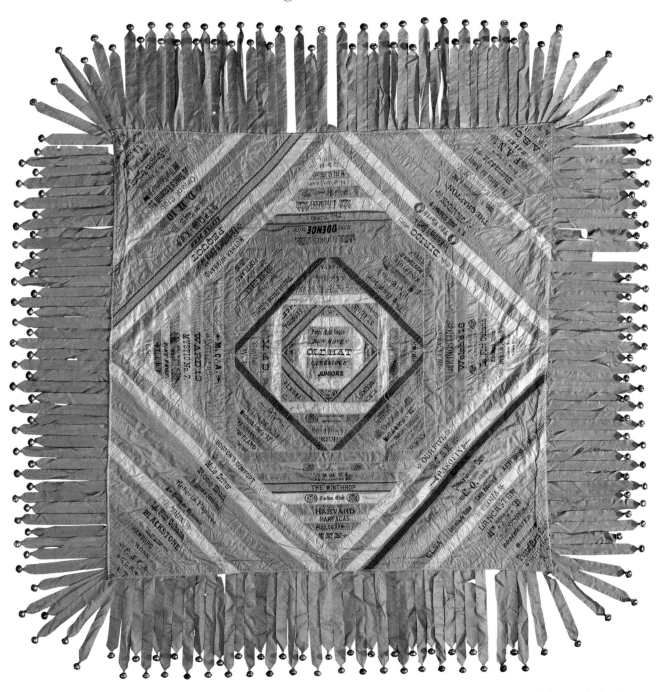

Caroline Tomfohrde collected silk ribbons from the boxes of cigars her father and his card-playing friends smoked. She made the throw, complete with silk fringe and small bells, for her father to drape over his revolving library rack.

PATTERN: *Cigar Ribbons*
DATE: *1895*
MAKER: *Caroline Marie Tomfohrde (1877–1969)*
ORIGIN: *Boston, Massachusetts*
FINISHED SIZE: *54" x 50"*

FABRIC: *Silk cigar ribbons*
OWNER: *Ardra W. Prescott, wife of the grandson of the maker*
LOCATION: *Milwaukee County, Wisconsin*

Tobacco Flannels, Flags, and Baseball

When Wilhelmina's grandson turned eighteen, she presented him with this quilt.

PATTERN: *Tobacco Flannels, Flags, and Baseball*
DATE: *c. 1920s–1930s*
MAKER: *Wilhelmina Weinke Layman (Mrs. William Layman, 1865–1944)*
ORIGIN: *La Crosse County, Wisconsin*
FINISHED SIZE: *76" x 80"*
FABRIC: *Cotton flannel*
OWNER: *Eleanor Waterman*
LOCATION: *Waukesha County, Wisconsin*

Quilt maker Minnie Weinke Layman, La Crosse, Wisconsin, c. 1940. (Photo courtesy of Eleanor S. Tikalsky.)

Wilhelmina "Minnie" Weinke Layman, her husband Bill, and their four children lived on the outskirts of La Crosse, close to the Mississippi River in west-central Wisconsin. Bill farmed and worked as a meatcutter to support their family. In 1920 Minnie's oldest daughter, Anna, and her baby son moved back to the farm to live with her parents. Minnie developed a close relationship with her grandson Dale Waterman and made him the special Tobacco Flannels, Flags, and Baseball quilt. She used advertising flannels saved from her husband's and sons' tobacco products. She grouped bright flags in the center of the quilt and surrounded them with blue-gray baseball prints. The names of the players read like an early-1900s lineup: St. Louis's Bobby Wallace and Miller Huggins, Cleveland's Willy Mitchell, and Washington's Eddie Ainsmith.

In 1936, when Dale turned eighteen, Minnie formally presented him with the quilt and encouraged him to go on to school to become a lawyer. Sixty-one years later, in 1997, Dale's widow wrote in a letter, "We are eternally grateful to Minnie for being a strong force in the history of our family."[26]

Crazy Signature Quilt

Clara signed her own and her husband's initials in the upper left block.

PATTERN: *Crazy Signature Quilt (four block section)*
DATE: *1920*
MAKERS: *Clara Belle Trumble Nimmo (1857–1934) and family and friends*
ORIGIN: *Jackson County, Wisconsin*
FINISHED SIZE: *70" x 65"*
FABRIC: *Velvet, silk*
OWNERS: *Muriel and Clifford Manthe, grandson of the maker*
LOCATION: *Monroe County, Wisconsin*

Clara Belle Trumble Nimmo. (Photo courtesy of Clifford Manthe.)

WCTU social meeting, Melrose, Wisconsin. Quilt maker Clara Nimmo is second from left; Agnes Nimmo, sixth from left in the first row. (Photo courtesy of Clifford Manthe.)

The Women's Christian Temperance Union (WCTU) was founded in Ohio in the early 1870s. It grew rapidly, especially in the Midwest. Wisconsin's WCTU was established in 1873 as the Women's State Temperance Alliance and recruited new members through "parlor meetings," a networking approach that perhaps laid the groundwork for twentieth-century in-home sales events. It also maintained a home for wayward women and studied the connections between men's intemperance and domestic violence, and between saloon keeping and prostitution.[27]

Clara Trumble Nimmo was thirty-three years old and the mother of two children when she joined a chapter of the WCTU in Melrose, near the Black River in the central part of the state, in 1890. The Melrose WCTU had started that very year with a group of seven women led by Lois Russel. Clara remained active in the organization's fund-raising and educational activities all her life, and her daughter Agnes also became a staunch member.

In Clara's diary entries of 1919 and 1920 she writes about "reciting" at the "Union" meetings, participating in bake sales, tying quilts for fundraisers, making crazy quilt blocks, and attending state meetings. She also took in boarders, cooked, baked, made her family's clothing, worked for her church, visited the sick—and wrote poetry. Many descriptions of her WCTU activities were written in verse.

Women's suffrage went hand in hand with the "stand against rum and beer." The following verses are from a song sheet Clara used at a state WCTU convention and were sung to the tune of "The Girl I Left Behind Me."

We ask the ballot as our right,
Now don't you think it time to
Step up like men and cast your vote
For the girls you've left behind you.
We help the laws and pay our taxes
To help in all we try to;
Now do you think you're dealing square
With the girls you've left behind you.
You've left us with the criminal:
And those with feeble minds, too,
Have you no more respect than this
For the girls you've left behind you?
We read and write, we cook and sew
To vote we're now inclined to.
Come show us that you love us still
The girls you've left behind you.[28]

WCTU parade wagon, Oshkosh, 1908. (Photo courtesy of the Oshkosh Public Museum.)

Clara Nimmo turned sixty-two years old on July 24, 1919. The following notations are from her diary.

1919

August 16, Saturday—I baked an apple pie and a pie plant pie. Agnes pieced 3 blocks for Minnie Wilson's quilt.

October 9, Thursday—Patched some on a quilt and fixed creamed potatoes and cabbage for the supper tonight. Agnes went and worked in my place.

October 17, Friday—We finished tying off the quilt.

November 24, Monday—I washed as usual. Began to piece some blocks for a small quilt for the bazaar.

December 8, Monday—Set piece on a block and went over to town to find some outing flannel to line my outing quilt. Went again and got some more. 19 cents per yard.

December 17, Wednesday—The day predicted for the end of the world and the coldest day on record. Neither happened.

1920

February 4, Wednesday—I set some crazy pieces on a block and began piecing some worsted stripe for a quilt.

February 5, Thursday—Went on piecing the stripe for the quilt. No Union today. Everything closed for "flue."

February 7, Saturday—I baked three pie plant pies and made fried cakes. Finished working my block with my mother's and my pieces on and did some mending.

February 18, Wednesday—I pieced crazy blocks all day.[29]

Many Wisconsin women became national leaders in the women's movement. Frances Willard of Janesville was president of the Women's Christian Temperance Union, and Carrie Chapman Catt of Ripon was a suffrage leader. Julia Grace Wales, known internationally in the World War I peace movement, taught English literature at the University of Wisconsin, Madison.[30]

In 1915, at a meeting of the International Committee of Women for Permanent Peace, Julia Wales presented a proposal addressing the immediate war crisis. Her plan for "continuous mediation" became known as the Wisconsin Peace Plan and involved bringing neutral nations together to study the disputes of warring nations and to offer feasible methods of resolving the conflicts. When President Wilson issued his famous Fourteen Points in 1917, one of them called for the creation of the League of Nations, which was modeled after Wales's peace plan.[31]

PATTERN: *Dresden Plate*
DATE: *1930s*
MAKER: *Agnes Nimmo Manthe (1884–1968)*
ORIGIN: *Jackson County, Wisconsin*
FINISHED SIZE: *68" x 84"*
FABRIC: *Cotton*
OWNERS: *Muriel and Clifford Manthe, son of the maker*
LOCATION: *Monroe County, Wisconsin*

Dresden Plate

Agnes Nimmo Manthe quilted with her mother, Clara Nimmo, and was also very active in the WCTU. She helped with Clara's crazy quilt and continued to make quilts after she married Ernest Manthe. Sometime in the 1930s she pieced a Dresden Plate quilt of scraps left over from dressmaking. This was a popular pattern during those years, when times were hard and every scrap needed to be used.

Melrose Ladies' Band, Melrose, Wisconsin, June 1916. Quilt maker Agnes Nimmo Manthe is front and center with the bass drum. The band played in WCTU parades and at other community events. (Photo courtesy of Clifford Manthe.)

This quilt was part of a fundraising effort for the Wisconsin Industrial School for Girls and was purchased by Nellie Roberts, a teacher at the school. See page 186–187 for pattern.

PATTERN: *Vase of Flowers*
DATE: *c. late 1920s*
MAKERS: *Girls from the Wisconsin Industrial School for Girls*
ORIGIN: *Milwaukee County, Wisconsin*
FINISHED SIZE: *80½" x 94½"*
FABRIC: *Cotton*
OWNER: *Mary E. Lemke, granddaughter of Nellie Roberts*
LOCATION: *Jefferson County, Wisconsin*

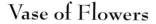

Vase of Flowers

Wisconsin Industrial School for Girls, 196 Prospect Avenue, Milwaukee, Wisconsin. (Photo courtesy of the Milwaukee County Historical Society.)

The Wisconsin Industrial School for Girls was organized by a group of concerned Milwaukee women in 1875. Their goal was to provide "wise and faithful" parenting and a self-supporting education for homeless, wayward, and abused girls. By 1912 nine buildings had been built on land designated by the city of Milwaukee. The school was situated on the city's east side, between Lake Drive and Prospect Avenue. Morals, discipline, and domestic skills were important aspects of the curriculum, which was presented in a combination home/school setting. Classes included cooking, dressmaking, millinery, weaving, quilting, and embroidery. Even the most elemental tasks—mending,

bed-making, laundering, ironing, sweeping, and dusting—were taught.[36]

In the late 1920s a group of young girls in the fancywork class made a pink and lavender Vase of Flowers appliqué quilt. Both the hand appliqué and hand quilting were well done. The quilt was donated to the school's fund-raising project, and Nellie Roberts, a teacher at the school, purchased it. She later gave it as a gift to her granddaughter, who still owns the quilt.[37]

Violet's quilt was made from remnants of dresses sewed for First Ladies.

PATTERN: *First Ladies Crazy Quilt*
DATE: *c. 1890–1920*
MAKER: *Violet Anne Nicholson McMillan (1853–*
    1926)
ORIGIN: *Washington, DC/Riverdale, Maryland*

FINISHED SIZE: *82¼" x 70½"*
FABRIC: *Velvet, silk*
OWNER: *James A. McMillan, grandson of the maker*
LOCATION: *Milwaukee County, Wisconsin*

Violet's husband wrote many years later, "The blue piece with spots was Mrs. Harrison's, and the yellow beside it was Ruth Cleveland's (the Clevelands' firstborn daughter)."

Quilt maker Violet Anne Nicholson McMillan, Riverdale, Maryland, 1920. (Photo courtesy of James A. McMillan.)

First Ladies Crazy Quilt

While Wisconsin women were working for the temperance movement and recording their lives in diaries, a woman in Washington, DC, was creating a quilt with a unique political connection. Violet McMillan and her physician husband, who worked for the government, lived in the middle of politics and power. One of Violet's close friends, a seamstress for the White House, saved the remnants from her sewing. She gave brocades and velvets to Violet from the dresses of Mary A. McElroy, President Chester A. Arthur's sister, who served as first lady for her widowed brother. Next came silks from Rose Cleveland, President Grover Cleveland's sister, who assumed the duties of first lady during his first year in office. Additional fabrics came from President Cleveland's wife, Frances, after their marriage in 1886, and from his elder daughter, Ruth.

In 1890 Violet began a crazy quilt with her historic remnants, including pieces from the dresses of President Benjamin Harrison's wife, Caroline. As Violet worked her quilt, she added embroidery around each patch.

From 1901 to 1909, Violet received additional pieces for the quilt from President Theodore Roosevelt's wife, Edith, and incorporated them into her design, embellishing several with embroidered spider webs and horseshoes. In 1920, thirty years after she began, Violet embroidered her initials on the finished First Ladies quilt. It is now in the possession of her grandson, who lives in Milwaukee, Wisconsin, and values both its beauty and its history.[32]

Five-Pointed Star

A rural grandmother's gift to her newborn grandson.

PATTERN: *Five-Pointed Star*

DATE: *c. 1920s*

MAKER: *Rose Wimmer (Mrs. Tony) Hubatch (1886–1977)*

ORIGIN: *Langlade County, Wisconsin*

FINISHED SIZE: *66" x 80"*

FABRIC: *Wool, corduroy*

OWNERS: *Carol and Bill Gresch, grandson of the maker*

LOCATION: *Unknown*

With a family of eleven, Rose Hubatch had a life story that could be told in the language of "making do." In the early 1900s, the Hubatches lived on a farm near Antigo in northern Wisconsin. Rose was used to saving, stretching, and reusing, whether the task was harvesting the garden, cooking, or sewing for her family. When Rose's daughter Helen gave birth to a baby boy, Rose made him the Five-Pointed Star quilt from used men's clothing and tied it over a wool batt.

Even though Rose's quilts were utilitarian and made from recycled pieces of fabric, the bright, orange-red diamonds slicing through the five star points creates a unique pattern that may have been her own design. The quilt, in the keeping of Rose's grandson Bill Gresch and his wife, serves as a reminder of this resourceful grandmother.[33]

Rose's daughter Helen wrote about their family's large garden: "As kids we crawled down the long rows, thinning carrots, beets, and onions. The beet greens we thinned were always cooked and seasoned with bacon and vinegar. Dandelion greens were also prepared in this manner…One of the few food items our parents did buy was barley coffee, which duly went through the coffee grinder behind the pantry door. Karo syrup came in two- and four-quart pails, and cornmeal, oatmeal, and flour were purchased in 100-pound bags. These bags were later turned into underwear, aprons, and material for 4-H projects. Those were the days when we carried our lunch to school in two-quart Karo syrup pails. Lunch was mostly butter and jelly, and sometimes meat sandwiches."[34]

Rose Wimmer Hubatch and her nine children, Antigo, Wisconsin, 1924. Back row, left to right: Helen, Rose holding Donald, and Edward; middle row, left to right: Caroline, Cecelia, and Jane; front row, left to right: Florence, Leonard, and Viola. (Photo courtesy of Bill Gresch.)

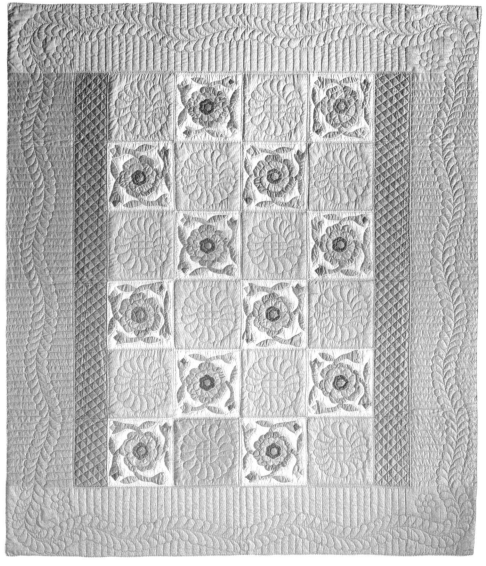

PATTERN: *Rose of Sharon*
DATE: *1922*
MAKER: *Effie (Mrs. Washington) Johnson, 1872–1945)*
ORIGIN: *Crawford County, Wisconsin*
FINISHED SIZE: *89" x 79"*
FABRIC: *Cotton sateen*
OWNER: *Gertrude Roth Wiseman, granddaughter of the maker*
LOCATION: *Outagamie County, Wisconsin*

Quilt maker Effie Johnson, Prairie du Chien, Wisconsin, 1936. (Photo courtesy of Gertrude Roth Wiseman.)

Effie was fifty when she made her Rose of Sharon quilt.

Rose of Sharon and Radiating Triangles

While she was in her fifties, Effie Johnson hand-stitched a classic Rose of Sharon appliqué quilt. Although this was a pattern often created as a wedding quilt, Effie made it solely for its beauty.

Five years later, Effie made another striking quilt. Each spring she and her husband, Washington, went by boat to swim their cattle from their farm, near the Villa Louis in Prairie du Chien, to a pasture on one of the islands in the Mississippi River. Every morning and evening in the summer of 1927, Effie and Washington made the trip by water to milk the cows. As Washington rowed the boat, Effie worked on a Radiating Triangles quilt top constructed of cotton sateen.

Besides milking cows, Effie helped raise hundreds of turkeys, boiled down the sorghum they grew to make syrup, and baked pies each week for nearby Campion College.

Effie's sense of color and placement gives this quilt a strong graphic impact.

PATTERN: *Radiating Triangles*
DATE: *1927*
MAKER: *Effie (Mrs. Washington) Johnson (1872–1945)*
ORIGIN: *Crawford County, Wisconsin*
FINISHED SIZE: *81½" x 91½"*

FABRIC: *Cotton sateen*
OWNER: *Gertrude Roth Wiseman, granddaughter of the maker*
LOCATION: *Outagamie County, Wisconsin*

Gold Star
(Lone Star or Star of Bethlehem)

Zoe made a version of this quilt for each of her three daughters, Gretchen, Gertrude, and Geraldine.

PATTERN: *Gold Star (Lone Star or Star of Bethlehem)*
DATE: *1934*
MAKER: *Zoe Johnson (Mrs. Frank) Roth (1893–1983)*
ORIGIN: *Crawford County, Wisconsin*
FINISHED SIZE: *80" x 90"*
FABRIC: *Cotton sateen*
OWNER: *Gertrude Roth Wiseman, daughter of the maker*
LOCATION: *Outagamie County, Wisconsin*

Zoe cut cardboard templates for quilting motifs from laundry, candy, and shoe boxes.

Effie Johnson's daughter Zoe Johnson Roth learned to quilt from her mother at an early age and duplicated her mother's energy and creativity. She made quilts, embroidered, crocheted, knitted, tatted, and even made herself a split skirt in order to drive a motorcycle. She had a seasonal job at a canning factory, where she became an inspector, and in later years waited on customers in a bakery.

Remnants from the dresses Zoe sewed for her three daughters, Gretchen, Gertrude, and Geraldine, were recycled into quilts. She waited patiently for Montgomery Ward and Sears catalog sales in order to purchase needed fabric at nine cents a yard. Catalogs were "wish books" for rural women in the early 1900s, and like other women, Zoe and her daughters loved to browse the pages. Zoe also purchased fabric from Greeley's Dry Goods Store in Prairie du Chien and followed the 1930's adage, "Use it up and wear it out, make it do or do without." She cut her templates from shoeboxes and cereal boxes and ordered quilting designs from the Needleart Guild. Zoe occasionally made three quilts from a favored quilt pattern, one for each of her daughters. In 1934, when she started her Gold Star quilt, she bought new, beautiful, mercerized broadcloth.

Zoe gave up housekeeping in 1975, at the age of eighty-three. About seventy of the family quilts were divided among her three daughters and her grandchildren—quilts that can be read as surely as if they were stories recorded in a family journal: Grandmother's Flower Garden, Pinwheel, Double Wedding Ring, Broken Dishes, Steps to the Garden, Ferris Wheel, Trip around the World, and Log Cabin.

Three generations of women carried on the quilting tradition: Effie, from 1912 through the 1929 stock market crash and depression; Zoe, from 1930 to the 1970s; and Gertrude, who quilted a Friendship quilt and a Tumbling Blocks quilt in the 1980s and 1990s. Artistic expression continues in the fourth generation as well. Gertrude's daughter Sherri Goudy designs and creates needlework on canvas and does ethnic embroidery and cross stitch.[35]

Quilt maker Zoe Johnson Roth, Prairie du Chien, Wisconsin, August 16, 1973. (Photo courtesy of the Telegraph Herald, Dubuque, Iowa.)

PATTERN: *Flower Basket*
DATE: *c. late 1920s*
MAKER: *Ada Hollabush
    Tousley (1878–1961)*
ORIGIN: *Jefferson County,
    Wisconsin*
FINISHED SIZE: *100" x 86"*
FABRIC: *Cotton*
OWNER: *Fort Atkinson
    Historical Society, Hoard
    Museum. Donated by Mrs.
    Marianna Dexter, niece of the
    maker*
LOCATION: *Jefferson County,
    Wisconsin*

*A simple arrangement of bluebells,
bleeding hearts, and other flowers.*

Ada created this Flower Basket quilt as a housewarming gift for her younger sister, Jessie.

Quilt edge detail.

Flower Basket

Ada Hollabush Tousley often helped her husband in his jewelry store in Fort Atkinson. In the late 1920s she made a Flower Basket quilt as a housewarming gift for her younger sister, Jessie Hollabush, who had purchased her own home in Fort Atkinson. The colors Ada selected—peach, lavender, blue, and green—reflected the prints and palette of the 1920s and early 1930s. The grouping of flowers is similar to patterns later published in a *Chicago Tribune* newspaper column under the byline of Nancy Cabot. Jessie placed the quilt on a small four-poster bed in her spare bedroom, where it remained until her death at the age of eighty-two.[38]

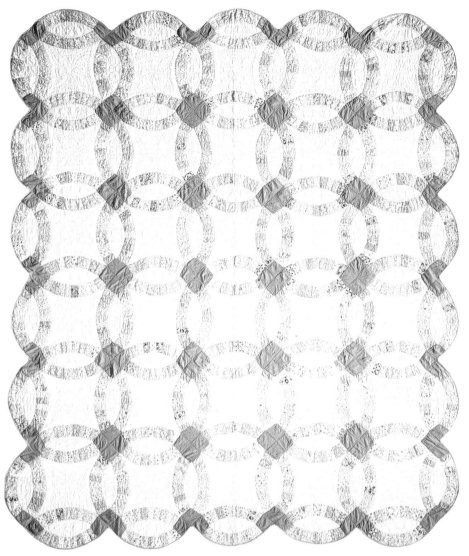

Mary fashioned her quilt from a picture featured in the October 1928 issue of Capper's Weekly.

PATTERN: *Double Wedding Ring*
DATE: *c. 1928*
MAKER: *Mary Poirier DeVoe
    Herscheid (1873–1945)*
ORIGIN: *Menominee, Michigan*
FINISHED SIZE: *75" x 87½"*
FABRIC: *Cotton*
OWNER: *Beatrice Eggener,
    granddaughter of the maker*
LOCATION: *Sheboygan County,
    Wisconsin*

*Quilt maker Mary Poirier DeVoe
Herscheid, Marinette, Wisconsin,
1944. (Photo courtesy of Beatrice
Eggener.)*

Double Wedding Ring

Women made gift quilts to commemorate special occasions, and in doing so they created keepsakes to be passed on to their descendants. Mary Poirier DeVoe Herscheid knew the value of such a gift. Born of French heritage in Bay Settlement in 1873, she was orphaned at the age of three and placed in the rotating care of several older brothers and sisters. She never learned to read or write, but was kept busy as a child with sewing and decorative needlework. By the time she was an adult, she could copy a pattern without being able to read the directions.

Mary constructed the Double Wedding Ring quilt from a picture that appeared in the October 1928 issue of *Capper's Weekly*. She used fabric from dresses and aprons to make little wedges for the interlocking rings. On June 12, 1944, Mary gave the quilt to her granddaughter Beatrice Devoe and Leonard Eggener on their wedding day. Mary died a year later, and Beatrice has kept the quilt as a tribute to a grandmother who taught her that a successful life is not measured by what is accomplished, but by what is overcome in order to accomplish it.[39]

Chapter 6

The Great Depression and End of WWII, 1930-1950

Irene L. Ray remembers her childhood days in Beloit between 1933 and 1936:

"We were victims of the Depression. When I was age ten, in 1933, my father had to start over as many did then. Shoes had cardboard liners to compensate for holes in the soles… At age thirteen I learned to sew. There was no money to buy any, so I sewed all my clothes on an old treadle machine. Mom cut leftover pieces from my sewing and made nine-patch blocks. Finally she put them together with a flannel backing. It was tied and was my pride and joy. I could find my sewing in those blocks."[1]

The two decades between World Wars I and II brought many changes, not only to Wisconsin but across the nation. Wisconsin rated slightly below the national average in population growth and urbanization. The state's residents, like those of much of the country, were moving off the farm and relocating in urban areas. A population that had been three-fifths rural in 1900 was now more than half urban.[2] Wisconsin was also no exception to the national trend of declining farm incomes and mounting debts.

The crash of the stock market in 1929 dealt a powerful blow to Wisconsin industries. Factories had to cut back or shut down. Unemployment rose sharply, and many of those who kept their jobs were forced to take pay cuts. The early 1930s are remembered as the Great Depression—dark days when even banks closed their doors. Families struggled to keep their farms, their jobs, and their homes. In 1932, Wisconsin became the first state to pass an unemployment compensation act.[3]

In spite of the grim times, there was good news. By 1930, eighty-four percent of Wisconsin farm families had cars; sixteen percent had water piped into their houses; and twenty-six percent had electricity, putting them in the market for home appliances and narrowing the gap between urban and rural lifestyles. The movies were already a powerful influence in American life by the 1920s, and radio wasn't far behind. The 1930 census showed that fifty-nine percent of Wisconsin urban families and thirty-eight percent of rural families had radios.[4]

Resourceful women continued to find ways to make quilts and to survive the aftermath of the Great Depression. The Works Progress Administration, one of President Roosevelt's agencies formed to aid economic recovery, spurred more quiltmaking through the Milwaukee Handicraft Project. The possibility of monetary prizes fueled Sears, Roebuck's Century of Progress quilt competition at the 1933 Chicago World's Fair. Newspaper quilt columns proliferated, inspiring women at the very least to paste intriguing designs into scrapbooks. And many of those patterns were pieced from the bright floral prints left over from the housedresses and aprons women sewed. Feed and flour sacks bloomed with calico prints, too, and found their way into quilts.

Sarah used a Ladies Art Catalog *pattern to make this quilt for her granddaughter.*

PATTERN: *Just a Quilt for Bunny (Double Four Patch or World's Fair Block)*
DATE: *1930*
MAKER: *Sarah Jane Elliott Lovell (1858–1940)*
ORIGIN: *Pierce County, Wisconsin*
FINISHED SIZE: *83" x 66"*
FABRIC: *Cotton*
OWNER: *Bernice L. Wolf, granddaughter of the maker*
LOCATION: *Unknown*

Just a Quilt for Bunny (Double Four-Patch or World's Fair Block)

Sarah Jane Lovell spent her early life as a schoolmistress and then a wife and mother of six in the rugged countryside of northwestern Wisconsin. When her husband died unexpectedly, she moved to River Falls in 1918 and became known as a fine quilter with an artist's eye. In her early seventies, Sarah made a quilt for her granddaughter Bernice Lovell, affectionately called "Bunny." Sarah used a *Ladies Art Catalog* pattern called World's Fair Block for the blue and gold four-patch quilt made mostly of old shirtings from her scrap bag.[9]

After she finished the quilt in 1930, Sarah went to live with the family of her son Byrne, who was Bunny's father. Times were hard in the thirties, and many people were out of work. The Lovells were more fortunate than some of their city friends, for they owned land and had a means of making a living and growing their own food. Bunny's quilt was well used and eventually met the fate of many worn quilts, becoming a pad between mattress and coil spring.

Bernice Lovell Wolf remembers rescuing the quilt when her parents, Byrne and Sadie Lovell, moved from the farm into the city. "I was married and had four children by then. The quilt had been mended with feed sack material and was being used to protect the mattress from the coil spring underneath."[10]

Wild Rose (French Basket)

Marie did all the intricate appliqué by hand and used a treadle sewing machine to join the completed blocks.

PATTERN: *Wild Rose (French Basket)*
DATE: *1929–1930*
MAKER: *Marie (Mrs. Edwin) Halmstad (1912–1998)*
ORIGIN: *Chippewa County, Wisconsin*
FINISHED SIZE: *72½" x 83½"*

FABRIC: *Cotton*
OWNER: *Richard Halmstad, son of the maker*
LOCATION: *Unknown*

Marie Webster, designer of the French Basket pattern, as well as the Red Poppy pattern (see page 163), spent most of the fifty-four years of her married life in Marion, Indiana. She lived in an elegant Colonial Revival home from which she operated a quilt pattern business. In 1921 Marie expanded the enterprise and, with Ida Hess and Evangeline Beshore, started the Practical Patchwork Company to market her patterns and kits. The cottage industry continued until the outbreak of World War II.[5]

Marie Walsdorf was seventeen years old in June 1929, when she graduated from Stanley High School in northwestern Wisconsin. With her mother's encouragement and the guidance of a neighbor, Marie made a quilt to add to the embroidered linens she had placed in her hope chest. The neighbor helped her copy a pattern onto brown butcher paper and calculate the yardage needed for the quilt. Peter Pan cottons were purchased from Korn's General Dry Goods Store in Stanley. Marie did all the intricate appliqué by hand and used a treadle sewing machine to join the completed blocks.

Marie worked on her quilt through the stock market crash of October 1929 and during the winter and summer of 1930. In September 1934, she married her high school classmate Edwin Halmstad, and the quilt was a welcome bedcover throughout the depression years.

Marie called this her Wild Rose quilt. It was not until many years later that she discovered the pattern had been designed by Marie Webster in 1915 for the *Ladies' Home Journal* and was called French Basket.

Marie died on September 12, 1998, at the age of eighty-six, shortly after her French Basket quilt was exhibited at the Pabst Mansion in Milwaukee. Her son, Richard, took photographs at the August 30, 1998, opening reception, and when Marie saw them, she considered the inclusion of her quilt her finest achievement in a lifetime of quilting.[6]

French Basket pattern from quilts and spreads: original designs by Marie D. Webster. (From the collection of Merikay Waldvogel.)

Quiltmaker Marie Walsdorf Halmstad, age sixty-nine, and her grandson R. Zachary Halmstad at Clearwater Quilter's Show, 1981. (Photo courtesy of Richard Halmstad.)

Alphabet

Carola's quilt is typical of the popular patterns featured in newspapers and magazines in the 1930s.

PATTERN: *Alphabet*
DATE: *1930*
MAKER: *Carola Witte Strehlow (1894–1961)*
ORIGIN: *Milwaukee County, Wisconsin*
FINISHED SIZE: *66½" x 93"*
FABRIC: *Cotton*
OWNER: *Ginny Reega, granddaughter of the maker*
LOCATION: *Waukesha County, Wisconsin*

Carola Witte Strehlow, c. 1940, who worked many quilts in the attic above her husband's paint and hardware store on South Kinnickinnic Avenue in Milwaukee, Wisconsin. (Photo courtesy of Audrey V. Reega.)

Jack in the Box

Florence La Ganke wrote a syndicated newspaper column, the "Nancy Page Quilt Club," from the late 1920s to the early 1940s. (From the collection of Merikay Waldvogel.)

Detail of Carola Strehlow's Alphabet quilt.

By the early 1900s women no longer had to rely solely on one another for the exchange of quilt patterns. Designs could be found in farm magazines such as *Successful Farming*, *Progressive Farmer*, and *Capper's Weekly*. Women's magazines, including *Needlecraft*, *Modern Priscilla*, *McCall's*, and *Good Housekeeping*, used quilt and other needlework patterns as a way of attracting readers. Daily newspapers became another rich resource, offering a variety of patterns several times a week or a series of single quilt block patterns that might run for several weeks. By the 1930s newspapers across the country offered syndicated quilt columns by Laura Wheeler, Jane Alan, Aunt Martha, and Nancy Cabot, to name a few. Most were fictitious names meant to romanticize the olden days of the colonial era.[7]

Sometime in the 1930s, for twenty-six consecutive weeks, the *Milwaukee Journal* featured the Alphabet quilt pattern in its Shopping News section. The pattern, created by Florence La Ganke as part of the fictional Nancy Page Quilt Club, was syndicated in newspapers throughout the country. The Milwaukee Journal featured a different letter of the alphabet weekly and offered prizes for those who completed the twenty-four-block quilt. La Ganke purposely left out the letters X and Z from her pattern and placed the letter Y in the last block to represent "You," the recipient of the quilt. She encouraged each quilter to place her initials in that block.

Alphabet was a very popular pattern in Wisconsin during the 1930s. Even though they used the same pattern, women set their blocks differently, in their own creative ways. Carola Strehlow created the quilt for her daughter. Eleanora Kiesslich Pabst, who married into the Pabst brewing family and whose husband worked at the brewery, made one for her granddaughter Elizabeth Ellen Williams. Arthra Clasen admired the pattern and used it to make a quilt for her nine-year-old niece, Ruth.[8]

Broken Star

Elda's quilt, made when she was thirteen, is a remarkable accomplishment, especially for a young girl.

PATTERN: *Broken Star*
DATE: *1931*
MAKER: *Elda Strahm (Mrs. Frank Schiesser, 1918–)*
ORIGIN: *Green County, Wisconsin*
FINISHED SIZE: *74" x 74"*

FABRIC: *Cotton*
OWNER: *Wisconsin Historical Society. Donated by Elda Strahm Schiesser*
LOCATION: *Dane County, Wisconsin*

Quiltmaker Elda Strahm, thirteen, holding up a crib quilt she made, Green County, Wisconsin. (Photo courtesy of Elda Strahm Schiesser.)

Elda Strahm lived on a farm in York Township, Green County, in 1931. She was thirteen years old and a member of a regional 4-H Club. Its pledge of "Head, Heart, Hands, and Health" was a way of focusing on every aspect of a young person's life. Farm families were experiencing hard times, and Elda contributed to her club's thrift project by making seventy-five articles, including a Broken Star quilt. As part of the project Elda was required to keep detailed records documenting the time and money spent on the quilt.

With the help of her mother, Ella (Mrs. Adolph Strahm), Elda used flour sacks from her aunt and uncle's bakery and chicken feed sacks donated by her father to make the quilt.

"It was quite a trick to know how to soak and rinse the sacks in bleach over a period of some weeks and open them so you wouldn't have 'Full O Pep' in the middle of your sewing project," wrote Elda. Using RIT® dye and boiling water, she transformed the bleached-white feed sacks into beautifully colored fabrics.

Elda used a diamond-shaped cardboard template to cut 1,152 pieces of yellow, red, white, pink, and green dyed fabrics. It took twenty-three hours of machine sewing to create the quilt top, whose pattern was popular among her mother's friends. Using a wooden frame, Elda hand-quilted cables and feather wreaths filled with cross-hatching.[11] In her record book she noted that it took 65 hours to make the quilt at a cost of $2.02. She estimated that she could sell it for $10, giving her a profit of $7.98, or a tidy 400 percent!

From the 1800s to the early 1900s, in both rural and urban America, quilts were often made from salvaged material, including feed and flour sacks. Women quiltmakers were resourceful, and when cotton sacks replaced wooden barrels as packaging for farm products, they recognized the sacks as a source of cloth for quilts, as well as for clothing, towels, curtains, and pillowcases. Many homemakers used the sack fabric as it came, with the printed labels intact. Some even used the colorful logos printed on the front of sacks as block designs for quilt tops. Others carefully bleached the sacks to remove the labeling and produce pristine white fabric that could be used for quilt backs, sashings, and foundations for appliqué, as well as other household items.

Rubber tire manufacturers also wrapped their product in cotton fabric, and in the 1920s Susie Harriman Grover bleached tire wrappers that had been brought to her by her son, who worked at the Ford garage in Rice Lake, Wisconsin. She used them to make a Double Wedding Ring quilt top.[12]

A popular Grandmother's Flower Garden quilt with a complicated border and edge is quilted along each "path."

Grandmother's Flower Garden Path

PATTERN: *Grandmother's Flower Garden Path*
DATE: *1932*
MAKER: *Ella Elizabeth Stoeckig Mink*
ORIGIN: *Adams County, Wisconsin*
FINISHED SIZE: *82" x 97"*
FABRIC: *Cotton*
OWNER: *Laura Weber, granddaughter of the maker*
LOCATION: *Unknown*

The Great Depression affected everyone, including women in the small railroad town of Adams in central Wisconsin. Many of the men had been laid off from their jobs or only worked part-time, and families struggled to make a living.

Ella Elizabeth Mink was among the young women invited by an older neighbor, Mrs. Anacher, to her home to make Grandmother's Flower Garden quilts. The pattern was a popular one in the early 1930s and could be made from scraps of fabric. No one could afford to purchase material from the general store in nearby Friendship, so the women shared what they had, whether leftover pieces of dresses or printed feed sacks. The quilt Ella made now reminds her three great-granddaughters of one woman's ability to persevere during times of hardship.[13]

Instructions for working hexagon blocks such as those in this elaborate quilt can be found on pages 182-183.

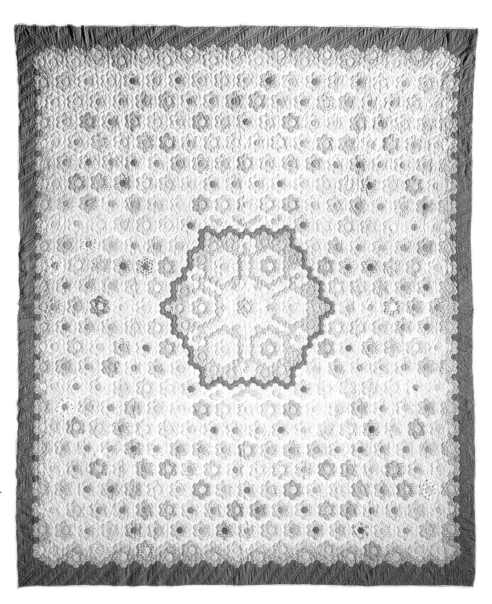

PATTERN: *Grandmother's Flower Garden with Center Medallion*
DATE: *1930s*
MAKER: *Prudence Downey Wood (1877–1955)*
ORIGIN: *Sauk County, Wisconsin*
FINISHED SIZE: *77" x 93½"*
FABRIC: *Cotton*
OWNER: *Catherine Wood Rinkob, daughter of the maker*
LOCATION: *Sauk County, Wisconsin*

Grandmother's Flower Garden with Center Medallion

Prudence Wood of Madison worked a unique rendition of a Grandmother's Flower Garden quilt during the 1930s. She was the wife of a railroad man and the mother of four grown children when, in her mid-fifties, she handpieced hundreds of tiny hexagons from her scrap bag. She was inspired to use the dramatic medallion set after seeing a picture of a quilt displayed in the Metropolitan Museum of Art in New York City.[14]

Prudence Downey Wood, Madison, Wisconsin, 1938. Prudence won many ribbons at county fairs for her knitting, tatting, crocheting, and quilting. (Photo courtesy of Catherine Wood Rinkob.)

PATTERN: *Grandmother's Flower Garden with Picket Fence Border*
DATE: *1932*
MAKER: *Eleanora Kiesslich Pabst*
ORIGIN: *Milwaukee County, Wisconsin*

FINISHED SIZE: *81" x 85"*
FABRIC: *Cotton*
OWNER: *Elizabeth Williams, granddaughter of the maker*
LOCATION: *Waukesha County, Wisconsin*

Grandmother's Flower Garden with Fenced Border

Eleanora Kiesslich Pabst of Milwaukee, daughter of Carola Strehlow (see page 146), made a Grandmother's Flower Garden quilt in 1932 to celebrate the birth of her granddaughter Elizabeth Ellen Pabst. She created a white picket fence as an outer border and embroidered the child's name and the date on the gate. A similar picket fence appeared in Ruby Short McKim's nationally syndicated newspaper column of January 1931, in what was called Pattern Number 27. Its description read, "A patchwork fence to put around the flower garden is quite optional with the 'gardner,' but really, it is not so hard to piece and does add much distinction to the assembled flowers."

Cecelia Wolf Wild remembers the value of quilts in rural Wisconsin during lean times. "In 1936 my husband took me as a bride to Hancock. I was a nurse and he was a physician. We pioneered medical care to that area. Everyone there was so poor. Our patients had no money, so they paid us with a chicken in a gunnysack, fresh vegetables, or eggs. Mrs. Gall was near eighty when she paid her bill with a Grandmother's Flower Garden quilt in 1936."[15]

Pearl Pauline Berton Konitzer, Appleton, Wisconsin, c. 1938. (Photo courtesy of Carol M. Werth Rank.)

Pearl won a merit award for her World's Fair Wreath entry.

PATTERN: *World's Fair Wreath (Chicago World's Fair, Sears "Century of Progress" Quilt Contest)*

DATE: *1933*

MAKER: *Pearl Pauline Berton (Mrs. Antone) Konitzer (1888–1940)*

ORIGIN: *Outagamie County, Wisconsin*

FINISHED SIZE: *78" x 91"*

FABRIC: *Cotton*

OWNERS: *Carol M. Werth Rank and NaVonne Werth Green, granddaughters of the maker*

LOCATION: *Outagamie County, Wisconsin*

World's Fair Wreath

Pearl Konitzer also entered the Sears quilt contest. She was forty-four years old and worked at Zwicker Knitting Mill in Appleton. She created a World's Fair Wreath quilt, an original design featuring an American flag encircled by wreaths of flowers and the words "1933 World's Fair, Chicago Ill. U.S.A." The appliqué was done with a buttonhole stitch, and a grid of quilting lines covered the surface. Pearl's twenty-year-old daughter, Louise, helped stitch the letters in order to meet the contest deadline. The D in the word World was stitched backwards, which could have been an error or may have been done deliberately, in keeping with the myth that quilters avoid making "perfect" quilts.

Pearl's quilt won a ribbon at the first level of competition.[23]

Post-Preparation (Whole-Cloth Block)

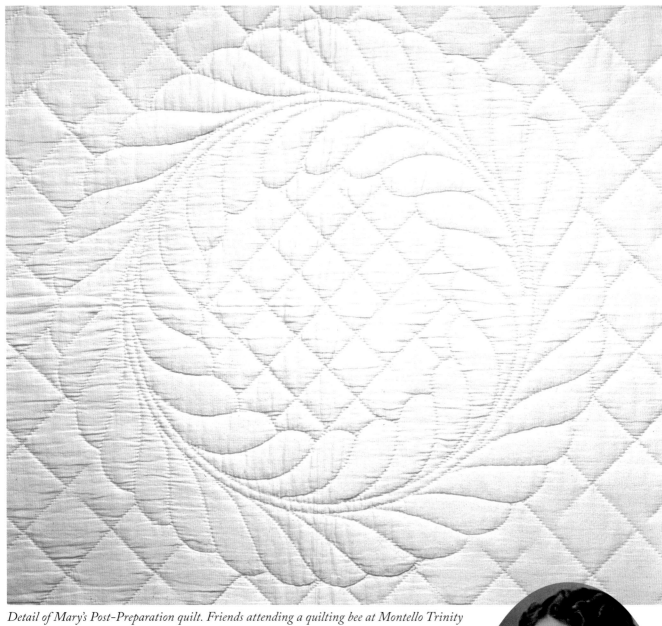

Detail of Mary's Post-Preparation quilt. Friends attending a quilting bee at Montello Trinity Methodist Church helped her complete the quilt and its feather wreath design. The fabric, originally pink, has faded to almost white.

PATTERN: *Post-Preparation (Whole-Cloth Block)*
DATE: *1933*
MAKER: *Mary Wells Cummings (1884–1981)*
ORIGIN: *Marquette County, Wisconsin*
FINISHED SIZE: *58" x 76"*
FABRIC: *Cotton sateen*
OWNER: *Mary Jean Thalacker, granddaughter of the maker*
LOCATION: *Marquette County, Wisconsin*

Mary Eliza Wells Cummings, Montello, Wisconsin. (Photo courtesy of Mary Jean Thalacker.)

The ladies of the Montello Trinity Methodist Church Quilting Bee Group, at Aseneth Brown's home in Montello, Wisconsin, c. 1930. Mary Cummings is at left in the back row. (Photo courtesy of Mary Jean Thalacker.)

Quilts have had strong emotional ties to ceremonies surrounding death. Making a mourning quilt for a deceased family member or friend has often been considered a mark of love and respect—and a comforting way for the quiltmaker to work through her grief.

Two pioneer Montello families were joined when Mary Eliza Wells married Clarence Cummings on Christmas Day 1904. Clarence worked for Evan Williams's furniture-undertaking business and in 1906 became the owner. There were no funeral homes at that time, so furniture merchants also sold caskets. Mary Cummings was well known as a quiltmaker and made whole-cloth quilts to be used as casket liners or to cover the deceased. She called them post-preparation quilts.

The preparation of the body, visitation, and funeral services were all conducted at the home of the deceased. Clarence then transported the lined casket to the cemetery in his black buggy, lit by kerosene side lamps and pulled by two black horses.

Mary and Clarence's daughter Eleanor recalled her father's house calls. "Trying times for the Cummings family were during the flu epidemic in 1918, when I would wake in the night to hear the door close and know father was going for another victim. Sometimes there would be more than one from a family. Many were close friends."

Mary was forty-nine years old in 1933 when she made a whole-cloth quilt that was given to her family rather than used as a casket liner. She gathered with friends at a quilting bee at Montello Trinity Methodist Church, and together they stitched the design of feather wreaths and straight lines that she had marked on the surface of a length of pink sateen, now faded to white. It had been purchased along with other fabrics at M. M. Smart's department store on Main Street. Mary made stitches that were neat and small—unlike one group member, whose stitches had to be removed before the quilt could be completed.[16]

String/Rolling Stone

Ellen Thomas Mason came to Wisconsin from the rural South after 1940, as did many black women, who brought with them their own quilting traditions and stories. As a young girl in the 1930s, Ellen Thomas helped her mother, Alice, make quilts on their farm near Utica, Mississippi. She picked cotton, fed the cows, weeded potatoes and peanuts, and shucked black walnuts to dye feed sacks for her mother's and grandmother's quilts. When her father sometimes returned from the cotton gin with some of the cleaned cotton, Ellen and her siblings sat cross-legged on the floor and beat the "white fluff" with paddles to make smooth batts for family quilts.

Ellen and her mother pieced their quilts by hand, using dressmaking scraps or pieces from large bags of cutaways ordered for one dollar from the Walter Field Company catalog.

Ellen's grandfather built a frame on pulleys in the "big room" of the house. It could be raised out of the way or lowered for making quilts. Ellen remembered using her imagination for the placement of curved lines of quilting. "You would quilt till you got sleepy or your neighbors went home."

Ellen also recalled the making of her mother's two-sided quilt. "Mother didn't have a lining for this, so she pieced one. She didn't piece nothing on the machine. See, this side is a string quilt. The other side—you call it the Rolling Stone? See this plaid and this fuchsia? They was from my dresses. Some of these pieces is old, old. Some of them I done forgot. All the people in the country—that's what they would do—make their own quilts. We didn't know nothing about buying blankets."[17]

Quiltmaker Alice Thomas Morris, Utica, Mississippi, c. 1940. (Photo courtesy of Ellen Thomas Mason.)

Quiltmaker Ellen Thomas Mason, Milwaukee, Wisconsin, 1998. (Photo courtesy of Ellen Thomas Mason.)

String
*Alice didn't have a lining for
this quilt, so she pieced one.*

PATTERN: *String/Rolling Stone (two-sided quilt)*
DATE: *1930s*
MAKER: *Ellen Thomas Mason (1919–) and her
    mother, Alice Thomas Morris (1900–1989)*
ORIGIN: *Hinds County, Mississippi*
FINISHED SIZE: *63" x 76"*
FABRIC: *Cotton*
OWNER: *Blessed and Giving Sewing (BAGS) of All
    Saints Parish, Milwaukee. Donated by Ellen Thomas
    Mason.*
LOCATION: *Milwaukee County, Wisconsin*

*Rolling
Stone*

PATTERN: *Map of the World—Chicago World's Fair, Sears "Century of Progress" Quilt Contest*

DATE: *1933*

MAKER: *Sophia Schoenike Krueger (Mrs. Herman) Clark (1899–1976)*

ORIGIN: *Marathon County, Wisconsin*

FINISHED SIZE: *68" x 89"*

FABRIC: *Cotton sateen*

OWNER: *The family of Sophia Clark—Marvin Krueger, Vila Klotzbuecher, Jim Clark, Anita Poepke, and Ganet Loberg*

LOCATION: *Marathon County, Wisconsin*

Map of the World

In January 1933, during the dark days of the Great Depression, Sears, Roebuck and Company announced a national quilting contest in conjunction with the Chicago World's Fair. With prize money totaling $7500, it was considered the greatest quilt competition ever held in the United States. The grand prize winner would receive $1000, and a $200 bonus would be added if the quilt was an original design featuring the fair's Century of Progress theme. That amount of money could go a long way toward a medium-size, three-bedroom house costing $3,000 or a luxury Dodge V-8 car that sold for $1,115. By today's standards the award would equal about $20,000.[18]

Families worked together to make quilts for the contest, neighbors helped one another, and women worked far into the night to place the last stitch before the deadline. Sears stores and mail-order centers throughout the country were overwhelmed with

Quiltmaker Sophia Krueger Clark, Plover, Wisconsin, 1933. (Photo courtesy of Jim Clark.)

entries—twenty-five thousand quilts by the May 15 deadline.[19]

Local winners won $10 and advanced to regional competition. Thirty regional winners received $200 each, and their quilts were displayed in the Sears Pavilion at the World's Fair.[20] The first-, second-, and third-place winners were chosen by a panel of judges. National judges for the final round of competition were Mary McElwain, owner of the Mary McElwain Quilt Shop in Walworth, Wisconsin; Anne Orr, quilt designer and needlework editor of *Good Housekeeping* magazine; contest organizer Sue Roberts of Sears, Roebuck and Company; and Beth Burnett, assistant director of the Chicago Art Institute. The quilt exhibit

became one of the fair's most popular attractions.[21]

Sophia Krueger made the headlines of the *Wausau Daily Herald* on May 19, 1933: "Plover Woman Is Designer of Quilt for World's Fair." Sophia was a widow in her mid-thirties who lived with her parents on their farm in the town of Plover, in east-central Wisconsin. She supported herself and her two children by doing custom sewing and alterations. Sophia's entire family encouraged her to enter the Sears competition. She designed a Map of the World quilt made of fifty-one different colors. A flag with stars representing all the nations of the world was stitched below the map and flanked by a quilted *Spirit of St. Louis* and *Graf Zeppelin*. The quilt was edged with six-inch-long, hand-tied fringe. Sophia entered the quilt in the original design division and received a green merit award at the local level."

Sophia later married Herman Clark and helped him operate a small grocery store west of Birnamwood until 1969. Her five children inspired her to become active in 4-H work. Her World's Fair quilt, which she entered in regional quilt competitions, won several prizes, and it continues to be a valued part of her legacy.[22]

Sophia's quilting awards.

Friendship and Family Crazy

Four generations of Abbie's family worked on this quilt.

PATTERN: *Friendship and Family Crazy. Displayed at the Chicago World's Fair, Sears "Century of Progress" Quilt Contest.*

DATE: *Begun December 7, 1897; completed April 1, 1933*

MAKER: *Abbie Elizabeth Hanson Diener (1878–1949)*

ORIGIN: *Begun in Winnebago County, Wisconsin; completed in Milwaukee County, Wisconsin.*

FINISHED SIZE: *66" x 84"*

FABRIC: *Velvet, wool; back is cotton sateen*

OWNER: *Betty Dean and Tom Diener, grandson of the maker*

LOCATION: *Dane County, Wisconsin*

Quiltmaker Abbie Elizabeth Hanson and Ernest Diener on their wedding day, Winnebago County, Wisconsin, September 1898. (Photo courtesy of Tom Diener.)

Quiltmaker Abbie Diener, Neenah, Wisconsin, 1940. (Photo courtesy of Tom Diener.)

Abbie Hanson of Neenah began making a quilt on December 7, 1897, when she was nineteen years old, in preparation for her marriage to Ernest Diener. Abbie was a Danish farm girl, the oldest of ten children, and she convinced her "city" husband to buy a farm in Winnebago County. Throughout the years of marriage, during which she gave birth to three sons, Abbie stitched the quilt piece by piece whenever she had spare time. Abbie and Ernest later divorced, and she moved to Milwaukee and bought the Raeborn Rooming House.

When the Sears quilt contest was announced, Abbie decided to finish her Friendship and Family Crazy quilt. During the thirty-six years that had passed, four generations of Abbie's family had worked on the quilt. Her elderly father called her a slave driver when she urged him to get his stitching finished. Each helper created his or her own block, and by 1933 a genealogy in cloth had emerged. It included Abbie's parents, Fred and Augusta Hanson, her brothers and sisters, three sons, grandchildren, nieces and nephews, in-laws, and friends. The eighty-six irregular blocks were joined, crazy-quilt style, and outlined with embroidery.

Abbie completed the quilt on April 1, 1933, and stitched the start and finish dates in red thread. She was fifty-five years old when she sent her wedding quilt, which was finally finished, to the contest. It won a green merit award.[24]

Linda and Clarence Rebenstorff of Caroline spent many weeks researching ideas for a quilt for the Sears competition. Clarence designed and cut each of the quilt's shaded pictorial blocks, including appliqué portraits of Abraham Lincoln, Charles Lindbergh, Franklin Roosevelt, and Thomas Edison. Linda did the piecing, quilting, and embroidery Even though it was a unique and stunning rendition of the Century of Progress theme, it didn't win a single prize.[25]

Fred Hanson, Clintonville, Wisconsin, 1930, who created a quilt block (right of center) for his daughter Abbie's competition quilt. (Photo courtesy of Tom Diener.)

PATTERN: *Muscatel Grape*
DATE: *Begun 1937, completed 1989*
MAKER: *Genevieve Peters Wainwright (1914–); appliqué and quilting done by a church group in Fontana, Wisconsin*
ORIGIN: *Walworth County, Wisconsin*
FINISHED SIZE: *83½" x 91½"*
FABRIC: *Cotton*
OWNER: *Wisconsin Quilt History Project. Donated by Genevieve and Richard Wainwright.*
LOCATION: *Ozaukee County, Wisconsin*

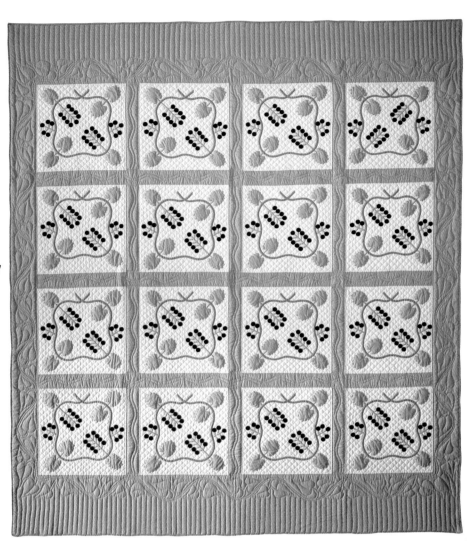

From left to right: Genevieve Peters, Mary McElwain, and Clareta Spencer in front of Mrs. Mac's home, 1935. (Photo courtesy of Genevieve Peters Wainwright.)

Muscatel Grape and Red Poppy

When William McElwain retired from the jewelry business in 1930, his wife, Mary, turned their Walworth store into a quilt shop, expanding her existing gift and needlework business. "Mr. Mac" did the shipping and bookkeeping, and their daughter DeEtte helped her mother in the store. Mary hired a high school student, Genevieve Peters, as her weekend typing assistant. After graduation Genevieve worked full-time—six eight-hour days at $10 per week. She duplicated patterns on the hectograph, learned to knit and crochet, and prepared fabric for the quilt kits sold in the shop.

The McElwain staff worked at a large table sewing two or three lengths of Peter Pan fabrics to create quilt backs in requested sizes. Yards of bias binding and Stiles Waxt thread were added to each kit. The patterns were varied—some pieced, some appliquéd, with many designed by Marie Webster. Mary also offered a design of her own: the Daisy Chain.

PATTERN: *Red Poppy*
DATE: *Begun 1937, completed 1986*
MAKERS: *Lydia Gates and Lucille Wainwright, appliqué and quilting done by a church group in Fontana, Wisconsin*
ORIGIN: *Walworth County, Wisconsin*
FINISHED SIZE: *80" x 103"*
FABRIC: *Cotton*
OWNER: *Wisconsin Quilt History Project. Donated by Genevieve and Richard Wainwright.*
LOCATION: *Ozaukee County, Wisconsin*

Richard Wainwright and Genevieve Peters, Walworth, Wisconsin, 1935. (Photo courtesy of Genevieve Peters Wainwright.)

Customers bought the kits and upon completion of the tops had the option of bringing them back to the shop for quilting. Mary hired skilled quiltmakers to do the quilting, including a woman in Kentucky by the name of Mrs. Scott. She also employed a group of area women to do basting, appliquéing, and quilting. Mary specialized in "one needle quilts," as was indicated in the catalog: "We are very glad to quilt any quilt tops sent to us, whether purchased from us or not. Our charges range from $10 to $21, depending on the type of quilting desired. Just one quilter works on a quilt so all the stitches are uniform. We do needle marking entirely so there are never any pencil lines to mar the beauty of the design."[26] Mrs. Schultz, the shop's cross-stitch expert, added a requested signature to complete each quilt.

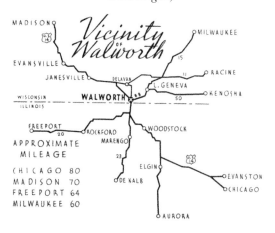

The McElwain shop was centrally located for customers from Chicago, Milwaukee, Madison, Beloit, and Janesville. The store attracted the wives of wealthy Chicago industrialists who had summer homes in nearby Lake Geneva. The McElwain name became synonymous with quiltmaking throughout the Midwest and was strengthened by a lucrative mail order business that distributed supplies and patterns all over the country.

One of Genevieve's favorite jobs at the shop was assisting Mary with quilt turnings. Quilts were layered on a black walnut four-poster bed. The two women turned them back one after another so customers could view the variety of quilts that could be made or purchased.

Genevieve recalls working for Mary McElwain: "Every day after lunch Mrs. Mac had her

Quilt pattern from Quilts and Spreads: Original Designs *by Marie D. Webster. (From the collection of Merikay Waldvogel.)*

Muscatel Grape pattern from Mary A. McElwain's catalog, The Romance of the Village Quilts. *(From the collection of Genevieve Wainwright.)*

'quiet time.' She always sat in her desk chair when she wasn't greeting customers. She would lean back in her chair, read her *Unity* magazine, and meditate. No one bothered her during this time. It was a pleasant place to work. We never had any 'words,' had a lot of laughs, and I learned a lot." [27]

Six months after Gen began working for Mrs. Mac, Richard Wainwright was hired to take charge of packages and mail. Five years later he asked Genevieve for a date, and they were married the following fall. Knowing the young couple would be leaving the store to move to Beloit, Mary suggested that they each choose a favorite quilt kit as a farewell gift. Genevieve chose the Muscatel Grape, described in the shop catalog as a design from a circa 1823 Kentucky quilt.[28] Dick chose the Red Poppy kit, a Marie Webster pattern. Gen's aunt Lydia Gates, who also worked for Mary McElwain, agreed to baste the intricate pieces into place for both quilt tops. Over the years, Gen did the appliqué stitches on her Grape quilt, and Dick's sister Lucile Wainwright completed the stitching on his quilt. In 1986, women of the Community Church in neighboring Fontana quilted the Red Poppy quilt, and in 1989, the Muscatel Grape.

Genevieve and Richard Wainwright celebrated their sixtieth wedding anniversary in October 1997.[29]

Mass-marketed quilt kits were available from needlework supply company catalogs, retail stores, women's magazines, newspapers, quilt shops, and even insurance companies and farm organizations. The time-and-labor-saving kits came in attractive packages with a variety of components. Women appreciated the efficiency of an already created design, cut pieces, and harmonious colors. The kit required basic sewing skills and was a simple and concise way to make a quilt.[30]

Mary McElwain's quilt shop, Walworth, Wisconsin, c. 1932. (Photo courtesy of Genevieve Peters Wainwright.)

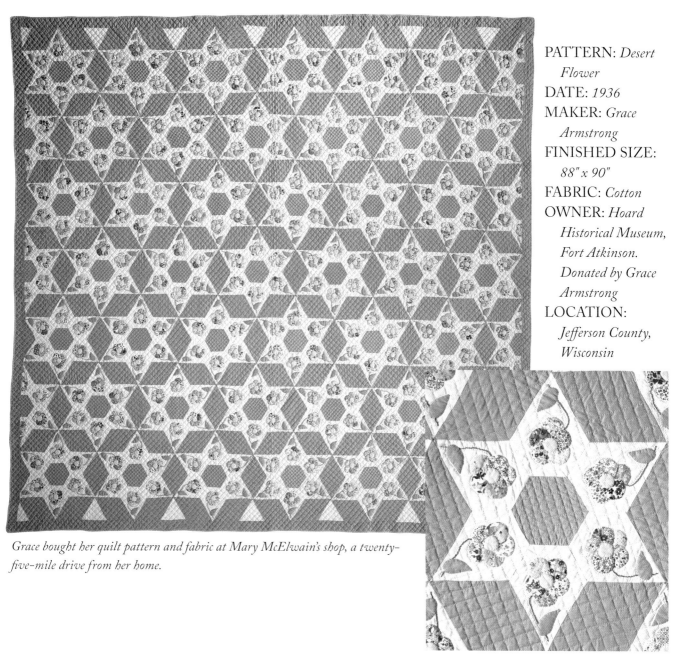

PATTERN: *Desert
    Flower*
DATE: *1936*
MAKER: *Grace
    Armstrong*
FINISHED SIZE:
    88" x 90"
FABRIC: *Cotton*
OWNER: *Hoard
    Historical Museum,
    Fort Atkinson.
    Donated by Grace
    Armstrong*
LOCATION:
    *Jefferson County,
    Wisconsin*

Grace bought her quilt pattern and fabric at Mary McElwain's shop, a twenty-five-mile drive from her home.

Desert Flower

Grace Armstrong lived with her unmarried brother and sister on their homestead farm in southern Jefferson County. Grace and her sister spent long winter evenings piecing quilts. In 1936 the two women made the twenty-five-mile trip to Mary McElwain's quilt shop in Walworth to choose fabric and a new pattern. Grace purchased a design called Desert Flower for thirty-five cents. She relied on her scrap bag for pastel floral prints with which to fashion the hundreds of flower petals. Her apple green setting

fabric was a hallmark shade of the thirties and a perfect background for the varied prints. She pieced every seam by hand, carefully appliquéing the petals and quilting the surface with stitches measuring ten to the inch.

The quilt, placed in Grace's hope chest, was never used. She donated it to the Hoard Historical Museum in Fort Atkinson, not far from the home where she lived all her life.[31]

Small Rocking Horse, Deer and Butterflies, and Wild Geese and Deer

One of three crib quilts purchased from a Beaver Dam, Wisconsin, school by Delores Sundeen.

PATTERN: *Small Rocking Horse*
DATE: *c. 1935–1940*
MAKER: *WPA Handicraft Project, Milwaukee State Teachers College*
FINISHED SIZE: *40" x 60"*
FABRIC: *Percale*
OWNER: *Delores Sundeen*
LOCATION: *Milwaukee County, Wisconsin*

PATTERN: *Deer and Butterflies*
DATE: *c. 1935–1940*
MAKER: *WPA Handicraft Project, Milwaukee State Teachers College*
ORIGIN: *Milwaukee County, Wisconsin*
FINISHED SIZE: *39" x 57"*
FABRIC: *Percale*
OWNER: *Delores Sundeen, purchased from a school in Beaver Dam, Wisconsin.*
LOCATION: *Milwaukee County, Wisconsin*

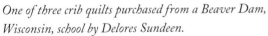

A child sleeping under a WPA quilt in Milwaukee. (Photo courtesy of the Milwaukee Public Museum.)

The stock market crash of 1929 precipitated a major depression of the US economy. By 1933, when Franklin Delano Roosevelt began his first term as president, millions of people had lost their jobs and had nowhere to turn for help. Within a hundred days Roosevelt had received congressional funding for his New Deal program, a collection of government agencies charged with providing relief and spurring recovery. The Works Progress Administration (WPA) was one such agency, created in 1935 to administer work relief jobs to provide income for the unemployed.

Working with the WPA, Milwaukee County developed a unique handicrafts project that garnered national recognition. Under the auspices of the Milwaukee State Teachers College (MSTC), the goal of the project was to employ all women on relief rolls in Milwaukee County. Another prime objective was to raise the standards of crafts and crafts education. The project began with industrial-type sewing of garments for inmates of county institutions. It evolved, with the help of Elsa Ulbricht, into such handicrafts as bookbinding; rug, doll, and quilt making; weaving; and the making of furniture and toys. Ulbricht was an art professor at MSTC, now the University of Wisconsin-Milwaukee, and her creative, determined spirit was a guiding force. Her philosophy was that anything worth doing was worth doing well. She employed young artists as designers and championed her belief in quality, cultural development, and education.[32]

WPA Handicraft Project identifying stamp.

Ulbricht appointed art student Mary June Kellogg, now Mrs. Rice, as art director, and the two of them designed the program. Women who took part were paid $50 a month and given medical care.[33] Later, Ulbricht described the early participants: "Many of them had had no work or very meager work experiences; many had been out of employment for so many months that they had become disheartened and depressed. They were of all ages, all nationalities… some could neither read nor write, Negro and white, of all degrees of intelligence and education."[34]

To avoid competing with private industry, the handicrafts project produced items that were sold only to tax-supported institutions for the cost of materials. Dolls, quilts, and wooden toys were made for children in government orphanages, schools, and WPA nurseries. Sample packets of crafts, such as block prints and quilt blocks, were sold at cost to school libraries and museums as educational items. Portfolios of quilt block designs were used by public institutions as marketing tools to stimulate the ordering of quilts.

Designers, instead of quilters, planned the quilt projects, and thus the construction of many of the patterns proved to be difficult. But time and labor were abundant, and the result was fine-quality piece-work and appliqué.[35] Mrs. Rice, the art director of the project, recalled, "The project quilts were made of 200 thread count percales in solid colors. It was the finest quality available. I had to fight to get it through the government system that was geared to buying construction materials for buildings and the like."[36]

The quilting of WPA quilts was of less importance than the graphic impact of their design. In fact, the quilting was minimal, usually surrounding large design elements, and batting was nonexistent except for special orders. Many of the quilts were meant to cover nondescript gray wool blankets already in use in orphanages and nurseries, so they needed only to provide cheerfulness, not warmth.[37]

As word of the project's success spread, educators from around the country toured its classrooms and workshops. Dr. Jane Betsey Welling, professor of education at Wayne State University, later described the spirit of the program. "I visited

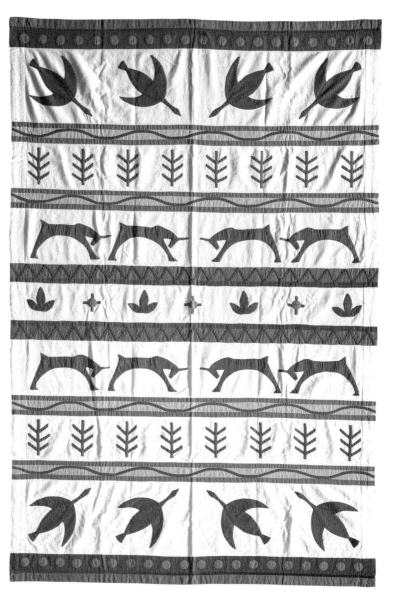

A cheerful crib quilt made to cover wool blankets and purchased by the state-owned Wisconsin Emergency Nursery Schools.

PATTERN: *Wild Geese and Deer*
DATE: *c. 1935–1940*
MAKER: *WPA Handicraft Project, Milwaukee State Teachers College*
ORIGIN: *Milwaukee County, Wisconsin*
FINISHED SIZE: *40" x 60"*
FABRIC: *Percale*
OWNER: *Delores Sundeen, purchased from a school in Beaver Dam, Wisconsin*
LOCATION: *Milwaukee County, Wisconsin*

this project in the late thirties. There in a great room with temporary partitions made functionally gay by their own wares and material, I saw people...working together earnestly and with that sort of joy in work and pride in workmanship which comes only when there is true identification with one's work. Here was that creative spark which makes hard work play and products craftsmanlike from start to finish."[38]

Eleanor Roosevelt, in her newspaper column "My Day," also wrote glowingly about the project. "Milwaukee has a handicraft project for unskilled women which gives one a perfect thrill. They are doing artistic work under most able teachers. The materials they use are of the least expensive variety, but...they are making dolls as attractive as any I have seen and much more original."[39]

As the WPA Handicraft Project became obsolete, school and institutional quilts either wore out or found their way into the homes of teachers and caregivers. Delores Sundeen taught fourth grade in Beaver Dam at the time the quilts were made and was able to purchase Small Rocking Horse, Deer and Butterflies, and Wild Geese and Deer quilts from the school.

Mrs. Quentin O'Sullivan purchased a Rocking Horse quilt similar to Delores Sundeen's from a Milwaukee schoolteacher. Mrs. O'Sullivan's mother, Elizabeth Danielson, was director of the program's hooked rug department and praised the WPA for the dignity, job skills, and sense of purpose it provided participants. In 1943 the program officially ended, leaving its legacy of quilts, toys, dolls, prints, and furniture to be discovered by a later generation.

Lillian Wolters tutored Mrs. Feldhahn's daughter. The quilt top was given to her in appreciation for her services.

Broken Star

PATTERN: *Broken Star*
DATE: *1936*
MAKER: *Mrs. Lily Feldhahn (1900–1990)*
ORIGIN: *Sauk County, Wisconsin*
FINISHED SIZE: *95" x 95"*
FABRIC: *Cotton*
OWNER: *Lillian Wolters*
LOCATION: *Sauk County, Wisconsin*

In the small town of Hillpoint, in Sauk County, Lily Feldhahn made quilts for pay and quilts for pleasure. In the 1930s she made Double Wedding Ring, Grandmother's Flower Garden, Broken Star, and Sunbonnet Baby quilts. Her husband made a quilt frame and metal templates. Lily used the templates and a darning needle to scratch quilting patterns onto cloth as a way of avoiding pencil markings.

Lily's daughter, Dorothy, often helped with the cutting, but Lily did the stitching. In the summer of 1936, Dorothy's eighth-grade history teacher, Lillian Wolters, came to the house to tutor Dorothy. In appreciation for her help, Lily made her a Broken Star quilt top. Several years later, Lillian took it to the ladies at nearby Ironton Methodist Church to have it quilted.[40]

Wreath of Leaves

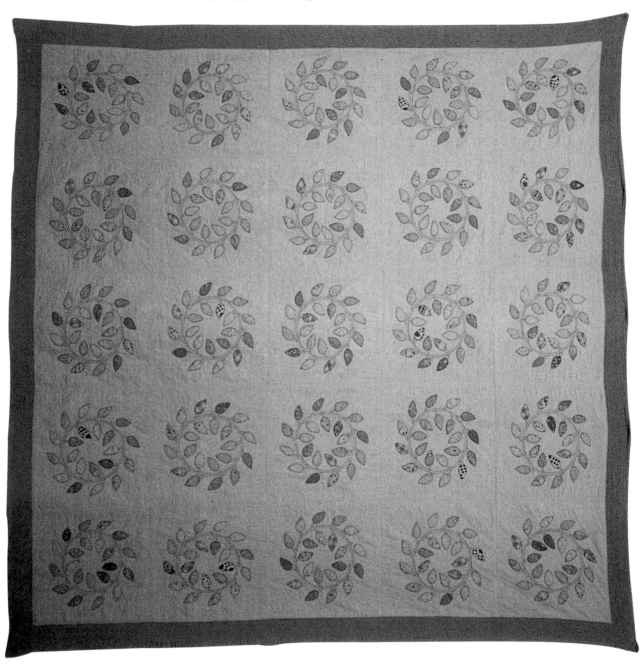

PATTERN: *Wreath of Leaves*

DATE: *c. late 1930s*

MAKER: *Corine Courture McLeod (1871–1960)*

ORIGIN: *Barron County, Wisconsin*

FINISHED SIZE: *85½" x 88"*

FABRIC: *Cotton*

OWNER: *Catherine Veitch, granddaughter of the maker*

LOCATION: *Barron County, Wisconsin*

Quiltmaker Corine Courture McLeod and her husband, John, in front of their home, Rice Lake, Wisconsin, c. 1939. (Photo courtesy of Pat Buchli.)

Corine McLeod lived in the small rural community of Rice Lake in northwestern Wisconsin. She arrived there as a child from Quebec with her French-Irish parents. After her daughters were grown, Corine used her horse, Barney, to drive a company-owned buggy through Barron County for the Grand Union Tea Company. She traveled country roads selling tea, coffee, and spices. The company offered ceramic dishes as a purchase premium, and women collected them piece by piece. Corine knew her customers well and often stayed overnight in their homes. She relinquished her tea route in 1922 in order to care for an infant niece whose mother had died in childbirth.

In the late 1930s, when Corine was in her sixties, she made a Wreath of Leaves quilt for her daughter Laura. The pattern, borrowed from a neighbor, allowed her to use small pieces of many colors for the leaves. The quilt is owned by Corine's granddaughter, who still lives in Barron County.[41]

The Wreath of Leaves pattern appeared in a Mary McElwain Quilt Shop catalog in 1936. The pattern could be ordered for thirty-five cents, and a ready-cut quilt top could be purchased for $12.50. In the Julia Fischer Force catalog, the pattern was listed "courtesy of Mary A. McElwain" and described in advertising copy as having been reproduced from an original quilt done in about 1830 in Racine. Boag, a kit company from Elgin, Illinois, did the packaging for the kit. Wreath of Leaves became a popular pattern among midwestern quilters.[42]

PATTERN: *Sunflower (The Green Quilt for Black Diamond)*
DATE: *1943*
MAKER: *Irene "Rena" Martel (Mrs. Hector) Sholette*
(1901–1956)
ORIGIN: *On the Great Lakes, aboard a Columbia*
Transportation Company steamship

FINISHED SIZE: *76" x 92"*
FABRIC: *Cotton*
OWNER: *Joyce Sholette Herringer, daughter of the*
maker
LOCATION: *Racine County, Wisconsin*

Sunflower (The Green Quilt for Black Diamond)

During World War II women served in the armed forces, entered the job force in ever-increasing numbers, took the places of men called away to war, and made baby quilts for the families of servicemen. Rena Sholette's husband, Hector, was one of five Sholette brothers sailing the Great Lakes for various steamship lines during the war. The five Sholette wives sailed and worked with their husbands.

Hector was a chef for Columbia Transportation Company, and Rena served as second cook. Each day she made doughnuts, bread, and other pastries for the thirty-five to forty men on board. After the baking was completed, she got out her prized Singer Featherweight machine and worked on quilts and other sewing projects.

In 1943 she made a green and white Sunflower quilt for her daughter Joyce. The Paragon Sunflower kit, sold as a *Woman's Day* "exclusive," was the perfect shipboard project. The appliqués were stamped on green-printed Quadriga cloth, and Rena did one block at a time, cutting, turning under, and whipstitching the small pieces to a white percale background. Joyce's nickname was Black Diamond, and the Sholette family called Rena's creation the Green Quilt for Black Diamond.

When the ship docked in Milwaukee or Racine, Rena enjoyed shopping trips ashore. The Sholettes returned to their winter home in upstate New York when the nine-month sailing season ended and the boat was dry-docked in Buffalo. On one of their journeys from the ship to their home, they boarded the New York Central train in Buffalo. Hector, who personally carried Rena's sewing machine, accidentally left it on the station platform. It was never recovered, and Hector willingly bought her a new one.

The Sunflower quilt now resides with Rena's daughter, Joyce, in Racine.[44]

Quiltmaker Rena Sholette and her husband, Hector, on the deck of a Great Lakes merchant marine vessel, c. 1944. (Photo courtesy of Joyce Sholette Herringer.)

Streak of Lightning

The December 7, 1941, Japanese attack on Pearl Harbor had a powerful effect on Pauline Kelly. Her son, Norbert, was stationed there, and she was thankful to receive the news that he had not been injured or killed. Other mothers were not as fortunate, so Pauline decided to form a Milwaukee chapter of the Navy Mother's Club of America. Members of the club invited sailors from the Great Lakes Naval Training Center to their houses for home-cooked meals. They also sponsored dances and met monthly to make baby quilts for navy families. Their intent was not to create beautiful, time-consuming pieces of needlework, but to make small, warm, tied comforters out of donated scraps of fabric. Their favorite quilts were the Log Cabin and Streak of Lightning.

Pauline Kelly became national commander of the Navy Mother's Club of America. In the early 1950s she gave some of the organization's extra quilts to her niece Audrey Yaeger to use for her own children. The Streak of Lightning quilt is one of those quilts that was packed away by Pauline and never used.[43]

PATTERN: *Streak of Lightning*
DATE: *1942*
MAKER: *Unknown member of the Navy Mother's Club of America*
ORIGIN: *Milwaukee County, Wisconsin*
FINISHED SIZE: *34½" x 57½"*
FABRIC: *Cotton*
OWNER: *Audrey Yaeger*
LOCATION: *Jefferson County, Wisconsin*

The Journey Continues, 1950-Present

World War II changed the country's political and domestic landscape forever. Women filled jobs left vacant by men out of necessity, but when peace came they remained an ever-growing presence in the work force. The measure of a woman's worth would never again be confined to how many quilting stitches she could place per inch.

Although quilt making seemed to make a retreat over the next twenty years, there was never really an interruption. Quilts continued to be made by a smaller number of women who still loved the craft. And even with the invention and marketing of the sewing machine and the mass production of blankets and ready-made bedcovers, women hand-sewed and stitched quilt tops and quilts.[1]

The Quilting Bee, *a Works Progress Administration wood engraving by Frank A. B. Utpatel, was exhibited at the 7th Wisconsin Salon of Art at the University of Wisconsin Memorial Union in 1940, where it won the $25.00 purchase award. It also appeared on the Salon poster and in the catalog. (Engraving property of the Wisconsin Union Galleries Collection.)*

The status of quilts was strengthened immeasurably in 1971, when the Whitney Museum of American Art showcased an exhibition of quilts from the collection of Jonathan Holstein and Gail van der Hoof titled *Abstract Design in American Quilts*. The emphasis was on the visual characteristics of pieced quilts.[2]

"As the 1976 bicentennial approached, a quilt-making renaissance emerged," according to Wisconsin quilt artist Ann Fahl. "History, nostalgia, and new technology combined to shape a vibrant quilt making explosion which moved quilts from the bed to the gallery wall. Now a new group of art quilters has emerged. They use the same components as found in traditional quilting: fabric, thread, batting, patchwork, and appliqué. Instead of the need to make a utilitarian item for the bed, these artists employ new technology and products to create an artistic medium to portray emotion and color."[3]

Judy Zoelzer Levine, another Wisconsin quilt artist, suggests that as the art quilt movement continues to evolve, there is a stronger emphasis on individuality in the form of personal expression and personal vision. She says: "Wildly vivid quilts with explosions of color and texture counterbalance quilts of simple, understated elegance. Today's art quilter uses dyes, paints, discharges, photo transfers, and embellishments, as well as appliquéing and piecing, to convey messages that range from the deeply introspective to the witty and frivolous. Materials range from traditional cotton, silk, and wool to lame, spandex, window screening, and recycled plastic bags. Quilt statements cover everything from war, poverty, abuse, and illness to personal impressions of birth, daily life, and nature. The concept of 'What is a quilt?' is constantly challenged as art quilters take familiar, everyday materials and reshape and mold them into something new and unexpected."[4] Quilt making continues to flourish as both art and fine needlework.

When read as a diary, a quilt becomes a portrait of the woman who made it, of those who came before her, and of those who follow. As women work on their quilts, the quilts themselves often become places of refuge and strength, places of belonging. Quilts serve as metaphors for memory, and the quilter is the messenger. What the quilt maker and her descendants ask us to do is remember the stories, tell them again and again, and pass back through the heart what it is that speaks to us, what it is that helps shape and connect our lives.

Creating Your Own Heirloom

Heirloom quilts lend themselves to creative re-interpretation. This section contains directions for making the blocks for eight of the quilts in the previous chapters. We have used modern fabrics and up-to-date techniques and equipment, but these aspects should not diminish the feeling of creating a piece of your own history.

The directions are presented step-by-step and are illustrated to provide information clearly and concisely. The constraints of space mean that we have in most cases provided directions for assembling one block. To make a full quilt, you will need to calculate yardage and decide on borders, sashing, setting blocks, etc., yourself. Directions for assembling quilt layers can be found in many general quiltmaking books and magazines.

 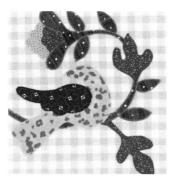  

Roman Stripe Block

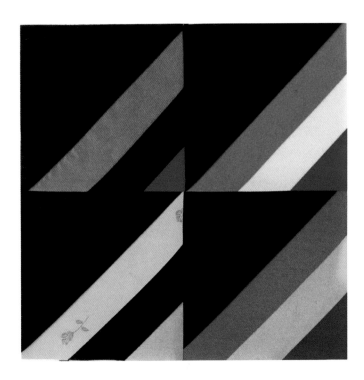

Sample made by Marion Wolfe

The original quilt, shown on page 110, shimmers with the highlights that come from the wonderful silks and satins used in its creation. Quilters know that working with fancy fabrics like silk and velvet requires some special handling. The Roman Stripe block provides a good introduction to using these fabrics, but this quilt would also be lovely made in cotton fabrics and might be an opportunity to reduce the size of a scrap basket.

Silk has a marked tendency to fray and can be tricky to handle, especially in narrow strips or small pieces. Increasing the seam allowances to ½" can help eliminate these dangers. Using a lightweight iron-on interfacing on the wrong side of the fabric before cutting is another good way to decrease raveling. While the interfacing will give the fabric more body, it may increase the stiffness of the finished quilt and be harder to hand quilt.

In Roman Stripe the square blocks are made from two right-angle triangles, one of which is pieced as diagonal stripes. In this version the pieced side of each block is made from three strips. Most of the corner triangles are red and the strips are multicolored, mainly brights. There is no border, only a light-colored binding.

Making the Roman Stripe Quilt

1 Cut eighty-four 6" squares. You can use the same fabric for each square or cut a variety. Ours are black. Cut each square on the diagonal to make 168 triangles.

2 Cut a selection of strips 1¾" wide. To stabilize fabrics that tend to fray, iron lightweight interfacing to the wrong side before cutting.

3 Cut the strips into lengths. You need 168 strips about 4" long, 168 strips at least 6" long, and 168 strips at least 8" long. Make sure to get a good range of lights and darks.

4 Sew one 8" strip to the long side of each triangle.

5 Center a 6" strip on the raw edge of the first strip and sew it in place.

6 Center a 4" strip on the raw edge of the second strip and sew it in place.

7 Using a square ruler, trim the ends of the strips to make 168 squares.

8 Join the blocks in rows of fourteen, then join the twelve rows to complete the quilt top. In the Roman Stripe pattern, the pieced strips all face in the same direction.

9 Layer the quilt top, batting, and backing, then quilt and bind the quilt.

Old Maid's Puzzle Block

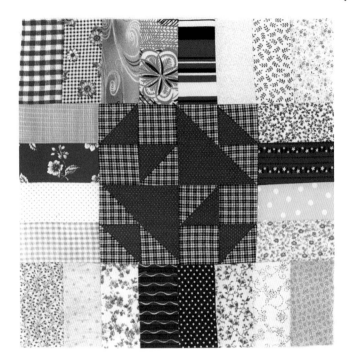

Sample made by Maggi Gordon

Old Maid's Puzzle is a classic four-patch block made from squares and triangles. It is not difficult, but requires careful piecing. The maker of the original quilt, shown on page 102, was Louisa Hanneman Gilow, who used mainly solid shirting and microprints to make her blocks. But in one case she pieced stripes so they run in different directions, making a fascinating eye-popper.

Several of Louisa's blocks combine checks and microdots, and we have used this combination for the sample shown here, together with scrap-basket sashing in the spirit of the original.

Making One Block and Sashing

    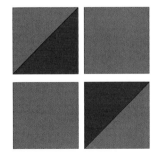 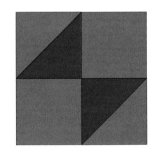

1 Cut three 2⅞" squares from the red microdot and the black-and-white check fabrics. Make six triangle squares as shown on page 192. Press.

2 Cut four 2½" black-and-white check squares. Join two squares to two triangle squares as shown. Make two of these units and sew them together, taking care to arrange the colors as shown.

3 Cut two black-and-white check 1⅞" squares and cut them in half along the diagonal.

4 Stitch them as shown to either side of the red triangles in the two remaining triangle squares made in step 1.

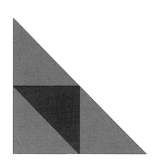

5 Cut one red microdot 4⅞" square and cut it in half along the diagonal. Stitch the long edge of one large red triangle to the long side of one of the pieced triangles made in Step 5. Make sure the small red triangle points toward the large red one. Repeat to make two units.

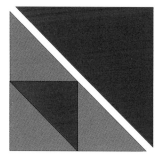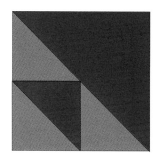

6 Combine the four units as shown. Join them in pairs, then join the pairs to make one block.

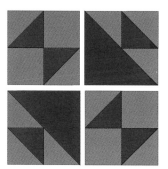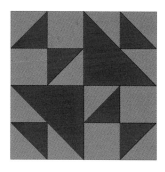

7 For the sashing cut strips 2½" x 4½". Join four strips along their long edges, repeat to make another sashing unit. Stitch these sashing units to opposite sides of the block. Join eight strips in the same way. Join these to the other sides of the block.

Tip: The original quilt has six rows of six blocks each. If you are making a full quilt, you will need to sash one side of each of five blocks with a four-strip unit. When you have joined these into rows with six blocks each, you will need five sash units of 34 strips each to join the rows together.

Grandmother's Flower Garden Path Block

Sample made by Mary Mauer

Grandmother's Flower Garden is a classic pattern made from hexagons. It is traditionally worked using the English paper piecing method. In this technique, heavy paper hexagons are cut to the finished size and fabric hexagons are cut ¼"–⅜" larger. Each fabric shape is basted to a paper pattern through the paper. The edges are then buttonhole-stitched or whipstitched to create rosettes of seven hexagons, one in the center and six around the edges. These rosettes can then be joined, usually with another row of hexagons of perhaps white or green to make a sort of path between them (fig. 1). Once the top is finished, the papers are removed.

There are several examples of Grandmother's Flower Garden quilts in this book. The sample shown here is unusual for its medallion center, shown on page 151. We have recreated a section of the medallion center to demonstrate the technique. We have used an up-to-date material for creating the hexagons. Brandy's® Mylar Pieces are precut plastic shapes that come in a selection of sizes and shapes. They can be used over and over, and make perfect pieces every time. See p. 183 for more information about this product.

Making Hexagon Patterns

1 Pin a Mylar shape to fabric through the hole in the center of the shape.

2 Cut a generous ¼" or larger seam allowance around the plastic piece. Cut fabric hexagons for several rosettes or rows.

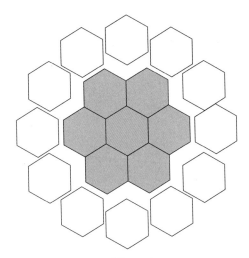

Figure 1

3 With the pin still in place, fold the fabric over one edge to the back at one corner. Miter the corner, and take a stitch with knotted thread and then a backstitch over the fold of the miter.

4 Move to the next corner with one long stitch and repeat.

5 Continue around the shape until one corner is left. Remove the pin, miter the corner, and stitch in the same way as the other corners. If you don't take out the pin before stitching the last miter, you get a little lump in the center of the shape. Take the final long stitch to the beginning corner. There, take the final stitch and backstitch. There will be seven backstitches in all. Make a good selection of basted hexagons before you begin assembling the quilt.

Assembling Grandmother's Flower Garden

1 Choose two adjoining hexagons and butt two edges together with right sides together. Make sure the corners on both edges are even. With a knotted thread start a few stitches in from the corner and whipstitch to the end. Go back over the first few stitches and buttonhole-stitch to the other end. Go back over the last few stitches, knot the thread, and tie off. If the knots are at the corners, they create bulk and lumps.

2 Continue to join pieces together in this manner. To make rosettes, join the six hexagons around the center first. Then remove the center plastic shape and stitch the adjoining sides. You can also sew hexagons in rows.

3 When the top is complete, remove all the plastic pieces. Press the entire top from the wrong side. The basting can be removed, but this is not absolutely necessary. In any case, because it holds the hexagon shapes so well, it should be left along the outside edges at least until you have applied your border.

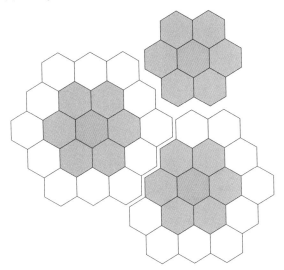

Note: There are fifty pieces in a pack. When you need more shapes, remove plastic pieces from hexagons that have already been surrounded by other pieces. The basted shapes retain their shape well, but removing the plastic shapes from pieces that have not been fully enclosed means you lose the rigid edge that makes sewing pieces together so simple and accurate. To set the edges, press joined sections with a cool iron before removing the plastic pieces. Leave the plastic pieces in place on all the outside edges until the top is finished. Then press again and remove the last row of pieces.

Brandy's Mylar Pieces are sold in packs. They can be purchased at quilt stores or by contacting Brandy's* at www.brandysquiltpatterns.com or by phoning 870-342-5005 or faxing 870-342-5030. Brandy's instructions for using the pieces differ slightly from ours. Try both to see which you prefer.

Feathered Star Block

16" finished block

Sample made by Sylvia Adair

Tiny bias squares like the ones that make the "feathers" surrounding the star and the narrow border that goes around the edges of the original quilt can be tricky to handle. Cutting strips on the bias and sewing them together before cutting the squares means that the outside edges of each 1" square will be on the straight of grain. The seam on the strips should be pressed open. All other seams should be pressed to one side. The original quilt, Mary Jane's Star, is shown on page 29.

Initial Cutting List:

Cut approximately 3½ to 4 yd. of 1" bias strips from blue fabric and the same amount from white fabric.

> Eight 1½" white squares
> Four 1½" blue squares
> Four 3¼" blue squares
> One 9¼" white square
> Four 4½" white squares
> One 8½" blue center square

Making the Feathered Star Block

1 Join 1" white strips to 1" blue strips lengthwise with a ¼" seam. Press the seams open.

2 Line up a small square acrylic ruler with the 45-degree line along the seam and trim the ends, creating a point. Then turn the ruler to face the other way and mark a 1" square with the diagonal seam along the diagonal mark on the ruler. Cut 120 1" squares.

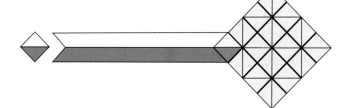

3 Join the bias squares in strips with the blues always facing in the same direction. Make eight strips of seven squares each, and eight strips of eight squares each.

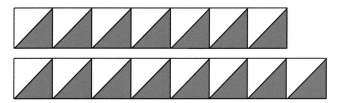

4 Cut the eight white 1½" squares in half along the diagonal to make 16 triangles. Add one white triangle to the blue end of each strip, making four left-hand and four right-hand versions. Cut the four blue 1½" squares in half along the diagonal to make eight right-angle triangles. Add one triangle to the white end of each eight-square strip, again paying close attention to make four left-hand and four right-hand versions.

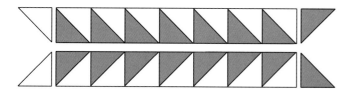

5 Cut the four 3¼" blue squares in half along the diagonal to make eight right-angle triangles. Add one eight-square strip of tiny triangles to the long bias edge of a blue triangle. Check the color position carefully.

6 Add one seven-square strip to each triangle unit along one straight edge. Make mirror images: that is, four right-hand and four left-hand versions. Again, check the color position carefully.

7 Cut the 9¼" white square twice along the diagonals to make four right-angle triangles. Join one blue and white feathered point from step 6 to each of the short edges of each white triangle to make double points.

8 Add a 4½" white square to each end of two of the completed double-point sections.

9 Add the other two (short) double-point sections to opposite sides of the 8½" blue center square.

10 Add the star-points-and-squares sections to the remaining opposite sides of the center square.

Vase of Flowers Appliqué Block

Sample made by Karen Moore

This charming block, shown here in bright colors, would also be very effective made from scraps. The scale of the block and the appliqué shapes is large enough to make this a suitable project for a beginner to hand appliqué, especially since there are no deep valleys or sharp points to contend with. It is relatively quick to make the thirty blocks needed to replicate the original quilt, shown on page 131.

Cotton fabric is usually preferred for hand appliqué because it is tightly woven and supple enough to make turning the seam allowances under easy.

Making One Block

1 Cut a 17" background square. We used a white tone-on-tone cotton. Fold the square in half twice and press lightly to mark the center.

2 Enlarge the pattern on page 187 and align the center of the pattern with the center of the background square. Trace the design lightly on the background fabric slightly inside the lines of the pattern to provide guidelines that can be easily hidden when the pieces are applied.

3 Cut out the shapes from the templates on page 187. You need one blue vase, nine pink petals, and three yellow flower centers. Mark the turn-under allowances on each piece and finger press. If you mark on the right side of the fabric, make sure the marks can be removed easily. Some people cut the finished shapes (without

turn under) from freezer paper. Iron this to the right side of the fabric and turn under the seam allowances by following the edge of the freezer paper shapes.

4 Cut 1½" green bias strips for the stems. Fold the edges of the strip in half to the wrong side lengthwise and stitch a ¼" seam. Trim the seam allowances slightly and fold the strip with the seam centered on the back to make a tube ⅜" wide. Press.

5 Position an 8" bias tube to make the center flower stem. Pin it in place and sew along the length of both long edges with tiny stitches. There is no need to turn under the raw edges on the ends, as these will be covered by other pieces.

6 Apply the two side stems in the same way. They should be approximately 6" long. Pin them carefully to create the slight curve.

7 Apply the pink flower petals. The center petal is worked first on each flower. They will cover one end of the bias stems.

Pin the piece in place, turning under the ¼" seam allowance as you work. Use the point of the needle to smooth out the edges as you sew.

8 Add the side petals, so they touch at their edges and cover part of the center petal. Do not sew through to the background where one piece covers another.

9 Add the yellow flower centers, again making sure you don't sew through to the background fabric.

10 Add the blue vase, covering the bottom end of the stems completely. Pin the piece in place and again use tiny stitches to apply it to the background.

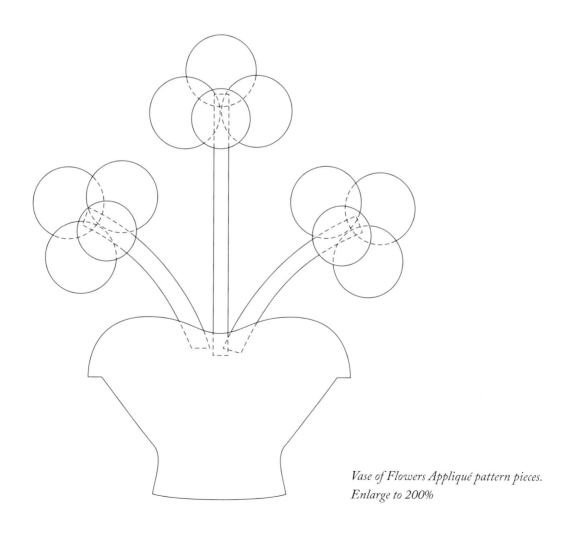

Vase of Flowers Appliqué pattern pieces.
Enlarge to 200%

Jo's Garden Appliqué Block

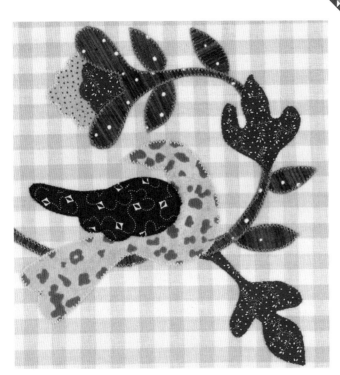

A pattern for Jo's Garden, featured on the cover and based on the quilt shown on page 118, can be obtained from the Wisconsin Museum of Quilts & Textiles, P.O. Box 562, Cedarburg, WI 53012, telephone 262-546-0300.

Appliquéing the Bird Motif

1 Trace the pattern onto fusible web using an ultra-fine permanent marker. Transfer the shapes to the wrong side of the relevant fabrics using a warm dry iron.

2 Cut out the shapes to be applied. To assemble the bird and its branch, use a leftover piece of the release sheet from the fusible web as a "holding place." Remove the paper backing from the appliqué pieces and iron the pieces in order on the sheet. Ironing the shapes onto a piece of the release sheet means that once they are assembled, they can be removed as one unit to be applied permanently to the background fabric.

Sample made by Jo Ann Jacobi
The quilt pictured on the cover was made by Jo Ann Jacobi of East Troy, Wisconsin. Jo used the Appliquéd Floral Medallion quilt by Alice Huebner Besau pictured on page 118 as inspiration for her quilt, Jo's Garden. It was quilted by Penny Gerds of Waterford on her household sewing machine, and when it was finished, it was offered to Wisconsin Quilters Inc. (WQI) as a fund-raiser. It was raffled in 2003 and now belongs to Ruth Ann Mathwig of Oshkosh, Wisconsin. Jo's version is machine appliquéd. The charming bird motif is found in the inner border of the quilt.

3 Apply the fused motif to the background fabric following the manufacturer's directions for using the fusible web. Because the motifs are already assembled and the background is made in units, Jo finds it easy to position the motifs on the background by "eyeballing" them. Remember, though, that once ironed, they will be bonded to the background permanently.

4 Stitch the motifs in place. Jo worked with 100-percent cotton thread with a zigzag stitch set at 1.5 width and 2.0 length. To tie off, she sewed a straight stitch along the edge of the shape about ¼" in a clockwise direction. Then she turned the piece and worked a zigzag counterclockwise all around the shape. When she got back to the starting place, she changed back to the straight stitch, made a tiny tack knot, pulled it to the back of the work, and clipped her thread.

Bird motif pattern

Appliquéd Flowers Block

Sample made by Maribeth Schmit
We have made this sample to represent the two major elements in the original quilt, shown on page 71. First are the diagonal rows of leaves with a stylized floral motif in the center. Second is the motif with four flowers arranged in a cross. The original quilt was made from nine large blocks with the diagonal leaf-and-vine motif, which can be joined and the four-flower motifs applied over the seams.

1 Cut a 30" background square. Fold the square in half twice to find the center, and align the pattern on the background. Transfer the design images to it using a water-soluble marker that you have tested first.

2 Trace the appliqué pieces on page 191 onto the paper side of freezer paper with a fine pencil or pen. You need 40 large green leaves, 8 small green leaves, 8 red flowers, and 4 yellow circles. Cut the motifs out leaving smooth edges on the paper. Iron the freezer paper shapes to the wrong side of the appropriate fabrics and cut them out, leaving a scant ¼" seam allowance all around. Then fold the seam allowance to the back. Using a toothpick to manipulate the fabric, and a glue stick, lightly glue the seam allowance to the paper side of the freezer paper. Clip the fabric as needed to achieve a smooth edge and sharp points.

3 Cut four strips of green fabric on the straight grain, each 1½" wide and 15" long. With wrong sides together, stitch a seam along the long edge of each strip to make a tube measuring ⅜" wide. Trim the raw edges to leave a ⅛" seam allowance. Insert a ⅜" bias rod into the tube and position the seam along the center back. Press firmly using starch to achieve a crisp stem. When it is cool, remove the bias bar and press again.

4 Appliqué the main stems first, either by hand or with an invisible machine-appliqué stitch. Repeat this step for the large leaves (there are ten per stem) and one large red flower to the outer end of each stem.

Appliquéd Flower pattern pieces.
Enlarge to 200%

5 To create the motif in the center of the block, cut a strip of yellow fabric 2" wide and approximately 15" long. Cut a strip of red fabric ¾" wide and 15" long. With right sides together, use a ¼" seam to sew the strips together along one long edge. Press the seam toward the red. Fold the red fabric to the back over the ¼" seam allowance and press. Then trim the excess red fabric to a scant ¼".

6 To make the trapezoid shapes, cut four freezer paper templates. Line up the widest side along the folded edge of the red strip and iron them to the right side of the pieced strip as shown, leaving an inch of space between each shape along the top edge. Cut them out leaving a seam allowance of ¼" along each slanted side.

7 Press the angled side seam allowances under and glue them in place on the back of the strip. Pin the shapes in place and stitch along the top fold and both sides. The bottom of the shape will be covered by the green center square.

8 Cut a green square measuring 1½". Turn under ¼" seam allowances on all four sides and pin the piece in place. Stitch along all four sides covering the raw edges of the trapezoid shapes.

9 Now apply the single flowers along the edges of the block in the same way. Make the stems by cutting strips ¾" wide and 12" long. Stitch and apply them as in step 3. Repeat this step to add a red flower to the top of each stem, then apply a yellow circle where the stems meet. Finally, add two small leaves to each flower.

10 To remove the freezer paper, cut a small slit in the background fabric behind each shape. Lightly mist each motif unit with water and let it soak in for a few minutes. Tease the paper out. Baste the slit closed with herringbone stitch.

Crown of Thorns Block

Sample made by Kay Walters

This traditional block looks more complex than it is, thanks to the triangle squares, which give movement. It is a simple block to construct and at the size shown, a quilt top can be assembled quite quickly. To make the blocks a different size, decide on the size of the square units. Add ½" seam allowance to the square units and cut the squares from which the triangle squares are made ⅞" larger than the finished size of the unit. So if you want a 15" block, each unit will be 3" square. Cut the plain squares 3½" and the squares for the triangle squares 3⅞".

The setting of the blocks in the original quilt, shown on page 47, with half-blocks along the edges and quarter-blocks in the four corners, is unusual and adds to the feeling of liveliness. The blocks are sashed and set on point, with a dark inner and light outer border, each 4" wide.

1 Cut eight dark and eight light 4⅞" squares. On the wrong side of each light square, draw a line across the diagonal using a fine pencil.

2 Place a dark and a light square right sides together, sew ¼" from each side of the diagonal line.

3 Cut along the pencil line with a rotary cutter or scissors.

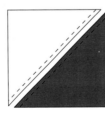

4 Press the triangle squares open with the seams toward the dark side. Make sixteen triangle squares.

5 Cut five light and four dark 4½" squares.

6 Sew the solid squares and triangle squares in rows, as shown in the diagram. Join the five rows to make a 20" block

NOTES

CHAPTER 1

1. Virginia Glenn Crane, "History and Family Values, a Good Wife's Tale: Mary Elizabeth Meade Grignon of Kaukauna, 1837-1898," *Wisconsin Magazine of History* 80, no. 3 (spring 1997): 180.

2. Ibid., 180, 184, 189.

3. Ibid., 185, 189-90.

4. Ibid., 179.

5. Barbara Brackman, *Clues in the Calico* (McLean, Va.: EPM Publications, 1989), 125.

6. Bradford genealogy records and oral family history.

7. Oral family history.

8. Family genealogy records.

9. Tandy Hersh, "Quilted Petticoats," in *Pieced by Mother: Symposium Papers*, ed. Jeannette Lasansky (Lewisburg, Pa.: Oral Traditions Project of the Union County Historical Society, 1988), 5-6.

10. Oral family history.

11. Robert C. Nesbit, *Wisconsin: A History*, ed. William F. Thompson, 2nd ed. (Madison: University of Wisconsin Press, 1989), 93.

12. Donald N. Anderson, "Wisconsin under Three Flags," in *Wisconsin's Historic Preservation Plan*, ed. Randal Wallar (n.p., 1973), 1:18.

13. Ronald Shaw, *Erie Water West* (Lexington, Ky.: University of Kentucky Press, 1966).

14. Nesbit, 103.

15. Ibid., 89.

16. Richard N. Current, *History of Wisconsin*, vol. 2, *Civil War Era, 1848-1873* (Madison: State Historical Society of Wisconsin, 1976), 62-63.

17. Nesbit, 91, 95.

18. Ibid., 166.

19. Ibid., 164.

20. Juliette (Mrs. John) Kinzie, *Wau-bun: The Early Days of the Northwest* (1856; reprint, Urbana and Chicago, Ill.: University of Illinois Press, 1992), introduction.

21. Ibid., x-xi, 61.

22. Frank A. Flower, *History of Milwaukee* (Chicago: Western Historical Co., 1881), 162-63.

23. Mrs. Rosaline Peck, "First House and First Resident Family of Madison," *Wisconsin Historical Collections*, ed. Lyman Copeland Draper and Reuben Gold Thwaites (1872; reprint, Madison: State Historical Society of Wisconsin, 1908), 6:350.

24. Kathleen Ernst, "Legendary Wisconsin Women," *Wisconsin Woman* (March 1989): 43.

25. Nesbit, 170.

26. Ibid., 168.

27. Ibid., 172.

28. Ethel McLaughlin Turner, Paul Boynton Turner, and Lucia Kate Page Sayre, *Wisconsin Page Pioneers and Kinsfolk* (Waterloo, Wisc.: Artcraft Press, 1953), 154-57, 159.

29. Lillian Krueger, "Motherhood on the Wisconsin Frontier," *Wisconsin Magazine of History* (December 1945-March 1946): 1.

30. Lawrence Merrill, *The Life of Queen Victoria*, memorial edition (England: D. Z. Howell, 1901), 80.

Elizabeth Longford, *Queen Victoria: Born to Succeed* (New York and Evanston, Ill.: Harper & Row, 1964), 79.
Cecil Woodham-Smith, *Queen Victoria: From Her Birth to the Death of the Prince Consort* (New York: Alfred A. Knopf, 1972),156-57.

31. Diary of Thomas Weekes, Old Wade House, Greenbush, Wisc.

32. Sarah Roberts, "The Welsh Pioneer Church, a Log Building, from 1848-1857." Privately held.
History of Columbia County, Wisconsin (Chicago: Western Historical Co., 1880), 605.

33. Brackman, 147.

34. Oshkosh Public Museum, textile department.

35. Anderson, 18, 20.

36. Nesbit, 116.

37. Ibid., 114-15.
Karel D. Bicha, "From Where Come the Badgers?" *Wisconsin Magazine of History* 76, no. 2 (winter 1992-93): 122, 124.

38. Daniel M. Parkinson, "Pioneer Life in Wisconsin," *Collections of the State Historical Society of Wisconsin*, ed. Lyman Copeland Draper and Reuben Gold Thwaites (1856; reprint, n.p., 1903), 2:332.

39. Family genealogy records.
Donald Hoke, *Dressing the Bed: Quilts and Coverlets from the Collections of the Milwaukee Public Museum*, exhibit catalog (Milwaukee Public Museum, 1986), 8-9.

40. Eleanor M. Tregonning, *Some Stalwart Cornish Immigrants: Henry and Susan Davies Tregonning and David and Lavinia Paul Bockerleg* (n.p.: privately printed, 1963).

41. Letters from family members and neighbors.
Betsey Seelye Sears diary.
History of Jefferson County, Wisconsin (Chicago: Western Historical Co., 1879), 521-22.
"A Memory Visit at Seeleyburg," *Viroqua (Wisc.) Broadcaster*, January 31, 1974.

42. Betsey Seelye Sears, *Original Poems and Other Selected Poems* (Rome, Wisc.: privately printed, n.d.).

CHAPTER 2

1. Barbara Wyatt, *Cultural Resource Management in Wisconsin*, vol. 1, *A Manual for Historic Properties* (Madison: State Historical Society of Wisconsin, 1986), Settlement Introduction Overview, (1-1), (1-2).
Larry Gara, *A Short History of Wisconsin* (Madison: State Historical Society of Wisconsin, 1962), 89.

2. Nesbit, 155, 157.

3. Jack J. Detzler, "I Live Here Happily: A German Immigrant in Territorial Wisconsin" (letter of George Adam Fromader, trans. by Mrs. Theka King Detzler, Mrs. Hedwig Leser, and Miss Theka Sack), *Wisconsin Magazine of History* 50, no. 3 (spring 1967): 259.

4. Nesbit, 158.

5. Johannes Saehle, September 28, 1847, in Theodore C. Blegen, *Immigrant Women and the American Frontier: Three Early America Letters* (n.p.: Norwegian American Historical Association Studies and Records, 1930), 5:18-22. As cited in Nancy Woloch,

Early American Women: A Documentary History 1600-1000 (Belmont, Calif.: Wadsworth Publishing Co., 1992), 267.

6. Nesbit, 151-52.

7. Ibid., 153.

8. Ibid., 154.

9. Ibid., 160.

10. Ibid.

11. Nancy Hornback, *Quilts in Red and Green: The Flowering of Fold Design in 10th Century America* (Wichita, Kans.: Wichita/Sedgwick County Historical Museum, 1992).

Rick Clarky et al., *Quilts in Community: Ohio's Traditions*, ed. Ricky Clark (Nashville: Rutledge Hill Press, 1991), 81-84.

Kathy Sullivan, "The Legacy of German Quiltmaking in North Carolina," *Bits and Pieces*, ed. Jeannette Lasansky (Lewisburg, Pa.: Oral Traditions Project of the Union County Historical Society, 1991), 70-71.

12. Oral family history.

13. Lydia Maria Child, *The American Frugal Housewife* (1836; reprint, New York, Evanston, Ill., San Francisco, and London: Harper & Row, n.d.), 9.

14. Hugo Ziemann and Mrs. F. L. Gillette, *The White House Cookbook*, ed. Janet Halliday (1887; reprint, Chicago: Follett Publishing Co., 1964), 298-99.

15. Oral family history.

16. Brackman, 128, 173.

17. Letters, genealogy by Edith Ring Welsh. Privately held.

Dennis O'Loughlin diary, sketch by Bryan F. O'Loughlin, 1849. Privately held.

18. Oral family history.

19. Orrin Guernsey and Josiah Willard, *History of Rock County and Transactions of the Rock County Agricultural Society and Mechanics Institute* (Janesville, Wisc.: William Doty Printers, 1856), 286.

20. State Historical Society of Wisconsin, textile department, Madison.

21. Oral family history.

22. Annie Waller, "The Story of My Father's Life," October 1, 1945, Burlington Historical Society.

23. Flower, 224-27, 240-46.

24. Anderson, 26.

25. Diaries of Nancy Derby, 1857-May 1869, Oshkosh Public Museum Archives.

26. Oral family history.

Rossiter Johnson, *Campfire and Battlefield* (Boston: Desmond Publishing Co., 1894), 297-303.

27. Nesbit, 257.

28. Adjutants general, comps., *Wisconsin Volunteers: War of the Rebellion 1861-65* (Madison: State-Democrat Printing Co., 1914), 907.

29. Reuben Gold Thwaites, ed., *Civil War Messages and Proclamations of Wisconsin War Governors*, reprint no. 2 (n.p.: Wisconsin History Commission, 1912), 52.

30. Virginia Gunn, "Quilts for the Union Soldiers in the Civil War," *Uncoverings 1985*, ed. Sally Garoutte (Mill Valley, Calif.: American Quilt Study Group, 1986), 6:104.

31. From the *Milwaukee Telegraph*, January 9, 1884, article reprinted in Ethel Alice Hurn, *Wisconsin Women in the War between the States* (Wisconsin History Commission, 1911), 26-27.

32. Ibid., 20, 25, 27, 29, 42-46.

33. Ernst, 43.

34. Flower, 759.

Margaret Ann Mott, "Lydia Ely Hewitt and the Soldiers' Home," *Historical Messenger of the Milwaukee County Historical Society* 22, no. 3 (September 1966): 101-11.

35. *Dane County Historic Quilts: Passing Through*, exhibit catalog (Madison: State Historical Society of Wisconsin, 1983).

36. Written family history.

37. Anderson, 26.

Lance J. Herdegen and William J. K Beaudot, *In the Bloody Railroad Cut at Gettysburg* (Dayton, Ohio: Morningside House, 1990), Official Records, Series 111, Vol. 1, Intro xix, 319.

38. Leona Torke Kane, trans., *The Torke Family Genealogy* (n.p.: self-published, 1985).

39. Thwaites, 107.

40. Diary of Traugott Umbreit. Sullivan, 70-71.

41. Oral family history.

42. Diary of Martha Ruth Hamilton. Privately held. *Work Family History* no. 608: 185.

Von Gail Hamilton, *Twelve Generations of Works in America: 1690-1969* (Park City, Utah: n.p., n.d.).

43. Oral family history.

44. J. B. Courtney, application for National Register of Historic Places, 1987, section no. 8, 1.

Frederic Merk, *Economic History of Wisconsin during the Civil War Decade* (Madison: State Historical Society of Wisconsin, 1916), 20.

45. Herdegen, 319.

CHAPTER 3

1. Robert C. Nesbit, *History of Wisconsin*, vol. 3, *Urbanization and Industrialization, 1873-1893*, ed. William Fletcher Thompson (Madison: State Historical Society of Wisconsin, 1985), 224, 246.

2. Ibid., 249.

3. Ibid., 250.

4. Elaine Hedges, *Hearts and Hands: Women, Quilts, and American Society* (Nashville: Rutledge Hill Press, 1987), 23, 39.

5. Rachel Maines, "Paradigms of Scarcity and Abundance: The Quilt as an Artifact of the Industrial Revolution," *In the Heart of Pennsylvania: Symposium Papers*, ed. Jeannette Lasansky (Lewisburg, Pa.: Oral Traditions of the Union County Historical Society, County Courthouse, 1986), 87.

6. Ibid., 86.

7. Ibid.

8. Suellen Meyer, "Early Influences of the Sewing Machine and Visible Machine Stitching on Nineteenth-Century Quilts," *Uncoverings 1989*, ed. Laurel Horton (San Francisco: American Quilt Study Group, 1990), 10:39-40, 51.

9. Ibid., 48-51.

10. Oral family history.

11. Written family history.

12. Eva Harold, "Krauss Family History," July 1964. Privately held.

13. Oral family history.

14. Rev. Peter Pernin, "The Great Peshtigo Fire: An Eye Witness Account," *Wisconsin Magazine of History* 54, no. 4 (summer 1971): 246, 256.

15. Robert Wells, *Fire at Peshtigo* (Englewood Cliffs, NJ.: Prentice-Hall, 1968), 167-68.

16. Pernin, 246, 271.

Wells, 87.

17. Wells, 218-19.

18. Pernin, 257.

 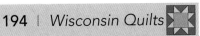

19. Louise Phelps Kellogg, "Wisconsin at the Centennial," *Wisconsin Magazine of History* 10, no. 1 (September 1926): 6,11-12.

20. *The State of Wisconsin: Embracing Brief Sketches of Its History, Position, Resources, and Industries, and a Catalogue of Its Exhibits at the Centennial in Philadelphia* (Madison: Atwood and Culver, 1876), 83.

21. Oral family history.

22. Oral family history.

23. Wendy Gamber, "The Female Economy: The Millinery and Dressmaking Trades, 1860-1930" (diss., Brandeis University, 1990).

24. Oral family history.

25. Morehouse, No. 4, Obituary, *Oshkosh Northwestern*, Oshkosh Public Museum Archives.

26. Oshkosh Public Museum, textile department.

27. State Historical Society of Wisconsin, textile department, Madison.

28. Fred L. Holmes, *Old World Wisconsin: Around Europe in the Badger State* (Eau Claire, Wisc.: E. M. Hale & Co., 1944), 303-18.

29. Autobiography of Martha Cecelia Jensen, n.d., Waupaca Historical Society.

"Carmen Barnes: Ancestors and Herself," transcription of taped interview printed in the *Waupaca County (Wisc.) Post*, April 1977 f.

30. Oral family history.

31. Victoria Brown, *Uncommon Lives of Common Women: The Missing Half of Wisconsin History* (n.p.: Wisconsin Feminists Project Fund, 1975), 56-57.

32. Dorothy Cozart, "The Role and Look of Fundraising Quilts, 1850-1930," in *Pieced by Mother: Symposium Papers*, ed. Jeannette Lasansky (Lewisburg, Pa.: Oral Traditions Project of the Union County Historical Society, 1988), 93.

33. Letter to WQHP, Elizabeth Bussell. Necedah United Methodist Church, Necedah, Wisc.

34. Family records and oral family history.

CHAPTER 4

1. Penny McMorris, *Crazy Quilts* (New York: E. P. Dutton, 1984), 10-11.

2. Ibid., 13, 15.

3. Ibid., 16.

4. Virginia Gunn, "Crazy Quilts and Outline Quilts: Popular Responses to the Decorative Art/Art Needlework Movement, 1876-1893," *Uncoverings 1984*, ed. Sally Garoutte (Mill Valley, Calif.: American Quilt Study Group, 1985), 5:131-32.

5. Written family history.

Richard Haney, "From Black Earth to Liverpool: Transatlantic Observations by George W. Bate," *Wisconsin Magazine of History* 65, no. 1 (autumn 1981): 3-10.

6. Oral family history.

7. McMorris, 75.

8. Jean M. Lamb, "Luther Clapp Family," *Historic Wauwatosa* no. 14 (1980).

9. *Good Housekeeping*, October 25, 1890.

10. Oral family history.

11. Oral family history.

12. Oral family history.

13. Jean Berns Jones, "Schools of Iowa County," *Dodgeville (Wisc.) Chronicle*, 1976.

14. Barbara Brackman, *An Encyclopedia of Pieced Quilt Patterns* (Lawrence, Kans.: Prairie Flower Publishing, 1979 and 1984), 110.

15. Oral family history.

16. Oral family history.

17. Oral family history, Kenosha County Historical Society and Museum, textile department.

18. *Telegraph-Courier*, Kenosha, Wisc., May 19, 1898.

CHAPTER 5

1. Norman K. Risjord, *Wisconsin: The Story of the Badger State* (Madison, Wisc.: Wisconsin Trails, 1995), 154.

2. Ibid., 177.

3. Excerpt, *The Milwaukee Journal*, April 17, 1955.

4. Frederick Hale, *Swiss in Wisconsin* (Madison: State Historical Society of Wisconsin, 1984).

5. Oral family history.

6. August Derleth, *Wisconsin: States of the Nation* (New York: Coward-McCann, 1967), 68-71.

7. Oral family history.

8. Oral family history.

9. Oral family history.

10. Oral family history.

11. Oral family history.

12. Oral family history.

13. *Quilt Pattern Book: Patchwork and Appliqué* (St. Louis: Ladies Art Co., 1922), no. 464.

Brackman, *Encyclopedia*, 246.

14. Dr. Merlin E. Horn, "A Look at Farming in 1900: The Johann B. Koch Homestead in Shawano County," *Voyager* (winter/spring 1997).

15. Diary of Norma Kruschke, Sheboygan County, Wisc., 1922. Privately held.

16. Nancy J. Rowley, "Red Cross Quilts for the Great War," *Uncoverings 1982*, ed. Sally Garoutte (Mill Valley, Calif.: American Quilt Study Group, 1983), 3:43.

17. R. B. Pixley, *Wisconsin in the World War* (Milwaukee: Wisconsin War History Co., 1919), 11.

18. Ibid., 242-43.

19. Ibid., 205.

20. Louise O. Townsend, "Red Cross Quilts," *Quilter's Newsletter* no. 132 (May 1981): 8. Mary A. McElwain, a well-known supplier of patterns and quilts in the 1930s, marketed this pattern through her quilt shop in Wal-worth, Wisconsin.

21. Cuesta Benberry, "The 20th Century's First Quilt Revival," *Quilter's Newsletter* no. 116 (October 1979): 10.

22. Oral family history.

23. Dorothy Cozart, "When the Smoke Cleared," *Quilt Digest* (San Francisco: Quilt Digest Press) no. 5 (1987): 50.

24. Ibid., 53, 55.

25. Oral family history.

26. Oral family history.

27. Barbara Wyatt, *Cultural Resource Management in Wisconsin*, vol. 3, *A Manual for Historic Properties* (Madison: State Historical Society of Wisconsin, June 1986), Social and Political, (2-4), (2-5).

28. Clara Belle Trumble Nimmo diary, 1919-20.

29. Ibid.

30. Wyatt, (4-1).

31. Ibid., (47), (48).

32. Oral family history.

33. Helen Hubatch Gresch, written family history.

34. Helen Hubatch Gresch, "Feeding a Farm Family of Eleven,"

Centennial Celebration Cookbook, comp. Antigo Junior Women's Club (Iowa Falls, Iowa: General Publishing and Binding, 1979), 11-12.

35. Oral family history.

36. Charles McKenny, ed., *Educational History of Wisconsin: Growth and Progress of Education in the State from Its Foundation to the Present Time* (Chicago: Delmont Co., 1912), 289-94.

37. Oral family history.

38. Oral family history.

39. Oral family history.

CHAPTER 6

1. Oral family history.

2. Nesbit, *Wisconsin: A History*, 478.

3. Justus and Barbara Dotts Paul, *The Badger State: A Documentary History of Wisconsin* (Grand Rapids, Mich.: William B. Eerdmans, 1979), 419-20.

4. Nesbit, *Wisconsin: A History*, 479-80.

5. Rosalind Webster Perry and Marty Frolli, *A Joy Forever: Marie Webster's Quilt Patterns* (Santa Barbara, Calif.: Practical Patchwork, 1992), 15, 35. For more information on cottage industries, see Cuesta Benberry, "Quilt Cottage Industries: A Chronicle," *Uncoverings 1986* (Mill Valley, Calif.: American Quilt Study Group, 1987), 7:83-100.

6. Judy Florence, *A Collection of Favorite Quilts* (Paducah, Ky.: American Quilters Society, 1990), 93.

7. Merikay Waldvogel, "Quilt Design Explosion of the Great Depression," *On the Cutting Edge*, ed. Jeannette Lasansky (Lewisburg, Pa.: Oral Traditions Project of the Union County Historical Society, 1994), 85, 90-91.

8. Oral family history.

9. Brackman, *Encyclopedia*, 136.

10. Oral family history.

11. Records of Elda Strahm.

12. Pat L. Nickols, "The Use of Cotton Sacks in Quiltmaking," *Uncoverings 1988* (San Francisco: American Quilt Study Group, 1989), 9:58-59.

13. Oral family history.

14. Oral family history.

15. Oral family history.

16. Oral family history.
Fran Spran, "Faces and Places," *Tribune*, Montello, Wisc., July 1982, 4.

17. Oral family history.
Jeanne Griesback, "Quilting Group Hopes to Help Homeless Piece Together Their Lives," *Catholic Herald*, Milwaukee, April 16, 1998.

18. Merikay Waldvogel and Barbara Brackman, *Patchwork Souvenirs from the 1933 World's Fair* (Nashville: Rutledge Hill Press, 1993), 34-35.

19. Ibid., 35-36.

20. Ibid., 35.

21. Barbara Brackman, "Quilts at Chicago's World's Fairs," *Uncoverings 1981*, ed. Sally Garoutte (Mill Valley, Calif.: American Quilt Study Group, 1982 and 1984), 2:70.

22. Violette Clark, "Plover Woman Is Designer of Quilt for World's Fair," *Wausau Daily Herald*, May 19, 1933.

23. Oral family history.

24. Written family history, Mrs. Thomas Diener.

25. For color photo and extensive research on the Rebenstorff quilt, see Waldvogel and Brackman, *Patchwork*, 65-69.

26. *Quilts and Spreads: Original Designs by Marie D. Webster* (Walworth, Wisc.: Mary McElwain Quilt Shop, c. 1930).

27. Oral family history.

28. *Romance of the Village Quilts*, catalog (Beloit, Wisc.: Daily News Publishing Co., 1936), 20.

29. Oral family history.

30. Xenia E. Cord, "Marketing Quilt Kits in the 1920s and 1930s," *Uncoverings 1995* (San Francisco: American Quilt Study Group, 1995), 16:139-73.

31. Oral family history.

32. Elsa Ulbricht, "The Story of the Milwaukee Handicrafts Project," *Design* (February 1944): 5-7, 11.

33. Merikay Waldvogel, "Quilts in the WPA Milwaukee Handicrafts Project, 1935-1943," *Uncoverings 1984*, ed. Sally Garoutte (Mill Valley, Calif.: American Quilt Study Group, 1985), 5:156.

34. Ulbricht, 7.

35. Waldvogel, "Quilts in the WPA," 156-57, 162.

36. Letter to WQHP, Mary June Kellogg Rice, May 4, 1996.

37. Waldvogel, "Quilts in the WPA," 161-62.

38. Ulbricht, 3.

39. Bea Bourgeois, "The WPA Project That Made Milwaukee Famous," *UWM Today* (winter 1998): 1.

40. Oral family history.

41. Oral family history.

42. *Romance of the Village Quilts*, catalog (Beloit, Wisc.: Daily News Publishing Co., 1936).
Julia Fisher Force, catalog (c. 1933), pattern no. 4410.

43. Oral family history.

44. Oral family history.

EPILOGUE

1. Patsy and Myron Orlofsky, *Quilts in America* (New York: Abbeville Press, 1992), 88.

2. Ibid., 86.

3. Letter to WQHP, Ann Fahl (award-winning Wisconsin quilt artist), Racine, Wisc., 1999.

4. Letter to WQHP, Judy Zoelzer Levine (award-winning Wisconsin quilt artist, lecturer, and current president of the Wisconsin Quilt History Project), Bayside, Wisc., 1999.

BIBLIOGRAPHY

Affleck, Diane Fagan. `Just New from the Mills." North Andover, Mass.: Museum of American Textile History, 1987.

Allen, Thomas B. "Remember the Maine." *National Geographic* 193 (February 1998).

Anderson, Donald N. "Wisconsin under Three Flags." In Vol. 1 of *Wisconsin's Historic Preservation Plan*, edited by Randal Wallar. Madison: State Historical Society of Wisconsin, 1973.

Austin, H. Russell. *The Wisconsin Story: The Building of a Vanguard State*. Milwaukee: Milwaukee Journal Publications, 1948.

Bacon, Lenice Ingram. *American Patchwork Quilts*. Bonanza ed. New York: Crown Publishers and William Morrow & Co., 1980.

Baranowski, Willa. *Historical Penny Squares*. Paducah, Ky.: American Quilter's Society, 1996.

Bath, Virginia Churchill. *Needlework in America: History, Designs, and Techniques*. New York: Viking Press, 1979.

Beaudot, William J. K., and Lance J. Herdegen. *An Irishman in the Iron Brigade*. New York: Fordham University Press, 1993.

Benberry, Cuesta. "The 20th Century's First Quilt Revival." *Quilter's Newsletter* (Leman Publications, Wheatridge, Colo.) no. 116 (October 1979).

Berenson, Kathryn W. "Origins and Traditions of Marseilles Needlework." In Vol. 16 of Uncoverings 1995, edited by Virginia Gunn. San Francisco: American Quilt Study Group, 1995.

Bicha, Karel D. "From Where Came the Badgers?" *Wisconsin Magazine of History* 76 (winter 1992-93).

Birch, Brian P. "From Southwest England to Southwest Wisconsin: Devonshire Hollow, Lafayette County." *Wisconsin Magazine of History* 69 (winter 1985-86).

Bishop, Robert, and Elizabeth Safanda. *A Gallery of Amish Quilts*. New York: E. P. Dutton & Co., 1976.

Boldtmann, Charlotte. "Patchwork Quilts of a Hundred Years Ago." *Woman's Home Companion* (January 1911).

Bottomley, Julia. *The Milliner's Guide: A Handy Reference Book for the Workroom*, edited by Emma Maxwell Burke. New York: The Illustrated Milliner Co., 1917.

Bourgeois, Bea. "The WPA Project That Made Milwaukee Famous." *UWM Today* (University of Wisconsin-Milwaukee Alumni Association, winter 1998).

Brackman, Barbara. "Buds and Blossoms: Nineteenth Century Album Patterns." *Quilter's Newsletter Magazine* 20 (June 1989).

___. *Clues in the Calico*. McLean, Va.: EPM Publications, 1989.

___. "Dating Old Quilts, Part One: Green Prints and Dyes." *Quilter's Newsletter Magazine* 15 (September 1984).

___. *Encyclopedia of Appliqué*. McLean, Va.: EPM Publications, 1993.

___. *An Encyclopedia of Pieced Quilt Patterns*. Lawrence, Kans.: Prairie Flower Publishing, 1979, 1984.

___. *Encyclopedia of Pieced Quilt Patterns*. Paducah, Ky.: American Quilters Society, 1993.

___. "Quilts at Chicago's World's Fairs." In Vol. 2 of *Uncoverings 1981*, edited by Sally Garoutte. Mill Valley, Calif.: American Quilt Study Group, 1982 and 1984.

___. "Signature Quilts: Nineteenth-Century Trends." In Vol. 10 of *Uncoverings 1989*, edited by Laurel Horton. San Francisco: American Quilt Study Group, 1990.

Brown, Victoria. "Uncommon Lives of Common Women." Project of the Wisconsin Feminists Project Fund, 1975.

Butterfield, C. W. *History of Dane County*. Chicago: Western Historical Co., 1880.

Carlisle, Lillian Baker. *Pieced Work and Appliqué Quilts at Shelburne Museum*. Shelburne, Vt.: Shelburne Museum, 1957.

Centennial Celebrations Cookbook. Iowa Falls, Iowa: Antigo Jr. Woman's Club, General Publishing and Binding, 1979.

Cerny, Catherine A. "Quilt Ownership and Sentimental Attachments: The Structure of Memory." In Vol. 18 of *Uncoverings 1997*, edited by Virginia Gunn. San Francisco: American Quilt Study Group, 1997.

Child, Mrs. *The American Frugal Housewife*, edited by Alice M. Geffen. New York, Evanston, Ill., San Francisco, and London: Harper & Row Publishers, 1972. Reprint, Boston: American Stationer's Co., 1836.

Christopherson, Katy. The Political and Campaign Quilt. Frankfort, Ky.: Kentucky Heritage Quilt Society, 1984.

Clark, Ricky. "Mid-19th-Century Album and Friendship Quilts, 1860-1920." In *Pieced by Mother: Symposium Papers*, edited by Jeanette Lasansky. Lewisburg, Pa.: Oral Traditions of the Union County Historical Society, 1988.

Coombs, Jan. "The Health of Central Wisconsin Residents in 1880: A New View of Midwestern Rural Life." *Wisconsin Magazine of History* 68 (summer 1985).

Cord, Xenia. "Marketing Quilt Kits in the 1920s and 1930s." In Vol. 16 of *Uncoverings 1995*, edited by Virginia Gunn. San Francisco: American Quilt Study Group, 1995.

Courtney, J. B. Courtney Woolen Mills application for National Register of Historical Places. Appleton, Wisc.: 1987.

Cozart, Dorothy. "The Role and Look of Fund Raising Quilts, 1850-1930." In *Pieced by Mother: Symposium Papers*, edited by Jeanette Lasansky. Lewisburg, Pa.: Oral Traditions Project of the Union County Historical Society, 1988.

___. "When the Smoke Cleared." *Quilt Digest* 5 (San Francisco: Quilt Digest Press, 1987).

Crane, Virginia Glenn. "History and Family Values, A Good Wife's Tale: Mary Elizabeth Meade Grignon of Kaukauna, 1837-1898." *Wisconsin Magazine of History* 80 (spring 1997).

"The Crazy Quilt." *Good Housekeeping Magazine* (October 25, 1890).

Cultural map of Wisconsin. Madison: University of Wisconsin Press, Board of Regents of University of Wisconsin System, 1996.

Current, Richard N. *History of Wisconsin*. Vol. 2, Civil War Era, 1848-1873. Madison: State Historical Society of Wisconsin, 1976.

Curtis, Ina. *Early Days at the Fox-Wisconsin Portage*. N.p.: Columbia County Historical Society, 1981.

Davis, Gayle R. "Women's Quilts and Diaries: Creative Expression as Personal Resource." Vol. 18 of *Uncoverings 1997*, edited by Virginia Gunn. San Francisco: American Quilt Study Group, 1997.

Delgado, Jeanne Hunnicutt. "Nellie Kedzie Jone's Advice to Farm Women: Letters from Wisconsin, 1912-1916." *Wisconsin Magazine of History* 57 (autumn 1976).

Derby, Nancy. Diaries of Nancy Derby. Oshkosh Public Museum Archives, Oshkosh, Wisc.

Derleth, August. *Wisconsin: States of the Nation*. New York: Coward-McCann, 1967.

Detzler, Jack J. "I Live Here Happily: A German Immigrant in Territorial Wisconsin." *Wisconsin Magazine of History* 50 (spring 1967).

Dopp, Pearl. *From the Top of a Secret Tree*. Chicago: J. Phunn Publishers, Adams Press, 1979.

Doudna, Edgar G. *The Thirtieth Star, 1848-1948*. Madison: Wisconsin State Centennial Sub-Committee on Education, 1948.

Dressing the Bed: Quilts and Coverlets from the Collections of the Milwaukee Public Museum, catalog edited by Mary Garity. Milwaukee: Bulfin Printers, 1985.

Early Ozaukee County Historical Sketches. Cedarburg, Wisc.: Ozaukee County Historical Society, n.d.

Eisenstat, Sharon L. "Small Sensations." The Great American Quilt Festival Special Souvenir Issue of The Clarion (New York: Museum of American Folk Art, spring–summer 1986).

Ernst, Kathleen. "Legendary Wisconsin Women." *Wisconsin Woman Magazine* (March 1989).

Essential Quilts, catalog of exhibit at the State Historical Society of Wisconsin, 1979-80. Madison: State Historical Society of Wisconsin, 1979.

Finley, Ruth E. *Old Patchwork Quilts and the Women Who Made Them*. McLean, Va.: EPM Publications, 1992.

Flower, Frank A. *History of Milwaukee*. Chicago: The Western Historical Co., 1881.

Force, Julia Fischer. *Die Cut Quilts Stamped*. N.p.: ca. 1933.

Fox, Charles Phillip. *Ticket to the Circus: A Pictorial History of the Incredible Ringlings*. New York: Bramhay House, 1959.

____. *Small Endearments: 19th Century Quilts for Children*. New York: Charles Scribner & Sons, 1985.

Fox, Sandi. *Wrapped in Glory: Figurative Quilts and Bedcovers, 1700-1900*. New York: Los Angeles County Museum of Art and Thames & Hudson, 1990.

Freeman, Roland L. *A Communion of the Spirits*. Nashville: Rutledge Hill Press, 1996.

Gamber, Wendy. *The Female Economy: The Millinery and Dressmaking Trades, 1860-1930*. Ann Arbor, Mich.: University Microfilms International and Madison: State Historical Society of Wisconsin.

Gara, Larry. *A Short History of Wisconsin*. Madison: State Historical Society of Wisconsin, 1962.

Gard, Robert E. *This Is Wisconsin*. Spring Green, Wisc.: Wisconsin House, 1969.

Gard, Robert E., and Maryo Gard. "My Land, My Home, My Wisconsin." *Milwaukee Journal* (Milwaukee, 1978).

Gardner, Marilyn. "Women's Quartet Stitches, Recalls Quilting Bees." *Milwaukee Journal* (April 17, 1955).

Garoutte, Sally. "Marseilles Quilts: Their Woven Offspring." In Vol. 3 of *Uncoverings 1982*. Mill Valley, Calif.: American Quilt Study Group, 1983.

Gebel, Carol Williams. "Quilts in the Final Rite of Passage: A Multicultural Study." In Vol. 16 of *Uncoverings 1995*, edited by Virginia Gunn. San Francisco: American Quilt Study Group, 1995.

Glad, Paul W. *History of Wisconsin*. Vol. 5, *A New Era, and Depression, 1914-1940*, edited by William Fletcher Thompson. Madison: State Historical Society of Wisconsin, 1990.

Grant, Marilyn. "The 1912 Suffrage Referendum: An Exercise in Political Action." *Wisconsin Magazine of History* (winter 1980-81).

The Great Avenue of History: The Green Bay Trail. Cedarburg, Wisc.: Osaukee County Historical Society, 1997. Published to commemorate the sesquicentennial of the statehood of Wisconsin, 1848-1998.

Greenaway, Kate. *Under the Window: Pictures and Rhymes for Children*. London and New York: F. Warne, 1878.

Guernsey, Orrin, and Josiah Willard. *History of Rock County and Transactions of the Rock County Agricultural Society and Mechanics Institute*. Janesville, Wisc.: William Doty Printers, 1856.

Gunn, Virginia. "Crazy Quilts and Outline Quilts: Popular Responses to the Decorative Art/Art Needlework Movement, 1876-1893." In Vol. 5 of *Uncoverings 1984*, edited by Sally Garoutte. Mill Valley, Calif.: American Quilt Study Group, 1985.

____. "Quilts for Union Soldiers in the Civil War." In Vol. 6 of *Uncoverings 1985*, edited by Sally Garoutte. Mill Valley, Calif.: American Quilt Study Group, 1986.

Hale, Frederick. *Swiss in Wisconsin*. Madison: State Historical Society of Wisconsin, 1984.

Harpers Bazaar (July 23, 1881).

Hedges, Elaine, and Ingrid Wendi. *In Her Own Image: Women Working in the Arts*. Old Westbury, N.Y.:

Feminist Press; New York, St. Louis, and San Francisco: McGraw Hill Book Co., 1980.

Herdegen, Lance J. *The Men Stood like Iron: How the Iron Brigade Won Its Name*. Bloomington, Ind.: Indiana University Press, 1997.

Herdegen, Lance J., and William Beaudot. *In the Bloody Railroad Cut at Gettysburg*. Dayton, Ohio: Morningside House, 1990.

Hersh, Tandy. "Quilted Petticoats." In *Pieced by Mother: Symposium Papers*, edited by Jeanette Lasansky. Lewisburg, Pa.: Oral Traditions Project of the Union County Historical Society, 1988.

 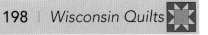

Hewitt, Nancy A. "Women, Families and Communities." Vol. 1, To 1877, of *Readings in American History*. Glenview, Ill., and London: Scott Foresman & Co., 1990.

Hilts, Victor, and Pat Hilts. "Not for Pioneers Only: The Story of Wisconsin's Spinning Wheels." *Wisconsin Magazine of History 66* (1982-83).

History of Jefferson County, Wisconsin. Chicago: Western Historical Co., 1879.

Holand, Hjalmar R. *History of Door County: The County Beautiful*. Vol. 1. Chicago: S. J. Clarke Publishing Co., 1917.

____. *Old Peninsula Days*. Madison: Wisconsin House, 1925.

Holmes, Fred L. *Old World Wisconsin: Around Europe in the Badger State*. Eau Claire, Wisc.: E. M. Hale, 1944; Minoqua, Wisc.: Heartland Press, 1990.

____, ed. *Wisconsin*. Vol. 2. Chicago: Lewis Publishing Co., 1946.

Holt, Margaret Ann. "Lydia Ely Hewitt and the Soldiers' Home." *Historical Messenger of the Milwaukee County Historical Society 22* (September 1966).

Hornback, Nancy. *Quilts in Red and Green: The Flowering of Folk Design in 19th Century America*. Wichita, Kans.: The Wichita/Sedgwick County Historical Museum, 1992.

Hurn, Ethel Alice. *Wisconsin Women in the War between the States*. Madison: Wisconsin History Commission, May 1911.

Jefferson County Union Newspaper (Fort Atkinson, Wisc.), July 7, 14, and 21, 1876.

Johnson, Rossiter. *Campfire and Battlefield*. Boston: Desmond Publishing Co., 1894.

Jones, Jean Berns. "Schools of Iowa County, Iowa County Bicentennial Education Committee." *The Dodgeville Chronicle* (Iowa County, Wisc.), 1976.

"Journal of Salmon Stebbins, 1837-1838." *Wisconsin Magazine of History* (Madison: State Historical Society of Wisconsin) 9, no. 2 (1925-26).

Keller, Patricia J. "To Go to Housekeeping: Quilts Made for Marriage in Lancaster County." *Bits and Pieces: Symposium Papers*, edited by Jeanette Lasansky. Lewisburg, Pa.: Oral Traditions Project of the Union County Historical Society, 1991.

Kellogg, Louise Phelps. "Wisconsin at the Centennial." *Wisconsin Magazine of History 10* (September 1926).

Kinzie, Mrs. John Quliette). *Wau-Bun: The Early Days in the Northwest*. Menasha, Wisc.: George Banta Publishing Co., 1930.

Kiracofe, Roderick. *The American Quilt: A History of Cloth and Comfort, 1750-1950*. New York: Clarkson Potter, 1993.

Klement, Frank L. "Milwaukee Women and the Civil War." *Historical Messenger of the Milwaukee County Historical Society 21* (March 1965).

____. *Wisconsin and the Civil War*. Madison: State Historical Society of Wisconsin for the Wisconsin Civil War Centennial Commission, 1963.

Kohler of Kohler News 42 (Kohler Village Issue, a special issue published by Kohler Co., Kohler Wisc., June 1963). Back cover tapestry map of Wisconsin by Lorentz Kleiser.

Kort, Ellen. *The Fox Heritage: A History of Wisconsin's Fox Cities*. Woodland Hills, Calif.: Windsor Publications, 1984.

Krone, Carolyn H., and Thomas M. Horner. "Her Grief in the Quilt." In Vol. 13 of *Uncoverings 1992*, edited by Laurel Horton. San Francisco: American Quilt Study Group, 1993.

Krueger, Lillian. "Motherhood on the Wisconsin Frontier." *Wisconsin Magazine of History* (Madison: State Historical Society of Wisconsin, December 1945-March 1946).

Krynski, Elizabeth, and Kimberly Little. "Hannah's Letters: The Story of a Wisconsin Pioneer Family, 1856-1864." Parts 1-3. *Wisconsin Magazine of History* (Madison: State Historical Society of Wisconsin) 74, no. 3 (spring 1991); 74, no. 4 (summer 1991); 75, no. 1 (autumn 1991).

"Ladies Aid Society of Milwaukee." *Home Fair Journal* (Milwaukee: Milwaukee County Historical Society, May 20 July 8, 1865).

The Ladies World. New York: S. H. Moore & Co., September 1892.

Lasansky, Jeanette. "The Colonial Revival." In *Pieced by Mother: Over 100 Years of Quiltmaking Traditions*, edited by Jeanette Lasansky. Lewisburg, Pa.: Oral Traditions Project of the Union County Historical Society, 1987.

____. "Myth and Reality in Craft Tradition: Were Blacksmiths Really Muscle-Bound? Were Basket Makers Gypsies? Were Thirteen Quilts in the Dowry Chest?" In *On the Cutting Edge*. Lewisburg, Pa.: Oral Traditions Project of the Union County Historical Society, 1994.

____. *Pieced by Mother*. Lewisburg, Pa.: Oral Traditions Project of the Union County Historical Society, 1988.

____. "The Role of Haps in Central Pennsylvania's 19th and 20th Century Quiltmaking Traditions." In Vol. 6 of *Uncoverings 1985*, edited by Sally Garoutte. Mill Valley, Calif.: American Quilt Study Group, 1986.

Leonard, Richard D. "Presbyterian and Congregational Missionaries in Early Wisconsin." *Wisconsin Magazine of History* (Madison: State Historical Society of Wisconsin, 1941).

Lesy, Michael. *Wisconsin Death Trip*. New York: Pantheon Books, 1973.

Lippard, Lucy R. "Up, Down, and Across: A New Frame for New Quilts." In *Feminism and Art History*, edited by Norma Broude and Mary D. Garrard. New York: Harper & Row, 1982.

Lipsett, Linda Otto. *Pieced from Ellen's Quilt: Ellen Spaulding Reed's Letters and Story*. Dayton, Ohio: Holsted & Meadows Publishing, 1991.

Longford, Elizabeth. *Queen Victoria: Born to Succeed*. New York and Evanston, Ill.: Harper & Row, 1964.

Lowe, Ed. "Blacks Have Long History in Wisconsin, Historian Says." *The Post Crescent* (Appleton, Wisc.), February 12, 1998.

Mainardi, Patricia. "Quilts: The Great American Art." In *Feminism and Art History*, edited by Norma Broude and Mary D. Garrard. New York: Harper & Row, 1982.

Marie Webster Quilts: A Retrospective (exhibit brochure). Indianapolis: Indianapolis Museum of Art, 1991.

Marquart, LaVerne H. *Wisconsin's Agricultural Heritage: The Grange, 1871-1071*. Lake Mills, Wisc.: Rural Life Publishing Co., 1972.

Mattern, Carolyn. *Soldiers When They Go: The Story of Camp Randall, 1801-1805*. Madison: State Historical Society of Wisconsin for the Department of History, 1981.

McBride, Genevieve. *On Wisconsin Women: Working for Their Rights from Settlement to Suffrage*. Madison: University of Wisconsin Press, 1993.

McCoy, Sue, Jill Dean, and Maggie Dewey, eds. "Yarns of Wisconsin." In *Wisconsin Trails*. Madison: Tamarack Press, 1978.

McCutcheon, Marc. *Writer's Guide to Everyday Life in the 1800s*. Cincinnati: Writer's Digest Books, 1993.

McDowell, Marsha. "Native North American Quilting Traditions: A Study and Exhibit of Native Quilts and Their Makers." *Lady's Circle Patchwork Quilts* (New York: October 1997).

McElwain, Mary A. *The Romance of the Village Quilts*. Beloit, Wisc.: Daily News Publishing Co., 1936.

McKenny, Charles A. M., ed. *Educational History of Wisconsin: Growth and Progress of Education in the State from Its Foundation to the Present Time*. Chicago: Delmont Co., 1912.

McMorris, Penny. *Crazy Quilts*. New York: E. P. Dutton, 1984.

McMorris, Penny, and Michael Kile. *The Art Quilt*. Lincolnwood, Ill.: Quilt Digest Press, WTC Publishing Group, 1996.

Merk, Frederick. *Economic History of Wisconsin during the Civil War Decade*. Madison: State Historical Society of Wisconsin, 1916.

Merrill, Lawrence. *The Life of Queen Victoria*. Memorial ed. N.p.: D. Z. Howell, 1901.

Modern Priscilla. Boston: Priscilla Publishing Co., 1917.

Morehouse, No. 4, Obituary, *Oshkosh Northwestern*. Oshkosh Public Museum Archives, Oshkosh, Wisc.

Mott, Margaret Ann. "Lydia Ely Hewitt and the Soldiers' Home." *Historical Messenger of the Milwaukee County Historical Society 22* (September 1966).

Moynihan, Ruth Barnes, Cynthia Russett, and Laurie Crumpacker. *Second to None: A Documentary History of American Women*. Vol. 1, From the 16th Century to 1865. Lincoln, Nebr.: University of Nebraska Press, 1993.

Munich, Adrienne. *Queen Victoria's Secrets*. New York: Columbia University Press, 1996.

Neft, David S., and Richard M. Cohen. *The Sports Encyclopedia: Baseball*. 17th ed. New York: St. Martin's Griffin, 1997.

Nesbit, Robert C. *History of Wisconsin*. Vol. 3, *Urbanization and Industrialization, 1873-1893*, edited by William Fletcher Thompson. Madison: State Historical Society of Wisconsin, 1985.

___. *Wisconsin: A History*, edited by William F. Thompson. 2nd ed. Madison: University of Wisconsin Press, 1989.

Nickols, Pat. "Mary A. McElwain: Quilter and Quilt Business Woman." In Vol. 12 of *Uncoverings 1991*, edited by Laurel Horton. San Francisco: American Quilt Study Group, 1992.

Nimmo, Clara Belle Trumble. Diary, notes from 1919-20. Privately held.

Nylander, Jane C. "Flowers from the Needle." *An American Sampler: Folk Art from the Shelburne Museum*, catalog of exhibit. Washington, D.C.: Board of Trustees, National Gallery of Art, 1987.

Oldane, John L. "Archiving and the American Quilt: A Position Paper." In Vol. 1 of *Uncoverings 1980*. Mill Valley, Calif.: American Quilt Study Group, 1984.

Oleson, Thurine. *Wisconsin, My Home: The Story of Thurine Oleson*. Madison: University of Wisconsin Press, 1950 and 1975.

Orr, William J. "Rasmus Sorensen and the Beginnings of Danish Settlement in Wisconsin." *Wisconsin Magazine of History 65* (spring 1982).

Outagamie County Historical Society Archives, Appleton, Wisc.

Parkinson, Daniel M. "Pioneer Life in Wisconsin." In Vol. 2 of *Collections of the State Historical Society of Wisconsin*, edited by Lyman Copeland Draper. Madison: State Historical Society of Wisconsin, 1903.

Parry, Linda, ed. *A Practice Guide to Patchwork from the Victoria and Albert Museum*. Pittstown, NJ.: Main Street Press, William Case House, 1987.

Paul, Justus F., and Barbara Dotts. *The Badger State: A Documentary History of Wisconsin*. Grand Rapids, Mich.: William B. Eerdmans, 1979.

Pernin, Rev. Peter. "The Great Peshtigo Fire: An Eyewitness Account." *Wisconsin Magazine of History* (Madison: State Historical Society of Wisconsin, 1971).

Perry, Lorinda. *Millinery as a Trade for Women*. New York, London, Bombay, and Calcutta: Longmans, Green, and Co., 1916.

Perry, Rosalind Webster, and Marty Frolli. *A Joy Forever: Marie Webster's Quilt Patterns*. Santa Barbara, Calif.: Practical Patchwork, 1992.

Petterson, Lucille. "Ephraim Is My Home Now: Letters of Anna and Anders Petterson, 1884-1889."

Parts 1-3. *Wisconsin Magazine of History 69* (spring 1986); 69, no. 4 (summer 1986); 70, no. 1 (autumn 1986).

Pixley, R. B. *Wisconsin in the World War*. Milwaukee: S. E. Tate Printing Co., 1919.

Quilts and Spreads: Original Designs by Marie D. Webster. Walworth, Wisc.: Mary A. McElwain Quilt Shop, n.d.

Rice, Mary June Kellog. Letter to Wisconsin Quilt History Project, 1996. Wisconsin Quilt History Project archives.

Rippley, LaVern J. *The Immigrant Experience in Wisconsin*. Boston: Twayne Publishers, 1985.

Risjord, Norman K "Wisconsin: The Story of the Badger State." In *Wisconsin Trails*. Madison: n.p., 1995.

Rowley, Nancy J. "Red Cross Quilts for the Great War." In Vol. 3 of *Uncoverings 1982*, edited by Sally Garoutte. Mill Valley, Calif.: American Quilt Study Group, 1983.

Schafer, Joseph. "The Yankee and the Teuton in Wisconsin." *Wisconsin Magazine of History 6* (June 1923).

Sears, Roebuck Catalogue. 1902. Replica, New York: Bounty Book, 1969.

Shaw, Ronald E. *Erie Water West*. Lexington, Ky.: University of Kentucky Press, 1966.

Smith, Alice E. *History of Wisconsin*. Vol. 1, *From Exploration to Statehood*, edited by William Fletcher Thompson. Madison: State Historical Society of Wisconsin, 1973.

Staniland, Kay. *In Royal Fashion: The Clothes of Princess Charlotte of Wales and Queen Victoria, 1796-1901*. London: Museum of London, 1997.

State Historical Society of Wisconsin Photo Archives, Madison.

 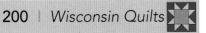

Taylor, Jean Federico. "White Work Classification System." In Vol. 1 of *Uncoverings 1980*. Mill Valley, Calif.: American Quilt Study Group, 1984.

Telegraph Courier (Kenosha, Wisc.), May 19 June 2, 1898.

Thompson, William F. *The History of Wisconsin*. Vol. 6, *Continuity and Change, 1040-1065*. Madison: State Historical Society of Wisconsin, 1988.

Thrasher, Tanya. "To Honor and Comfort: Native American Quilting Traditions." *Native Peoples Magazine* (Phoenix: Media Concepts Group, summer–October 1997).

Thwaites, Reuben Gold. *Civil War Messages and Proclamations of Wisconsin Governors*. Madison: Wisconsin History Commission, 1912 (reprint no. 2).

Townsend, Louise O. "The Great American Quilt Classics: New York Beauty." *Quilter's Newsletter 12* (April 1981).

___. "Red Cross Quilts." Quilter's Newsletter 12 (May 1981).

Trask, Kerry A. *Fire Within: A Civil War Narrative from Wisconsin*. Kent, Ohio, and London: Kent State University Press, 1995.

Trechsel, Gail Andrews. "Mourning Quilts in America." In Vol. 10 of *Uncoverings 1080*, edited by Laurel Horton. San Francisco: American Quilt Study Group, 1990.

Turner, Ethel McLaughlin, Paul Boynton Turner, and Lucia Kate Page Sayre. *Wisconsin Page Pioneers and Kinsfolk*. Waterloo, Wisc.: Artcraft Press, 1953.

Ulbricht, Elsa. "The Story of the Milwaukee Handicraft Project." *Design* (Columbus, Ohio: Design Publishing Co., February 1944).

Umbreit, Traugott. Diary of Traugott Umbreit. Translated from the German (translator unknown) and edited by M. James Simonsen. 1865. Privately held.

Waldvogel, Merikay. "Quilt Design Explosion of the Great Depression." In *On the Cutting Edge*, edited by Jeanette Lasansky. Lewisburg, Pa.: Oral Traditions Project of the Union County Historical Society, 1994.

___. "Quilts in the WPA Milwaukee Handicrafts Project, 1935-1943." In Vol. 5 of *Uncoverings 1984*, edited by Sally Garoutte. Mill Valley, Calif.: American Quilt Study Group, 1985.

___. *Soft Covers for Hard Times*. Nashville: Rutledge Hill Press, 1990.

Waldvogel, Merikay, and Barbara Brackman. *Patchwork Souvenirs from the 1033 World's Fair*. Nashville: Rutledge Hill Press, 1993.

Walters, Kay. "Preservation of a Historic Woolen Mill." In *Colored Sheep and Wool: Exploring Their Beauty and Function*, edited by Kent Erskine. Ashland, Ore.: Black Sheep Press, 1989.

Wells, Robert W. *Fire at Peshtigo*. Englewood Cliffs, NJ.: Prentice-Hall, 1968.

___. *This Is Milwaukee: A Colorful Portrait of the City That Made Beer Famous*. Garden City and New York: Doubleday, 1970.

Wessel, Thomas, and Marilyn Wessel. *4-H: An American Idea 1000-1080, A History of 4-H*. Chevy Chase, Md.: National 4-H Council, 1982.

Winkler, Kathleen. "Preserving Wisconsin's Wooly Heritage." *Wisconsin Country Life*, edited by Ed Liermann (Milwaukee, fall 1991).

Wisconsin Women: A Gifted Heritage. Neenah, Wisc.: American Association of University Women, Wisconsin State Division, 1982.

Woloch, Nancy. *Early American Women: A Documentary History, 1600-1900*. Belmont, Calif.: Wadsworth Publishing Co., 1992.

Woodard, Thomas K. *Twentieth Century Quilts, 1000-1050*. New York: E. P. Dutton, 1988.

Woodham-Smith, Cecil. *Queen Victoria: From Her Birth to the Death of the Prince Consort*. New York: Alfred A. Knopf, 1972.

Woodward, Thomas K., and Blanche Greenstein. *Crib Quilts and Other Small Wonders*. New York: Bonanza Books, 1988.

"Woolen Industry Here Dates from Civil War." *Appleton (Wisc.) Post Crescent*, April 30, 1932.

Wyatt, Barbara, and the Resource Protection Planning Project. *Cultural Resource Management in Wisconsin*. Vols. 1-3. Madison: State Historical Society of Wisconsin, Historic Preservation Division, 1986.

Zeitlin, Richard H. *Germans in Wisconsin*. Madison: State Historical Society of Wisconsin, 1977.

Ziemann, Hugo, and Mrs. F. L. Gillette. *White House Cookbook*. Chicago: R. S. Peale, 1887, 1899, and 1913; Minneapolis: Chronimed Publishing, 1996.

INDEX

Quick Quilting Tips for Savvy Stitch

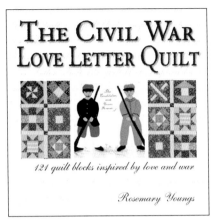

The Civil War Love Letter Quilt

121 Quilt Blocks Inspired by Love and War

by Rosemary Youngs

Get wrapped up in the loves and lives of 11 Civil War soldiers and the beautiful quilt their stories inspired. Using 121 different blocks, you can create any of the 14 projects, including a full-size quilt, lap quilts, wall hangings and table runners. Full-size patterns included.

Softcover • 8 x 8 • 288 pages • 20 color photos, 300 color illus.
Item# Z0751 • $24.99

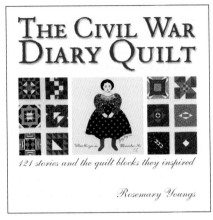

The Civil War Diary Quilt

121 Stories and The Quilt Blocks They Inspired

by Rosemary Youngs

This book helps you bring the past alive with distinctive and exquis quilt blocks that tell the stories of 10 women living and surviving the Ci War. Explore diary entries of each woman, plus instructions for 121 relat quilt blocks.

Softcover • 8 x 8 • 288 pages • 121 color illustrations
Item# CWQD • $22.99

Quilt As Desired

Your Guide to Straight-Line and Free-Motion Quilting

by Charlene C. Frable

Take your quilting skills to new heights with the six projects, using straight-line and free-motion techniques, featured in this revolutionary new guide. Discover what it means to truly quilt as desired.

Hardcover • 8¼ x 10⅞ • 128 pages
150 color photos
Item# Z0743 • $24.99

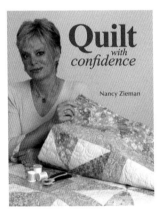

Quilt With Confidence

by Nancy Zieman

Through her inviting and inspiring writing style, and detailed directions, America's favorite sewing teacher walks you through the tools to get started, organizing an effective quilting area and practicing rotary cutting techniques.

Softcover • 8¼ x 10⅞
144 pages
Item# Z1549 • $24.99

Caliente Quilts

Create Breathtaking Quilts Using Bold Colored Fabrics

by Priscilla Bianchi

Learn five methods for mixing and matching ex fabrics from around the world for a fresh approach contemporary quilts.

Softcover • 8-¼ x 10-7/8 • 144 pages
200+ color photos and illus.
Item# Z0103 • $24.99

krause publications
An imprint of F+W Publications, Inc.

P.O. Box 5009, Iola, WI 54945-5009
www.krausebooks.com

Order directly from the publisher by calling **800-258-0929**
M-F 8 am - 5 pm

Online at **www.krausebooks.com**,
or from booksellers and craft and fabric shops nationwide.

Please reference offer **CRB8** with all direct-to-publisher orders.